BOEING
747
A HISTORY

DELIVERING THE DREAM

This book is dedicated to the memory of the late Barry Reeve

BOEING
747
A HISTORY

DELIVERING THE DREAM

MARTIN W. BOWMAN

Pen & Sword
AVIATION

First Published in Great Britain in 2014 by
Pen & Sword Aviation
an imprint of
Pen & Sword Books Ltd
47 Church Street, Barnsley, South Yorkshire S70 2AS

Copyright © Martin W Bowman
ISBN 9781783030392

The right of Martin W Bowman to be identified as author of this work
has been asserted by him in accordance with the Copyright,
Designs and Patents Act 1988.

A CIP catalogue record for this book is
available from the British Library.

Typeset in 9/11 Times
by GMS Enterprises

Printed and bound in India by Replika Press Pvt Ltd

Pen & Sword Books Ltd incorporates the Imprints of Pen & Sword Aviation,
Pen & Sword Family History, Pen & Sword Maritime, Pen & Sword Military,
Pen & Sword Discovery, Pen and Sword Fiction, Pen and Sword History,
Wharncliffe Local History, Wharncliffe True Crime, Wharncliffe Transport,
Pen & Sword Select, Pen & Sword Military Classics, Leo Cooper, The Praetorian Press,
Seaforth Publishing and Frontline Publishing

For a complete list of Pen & Sword titles please contact
PEN & SWORD BOOKS LIMITED

47 Church Street, Barnsley, South Yorkshire, S70 2AS, England
E-mail: enquiries@pen-and-sword.co.uk
Website: www.pen-and-sword.co.uk

Contents

Acknowledgements 4

Bibliography 7

747 Programme Chronology 9

Introduction 15

Chapter 1   The Start of It All 25
Chapter 2   The Dream Becomes Reality 39
Chapter 3   The Spacious Age 51
Chapter 4   Pilot Error 73
Chapter 5   Continuing The Classic Line 89
Chapter 6   Off Course To Disaster 107
Chapter 7   Baby Boeings 117
Chapter 8   Pan Am Flight 103 133
Chapter 9   Long Haul 137
Chapter 10   Freighters 147
Chapter 11   Military And Multifunctional 161
Chapter 12   'Megatop' - the 747-400 Series 173
Chapter 13   A Day in Schiphol 197
Chapter 14   'Cathay 403, Will You Accept A Visual?' Captain Mike Rigg 203
Chapter 15   Wings Across The Prairie: From the Flight Deck 213
Chapter 16   Towards the Eight 225

Appendix I   747-100 Characteristics 241
Appendix II   Specification - 747-100 241
Appendix III   747-100 Total Production List 241
Appendix IV   747-100B Total Production List 242
Appendix V   Characteristics with JT9D-7A engines 242
Appendix VI   Model 747-100SR Production List 242
Appendix VII   Specification 747-200B 243
Appendix VIII   747-200B Characteristics with JT9D-7AW engines 243
Appendix IX   Specification 747-300S 243
Appendix X   Specification 747-200SP 244
Appendix XI   747SP Characteristics with JT9D-7 Engines 244
Appendix XII   47SP Production 245
Appendix XIII   Iranian Air Force 747s 245
Appendix XIV   USAF E-4 E-4/C-25A/SP (Military/VIP) Series ... 245
Appendix XV   Specification 747-400 245
Appendix XVI   747-100B-747-8I 246
Appendix XVII   Specification 747 Dreamlifter 247
Appendix XVIII   747 Orders and Deliveries 247
Appendix XIX   747-8 Firm Orders and Deliveries 248
Appendix XX   Airframe Losses and Incidents 248
                 Index 253

Acknowledgements

I would like to thank Peter Middleton, media relations manager at British Airways for his superb and unstinting help with material and for very kindly arranging my flight to Denver to experience 747-436 flight-deck operations. In turn, I am equally grateful to Captain John Downey, Senior 1st Officer Alan Emery, 1st Officer Dominic Boyle and all the cabin crew of G-BNLR *Rendezvous/Speedbird 2019* and G-CIVM *Nami Tsumu/Speedbird 2018*. Special mention must be made to Graham M. Simons of GMS Enterprises for compiling the book to press-ready standard and for his relentless pursuit of information and kind loan of several notable reference works on the 747. The majority of data and individual aircraft histories for the aircraft have been obtained from *Jet Airliner Production List*, produced by Messrs John R. Roach and A.B. Tony Eastwood. Copies are available from The Aviation Hobby Shop, 4 Horton Parade, Horton Road, West Drayton, Middlesex UB7 8EA. I am also indebted to Phil Kemp, an Air Britain historian, who very kindly supplied much information and photographs and who also 'beat the bushes' to find additional material and valuable contributors for me. The account entitled *Down to a Sunless Sea* is by kind permission of *The Log,* the BALPA journal, which very kindly allowed me to reproduce parts of the excellent article by Jack Diamond. Mike Rigg, a retired Cathay captain, kindly provided me with a most interesting account of flying into Kai Tak. I am no less grateful to all the following people, each of whom supplied me with an embarrassment of riches, time and expertise: Michael Austen; Dean Bantleman, Swissair; Philip J. Birtles: Chris Chatfield; Bryn Colton; Graham Dinsdale of Ian Allan Aviation Tours; Brian Foskett, chief photographer and Terry Holloway FRAeS, group support executive, Marshall Group of companies; Ron Green; Terry Grover, public relations officer, Singapore Airlines; Derek Harknett; Thomas Hempel, Assistant Manager PR, Cargolux; Robert Holder; Tom Hulse, Saltmarsh Partnership; Tim Kerss; David Lee; Tom Lubbesmeyer, Boeing archivist; Hans Leijte, KLM; Emma Med-Sygrove, Rolls-Royce plc; Gerry Manning; Scott M. McGuire, CSR, America West Airlines; Captain Eric Moody; Mrs Pat Moody; Tim Moore; Pascale Noordam, Public Relations, KLM Royal Dutch Airlines; Dennis Norman; Sergeant Jack Pritchard RAF PR; Barry Reeve; Mike Rondot; Jerry C. Scutts; Walt Truax; Judith Watson, public relations officer, Air New Zealand; and Camilla Wrey. Lastly, I must not forget the dedicated staff at the US Memorial Library in Norwich nor my good friend, Nigel McTeer who scanned a multitude of transparencies and devoted much of his time and unstinting energies in helping track down photos and stories.

All contributions, however large or small, have played an equal part in helping to produce what I hope is a fitting tribute to one of the world's greatest aircraft.

Martin W. Bowman

Bibliography

Baum, Brian. *Boeing 747-SP* (Great Airliners, Vol. 3). Osceola, WI: Motorbooks International.

Bauer, Eugene E. *Boeing: The First Century & Beyond,* TABA Publishing Inc, Issaquah, Washington 2006.

Birtles, Philip. *Boeing 747-400,* Hersham, Surrey: Ian Allen, 2000.

Bowers, Peter M. *Boeing Aircraft Since 1916.* London: Putnam Aeronautical Books, 1989.

Bowman, Martin. *Boeing 747* (Crowood Aviation Series). Marlborough, Wilts: Crowood, 2000.

Davies, R.E.G. *Delta - An Airline and Its Aircraft: The Illustrated History of a Major V.S. Airline and the People Who Made It.* McLean, VA: Paladwr Press, 1990.

Dorr, Robert F. *Boeing 747-400* (AirlinerTech Series, Vol. 10). North Branch, MN: Specialty Press, 2000.

Falconer, Jonathan. *Boeing 747 in Color,* Hersham, Surrey: Ian Allen, 1997.

Faith, Nicholas *Black Box: Inside the World's Worst Air Crashes* (Boxtree 1996).

Gesar, Adam. *Boeing 747: The Jumbo.* New York: Pyramid Media Group, 2000.

Gilchrist, Peter. *Boeing 747-400* (Airliner Color History). Osceola, WI: Motorbooks International, 1998.

Gilchrist, Peter. *Boeing 747 Classic* (Airliner Color History). Osceola, WI: Motorbooks International, 2000.

Graham, Ian. *In Control: How to Fly a 747.* Somerville, MA: Candlewick, 2000.

Haenggi, Michael. *Boeing Widebodies.* St. Paul, MN: MBI Publishing Co., 2003.

Henderson, Scott. *Boeing 747-100/200 In Camera.* Minneapolis, MN: Scoval Publishing, 1999.

Ingells, Douglas J. *747: Story of the Boeing Super Jet.* Fallbrook, CA: Aero Publishers, 1970.

Irving, Clive. *Wide Body: The Making of the Boeing 747.* Philadelphia: Coronet, 1994.

Itabashi, M. K. Kawata and S. Kusaka, '*Pre-fatigued 2219-T87 and 6061-T6 aluminium alloys.*' *Structural Failure: Technical, Legal and Insurance Aspects.* Milton Park, Abingdon, Oxon: Taylor & Francis, 1995.

Jenkins, Dermis R. *Boeing 747-100/200/300/SP* (AirlinerTech Series, Vol. 6). North Branch, MN: Specialty Press, 2000.

Jet Airliner Production List, Messrs John R. Roach and A.B. Tony Eastwood

Kane, Robert M. *Air Transportation: 1903-2003.* Dubuque, IA: Kendall Hunt Publishing Co., 2004.

Lee, David *Boeing, from Peashooter to Jumbo,* Chartwell Books, 1999.

Lucas, Jim. *Boeing 747 - The First 20 Years.* Browcom Publishing Ltd.

Lawrence, Philip K. and David Weldon Thornton. *Deep Stall: The Turbulent Story of Boeing Commercial Airplanes.* Burlington, VT: Ashgate Publishing Co., 2005.

March, Peter. *The Boeing 747 Story.* Stroud, Glos: The History Press, 2009.

Norris, Guy and Mark Wagner. *Boeing 747: Design and Development Since 1969.* St. Paul, MN: MBI Publishing Co., 1997.

Minton, David H. *The Boeing 747* (Aero Series 40). Fallbrook, CA: Aero Publishers, 1991.

Nicholls, Mark. *The Airliner World Book of the Boeing 747.* New York: Osprey Publishing, 2002.

Norton, Bill. *Lockheed Martin C-5 Galaxy.* North Branch, MN: Specialty Press, 2003.

Orlebar, Christopher. *The Concorde Story.* Oxford: Osprey Publishing, Fifth edition, 2002.

Pealing, Norman, and Savage, Mike. *Jumbo Jetliners: Boeing's 747 and the Widebodies* (Osprey Color Classics). Osceola, WI: Motorbooks International, 1999.

8

Pelletier, Alain *Boeing The Complete Story* Haynes Publishing 2010.
http://en.wikipedia.org/wiki/Boeing747
Seo, Hiroshi. *Boeing 747*, Worthing, West Sussex: Littlehampton Book Services Ltd., 1984.
Shaw, Robbie. *Boeing 747* (Osprey Civil Aircraft series). London: Osprey, 1994.
Shaw, Robbie. *Boeing 747-400: The Mega-Top* (Osprey Civil Aircraft)! London: Osprey. 1999.
Sutter, Joe 747: *Creating the World's First Jumbo Jet and Other Adventures from a Life in Aviation*. Washington. DC: Smithsonian Books, 2006.
Stanley Stewart *Air Disasters* (Ian Allan Ltd 1986, Arrow 1988).
Wilson, Stewart. *Boeing 747* (Aviation Notebook Series). Queanbeyan, NSW: Wilson Media Pty. Ltd.
Wilson, Stewart. *Airliners of the World*. Fyshwick, Australia: Aerospace Publications Pty Ltd., 1999.
Wright, Alan J. *Boeing 747*, Hersham, Surrey: Ian Allen, 1989.
The Great Gamble: The Boeing 747. The Boeing - Pan Am Project to Develop. Produce and Introduce the 747. Tuscaloosa: University of Alabama Press, 1973
Yenne, Bill *The Story of the Boeing Company,* Zenith Press, St Paul, MN 2005.

Anchorage Airport, Alaska on 8 August 1989. (Author)

747 Programme Chronology

1963

Spring — Engineering group is organized to plan an aircraft which will meet passenger and cargo growth predicted for the 1970s.

1966

March — Boeing board of directors decide to proceed on the 747 programme.

13 April — Pan American World Airways announces $525 million order for twenty-five Boeing 747s.

June — 780 acres acquired adjacent to Paine Field, Everett, Washington, for 747 manufacturing plant.

September — Airline orders for the 747 reach $1.8 billion.

1967

3 January — Production operations for 747 begin at the Everett plant.

1 May — Everett assembly building - the World's largest - is activated.

21 November — First nose section arrives at Everett from Wichita, Kansas. Components manufactured by major subcontractors begin to arrive.

1968

Mid-June — JT9D test engine flown by Pratt & Whitney on B-52 test-bed.

30 September — First 747 completed and rolled from factory.

November — Boeing announces a longer-range 747 capable of greater payloads, to be designated 747B. Freighter and convertible versions also to be offered.

1969

9 February — First flight of the 747-100 completed. Flight-test programme begins.

June — First 747-100 participates in the Paris Air Show.

30 December — Boeing 747 certificated by US Federal Aviation Administration for commercial passenger service.

1970

21 January — Boeing 747 commercial service by Pan American World Airways begins on the New York-London route.

16 July — Millionth passenger carried on 747s.

10 September — First 747-200B, the eighty-eighth 747 produced, rolled out at Everett.

11 October — First flight of the first 747-200.

12 November — 747-200B sets world heavyweight record, taking off from Edwards AFB, California at 820,700lb gross weight, 500,700lb being fuel, flight-test equipment and payload.

23 December — 747B certificated.

1971

January — 747 worldwide fleet accumulates 71 million miles in first year.

11 February — Boeing delivers line No.100 to US-based Braniff Airlines.

12 February — Boeing 747 equipped with fail-operative triple-autopilot system certificated for operation in Category IIIA conditions, with runway visual range only 700 feet or about three aircraft lengths.

26 February — One-hundredth 747 delivered.

June — 727-200 enters commercial service with KLM Royal Dutch Airlines.

July — First 747 to have extended upper deck (line number 147) handed over to QANTAS.

23 November — First 747-200 Freighter rolls out of the factory.

30 November — First flight of the first 747-200 Freighter.

December — Delivery of 747s with new sound-suppressing nacelles begins.

1972

8 March — First 747F freighter, for Lufthansa German Airlines, certificated.

19 April — 747-200 Freighter enters commercial service with Lufthansa.

| September | 747s log one million flight hours. |
| 30 October | Boeing announces it will produce short-range version of the 747, Japan Air Lines (JAL announces order for four of the new version, designated 747SR. |

1973

28 February	First 747-200 Convertible rolls out of the factory.
23 March	First flight of the first 747-200 Convertible.
17 April	747C convertible passenger-cargo airliner certificated by FM and delivered to World Airways, largest charter carrier.
18 April	First delivery of a JT9D-7 AW engine, capable of 46,950lb thrust (dry) or 48,750lb with water injection, fitted to -200B line number (the 200th 747 built) for El Al.
May	747-200 Convertible enters commercial service with US-based World Airways.
August	Boeing announces it is proceeding with development of a 'Special Performance' 747.
10 September	Pan American World Airways becomes the first airline to order the 747SP (Special Performance) extra-long-range jetliner.
7 October	First 747SR (Short Range) enters service with Japan Air Lines (JAL) between Tokyo and Naha, Okinawa.
30 October	First 747-200 Combi rolls out of the factory.

1974

15 February	SABENA Belgian World Airways is first carrier to get 747 with side cargo-door modification.
5 July	KLM-Royal Dutch Airlines orders first 800,000 lb gross weight 747B powered by General Electric CF6-50E engines.
11 November	First flight of the first 747-200 Combi.
29 December	QANTAS 747-238B City of Melbourne (fitted with 369 seats) evacuates 674 passengers (306 adults, 328 children and 40 infants) from Darwin to Sydney, following the devastation caused by Cyclone Tracy.

1975

7 March	747-200 Combi enters commercial service with Air Canada.
8 April	747 approved for thirty-two passengers on upper deck when fitted with left side upper deck emergency exit.
19 May	First 747SP (Special Performance) airliner rolls out.
27 June	British Airways orders 747s powered by Rolls-Royce RB211.524 engines rated at 50,100lb the third 747 engine-type option.
4 July	First 747SP makes initial flight, completing the 'most ambitious' test series ever by a Boeing jetliner. Top speed attained is Mach 0.92.
October	747 fleet carries 100-millionth passenger.
10 December	Boeing 747SP lands at Boeing Field, Seattle, completing a twenty-nine day, 72,152-mile worldwide demonstration tour with visits to eighteen cities in eighteen countries and three non-stop flights of more than 7,000 miles.

1976

4 February	747SP is certificated by the Federal Aviation Administration for commercial use.
5 March	First 747SP delivered, to Pan American World Airways.
24 March	A South African Airways 747SP lands in Cape Town following a 10,290-mile non-stop flight from Paine Field, Washington, setting a world distance record for commercial aircraft.
25 April	747SP enters commercial service with Pan Am
1-3 May	A new around-the-world record is set by a Pan American World Airways 747SP (*Clipper Liberty Bell*) when it lands at New York JFK airport after a two-stop, 22,864-mile flight. Elapsed time totalled 39 hours 26 minutes. En route stops were made at Delhi and Tokyo.
1 November	A new world record for maximum mass lifted to 6,562 feet was claimed for the 747 when a 747B powered by Rolls-Royce RB211 engines takes off from Lemoore Naval Air Station,

California, at 840,500lb and climbed to the required altitude in 6 minutes 33 seconds.

1977

18 February   Specially equipped 747 carries US space shuttle for the first time.

30 September   The worldwide fleet of more than 300 747s passes the five million flight-hours' mark.

28-30 October   Pan Am 747SP *Clipper New Horizons,* to mark Pan Am's fiftieth anniversary, sets a new speed record for an around-the-world flight, passing over both poles, in 54 hours 7 minutes and 12 seconds for the 26,706 mile flight, from John F. Kennedy Airport, New York and return, breaking the previous record established twelve years earlier by a modified 707 by 8 hours 20 minutes.

1978

21 December   First 747-100B delivered, to All Nippon Airways.

1979

11 October   400th delivery, a 747-200B to Aerolineas Argentinas.

21 December   100th main deck cargo 747 delivered; a 747C to Transamerica Airlines.

1980

31 January   First 550-passenger 747 delivered, an SR to Japan Air Lines (JAL).

11 June   Boeing announces a new version; the 747-300 (extended upper deck). First deliveries begin in 1983, to Swissair.

19 November   Boeing rolls out line No.500 from the factory, a 747-200 Combi delivered 17 February 1981 to Scandinavian Airlines System (SAS).

1981

15 December   Largest 747-300 order; eight for Singapore Airlines.

1982

21 September   First 747-300 rollout (Swissair livery); enters five-month flight-test.

5 October   First flight of the first 747-300.

1983

March   747-300s enter commercial service (Swissair and UTA - Union de Transportes Aeriens).

1984

July   Captain Lynn Rippelmeyer of PeoplExpress becomes the first woman to captain a 747 across the Atlantic.

1985

October   Boeing announces twelfth commercial version of the aircraft; the advanced-technology 747-400 will-roll out in early 1988, with first deliveries in late 1988.

1986

9 April   Boeing announces a 747-400 Combi version.

5 June   US Air Force orders two specially equipped 747-200s to transport the president of the United States.

1988

26 January   Roll out of the first 747-400 on same day as first 737-400.

January   Clay Lacy sets a 36 hour 54 minute around-the-world speed record in 747SP-21 N147UA (c/n. 21548) christened Friendship-One. The flight (routing through Seattle-Athens-Taipei-Seattle) raises more than $500,000 for children's charities of the world.

29 April   First flight of the PW4056-powered 747-400.

27 June   The first 747-400 set a new world record by taking off at a gross weight of 892,450lb.

1989

9 January   PW4056-powered 747-400 certificated by the FAA.

26 January   PW4056-powered 747-400 delivered to Northwest Airlines, entering service on the Phoenix-Minneapolis route on 9 February.

23 March   First 747-400 Combi rolls out of the factory.

18 May   First GE-powered 747-400 delivered to KLM.

26 May	747-400 completes the longest engineering flight in Boeing Commercial Aircraft history, lasting more than fourteen hours as cruise performance is evaluated.
8 June	Cathay Pacific received first Rolls-3oyce-powered 747-400.
June	First 747-400 Combi completed. First flight completed on 30 June.
12 September	747-400 Combi enters commercial service with KLM.
13 September	747-400F programme launched.

1990

28 March	First 747-100 enters semi-retirement at Museum of Flight in Seattle.
August	Boeing delivers first of two presidential 747-200s to the US Air Force.
August 1990- March 1991	747s participate in operation 'Desert Storm', carrying 644,000 troops and 220,000 tons of equipment to and from the Middle East as part of a United Nations' effort to restore peace in the region.

1991

18 February	First 747-400 Domestic rolls out of the factory.
18 March	First 747-400D (Domestic) (for JAL), the 844th 747 built, flies for the first time.
22 March	747-400D enters commercial service with JAL.
During the year	As part of Operation 'Solomon' El Al 747-200C Combi, specially converted to passenger configuration with 760 seats, carries more than 1,200 Ethiopian Jewish settlers from Addis Ababa to Tel Aviv, Israel in Operation Solomon, a top secret operation to airlift 14,000 Ethiopian Jews to Israel before the Ethiopian capital fell to rebel troops. Two other standard passenger-configured El Al 747s, with normal seating for 454, carry 920 passengers each. The rest of the operation is carried out using four 767s, two 757s and eight Israeli Air Force 707s.

1992

December 1992-	747s participate in Operation 'Restore Hope', transporting 13,609 troops on a United Nations' mission to Somalia.
January 1993-	

1993

25 February	First 747-400F (the 968th 747 built) rolled out at Everett.
8 March	First 747-400 Freighter rolls out of the factory.
4 May	First flight of the 747-400F (for Cargolux).
10 September	Rollout for the 1,000th 747 (a 747-400 for Singapore Air Lines) at Everett.
12 October	Boeing delivers line No.1000 to Singapore Airlines.
17 November	747-400 Freighter enters commercial service with Luxemburg's Cargolux Airlines.

1996

January	Boeing delivers 1,100th 747, a 747-400, to Virgin Atlantic Airways and Los-Angeles-based International Lease Finance Corp.

1997

23 April	Boeing and Lufthansa celebrate the 25th anniversary of the first 747-200 Freighter delivery.

1998

6 July	Cathay Pacific's 747-467 B-HUJ first airliner to land at Hong Kong's new Chek Lap Kok International Airport, after a record-breaking world distance record for the longest commercial flight, from New York, over the North Pole, a distance of over 6,582 miles, lasting 15 hours and 24 minutes.
30 September	Boeing celebrates 30th anniversary of the first 747-100 to roll out of the Everett factory. A new 747 slogan is revealed at the ceremony: *'Boeing 747 - The Leader, The Legend.'*
30 October	Boeing and British Airways celebrate the delivery of the airline's 50th 747-400.
19 November	Boeing and Japan Airlines celebrate the delivery of the airline's 100th 747.

1999

15 February	Boeing celebrates completion of digitizing the 747 fuselage and utilizing new fuselage tooling, a four-year effort that results in simplified assembly and improved quality.
17 February	Boeing delivers 1,200th 747, a 747-400 to British Airways.
22 April	United Airlines takes delivery of its 75th 747.
10 August	Major assembly begins on first 747-400 Freighter to be used as platform for US Air Force's Airborne Laser programme.
15 November	US Postal Service unveils 747 postage stamp, which Boeing places on its factory doors: world's largest stamp on world's largest building that produces world's largest commercial aircraft.

2000

28 November	Boeing launches newest member of the 747 Family, the Longer-Range 747-400, with an order from QANTAS.
14 December	Factory rollout of China Airlines 747-400 Freighter, 2000's 15th 747-400 Freighter, a new single-year record.

2001

30 April	Boeing launches second member of its Longer-Range 747-400 Family - the 747-400ER Freighter - with an order from International Lease Finance Corporation (ILFC).
15 May	ANA selects Boeing to convert two ANA 747-400s from its International three-class 367-seat configuration to its two-class, 569-seat domestic configuration.
18 December	Boeing engineers complete 90 percent of the design work for both the passenger and freighter versions of the new Longer-Range 747-400 family.

2002

11 February	Boeing workers load the 747's forward section floor grid into an assembly tool, marking the start of major assembly for the 747-400ER.
17 June	Thousands of Boeing employees gather in the world's largest building to celebrate rollout of the first 747-400ER.
18 July	First flight of the YAL-1A, a 747-400F modified by Boeing for the US Air Force as a platform for a powerful airborne chemical oxygen iodine laser (COIL) that can potentially be used to destroy enemy missiles flying at several times the speed of sound.
31 July	First flight of the 747-400ER begins a three-month flight test programme that will culminate with certification and delivery to launch customer QANTAS Airways.
17 October	Delivery of first 747-400ER freighter to Air France (financed by International Finance Lease Corporation).
31 October	Delivery of first 747-400ER passenger version to QANTAS Airways.

2005

14 November	Boeing launches the 747-8 Family -- the 747-8 Intercontinental passenger airliner and the 747-8 Freighter - with orders from Cargolux and Nippon Cargo Airlines.

2006

31 October	Boeing completes firm configuration for 747-8 Freighter.
6 December	Lufthansa becomes first airline to order 747-8 Intercontinental.

2007

10 March	Orders for Boeing 747 surpass 1,500.
7 November	Boeing completes firm configuration for 747-8 Intercontinental.

2008

28 February	Boeing delivers 1,400th 747 to GECAS for lease to AirBridgeCargo Airlines.
8 August	Boeing starts major assembly of the first 747-8 Freighter.
12 November	First 747-8 Freighter rolls out of the factory.

2010

8 February	First 747-8 Freighter completes first flight.

14

| 8 May | Assembly begins on first 747-8 Intercontinental. |

2011

| 20 March | 747-8 makes first test flight. |
| 12 October | -8F first delivered, to Cargolux |

2012

| May | First 747-8I delivered, to Lufthansa. |
| 2012 | Boeing buybacks help 747-8 customers avoid recording losses on older planes they would otherwise struggle to sell amid a global glut of used jumbos. About 75 747s are parked in deserts around the world and valuations tumble. A 1992-vintage 747-400 that was appraised at $41.6 million in January 2008 is valued at $16.7 million now. Boeing buys Airbus A340s no longer in production from China Eastern Airlines (CEA), which is taking 20 Boeing 777s in a $6 billion deal. |

2013

| June | Korean Air, which has sold six 747400s to Boeing since 2010 agrees to buy five 747-8s as part of a planned $3.6 billion aircraft purchase. The carrier is the second-largest global operator of the 747-400 and one of the biggest buyers of the latest version of the 747-8. |
| August | Businessweek reports that potential buyers for the 747-8 are dwindling as cargo companies increasingly ship freight by rail or in the bellies of passenger versions of large twin-engine jets such as Boeing's 777s. With 53 unfilled 747-8 orders, Boeing has enough work to keep the 747-8 production line busy through the end of 2015. Boeing acquires previous versions of the 747 from airlines ordering the 747-8 (Korean Air Lines, Cathay Pacific Airways, Cathay's Dragonair and its cargo joint venture with Air China). Of the 19 older 747s that change hands, Boeing snaps up seven, which makes Boeing the biggest buyer of the used jets in 2013. |

Introduction

If It Isn't Boeing, We Aren't Going!

The Boeing Company was founded by William E. Boeing, the son of a wealthy timberman. At the age of thirty-four, Boeing took up flying for his own amusement, but after a couple of rides he became convinced that he could build a better aeroplane. He and Commander G. Conrad Westervelt, a Navy officer assigned to engineering work at a Seattle shipyard, Washington, decided to build a pair of seaplanes. By December 1915, an aeroplane called the 'B & W Seaplane' was under construction in a hangar on the east shore of Lake Union. Bluebird, the first B & W, was completed in early 1916, marking the modest beginning of aircraft production at the Boeing Company; it flew for the first time on 29 June.

Although aircraft work had been in progress since 1915, corporate identity was not achieved until the Pacific Aero Products Company was incorporated on 15 July 1916 and a new airline subsidiary, Boeing Air Transport, was formed. On 26 April 1917 the name was changed to The Boeing Airplane Company. The Seattle factory redesigned their 1925 Model 40 to take the new, air-cooled Wasp engine and built twenty-four Model 40As in just six months, ready for service with the new airline. Its competitors, meanwhile, continued to use the heavier, water-cooled Liberty-engined aircraft for mail service. In addition to having space for 1,200lb of air mail, the Model 40A had room for two passengers in a small cabin ahead of the pilot's open cockpit; later models carried four passengers. A total of eighty-two Model 40s were built. Their introduction signalled the beginning of regular commercial passenger service over long distances and served as the vehicle for the first regular passenger and night mail flights.

The success of the passenger operations with Model 40s on the San Francisco-Chicago route encouraged expansion of the business through the addition of larger aircraft designed specifically for passenger convenience and comfort. In 1928 Pacific Air Transport (PAT), a San Francisco to Seattle airline was purchased and the two airlines were merged to become 'The Boeing System'. The first of four Model 80 tri-motor biplanes, the last word in air transportation, was delivered to Boeing Air Transport in August 1928, only two weeks after its first flight. Twelve passengers - and later, eighteen - were carried in a large cabin provided with hot and cold running water, a toilet, forced air ventilation, leather upholstered seats and individual reading lamps. The needs of a dozen or more passengers during long flights soon indicated the desirability of a full-time cabin attendant who could devote all his/her attention to their comfort. While some European airlines used male stewards, Boeing Air Transport hired female registered nurses who became the first of the now-universal stewardesses. The pilot and co-pilot were enclosed in a roomy cabin ahead of and separate from the passenger cabin.

In 1909, Edward Heath constructed a wooden boat shipyard on the Duwamish River in Seattle. Heath soon became insolvent, and William Boeing, for whom Heath was building a hugely expensive and luxurious yacht, bought the shipyard and land for ten dollars during 1917, in exchange for Boeing's acceptance of Heath's debts. Building No. 105, also known as the Red Barn was part of that package. The Boeing Company began producing aircraft from the simple barn-like structure.

Boeing, meanwhile, expanded rapidly. In February 1929 it acquired the Hamilton Metalplane Co. of Milwaukee, Wisconsin and that summer established a Canadian subsidiary (Boeing Aircraft of Canada) in Vancouver, Canada, where it began building C-204 flying boats. A powerful holding company was formed with the merger of the Boeing airplane and airline operations and Pratt & Whitney, a leading airplane engine manufacturer, Hamilton Aero Manufacturing Company and another airplane manufacturer, Chance Vought Corporation, to form United Aircraft and Transport Corporation. Each company continued to produce its own specialized product under its own name, while the airlines operated under their own names within a holding company known as United Airlines. Three airlines were acquired and added to the existing operation, while the manufacturing companies Sikorsky Aviation and Standard Steel Propeller Co. were bought up. On 1 April 1938 the Boeing Aircraft Company bought the Wichita, Kansas-based Stearman Aircraft Co. to create the Stearman Aircraft Division (renamed the Wichita Division in 1941).

When markets for new airplane designs developed, Boeing was ready with new models and processes. It was the first American manufacturer to use welded steel tubing for fuselage structure, a feature that soon became standard throughout the industry until generally replaced by monocoque sheet-metal structures in the mid-1930s. Boeing again demonstrated its technological leadership by introducing this new construction, matched to aerodynamically advanced airplanes, in both commercial and military production with the Monomail, B-9 and 247 models of 1930-1933.

The all-metal Model 200 Monomail mail and cargo carrier first flew on 6 May 1930: it was one of the most revolutionary airplanes in commercial aviation history. Designed initially as a combination mail and passenger airplane, its increased performance resulted from structural and aerodynamic refinements, not from the addition of brute horsepower. The traditional biplane design with drag-producing struts and wires was replaced by a single, smooth, all-metal low wing of clean cantilever construction. The wheels were retracted into the wing during flight and the drag of the air-cooled 'Hornet' engine was greatly reduced by enclosing it in a newly developed anti-drag cowling. However, the Monomail's sleek aerodynamic design was too advanced for the power-plants of the day. Efficient use of its full

The Boeing 247 is often claimed to be the first modern airliner, which first took to the air on 8 February 1933. The first Model 247 is seen below, carrying the experimental registration X-13301 and the Boeing Air transport logo. The interior of the 247 featured a pair of steps over the main wing spar which passed through the passenger cabin.

performance range required a variable-pitch propeller and when one was eventually installed, the aircraft was already on the verge of being replaced by the newer, multi-engined designs it had inspired.

Boeing Models 214 and 215, which became the US Army Y1B-9 and YB-9, were logical military developments of the Monomail. Boeing embarked on the two B-9 projects as a private venture in the hope that they would produce the same performance advance in the area of heavy bombers as the Monomail had done in the commercial sector; but the type was not ordered in quantity. The B-9 did, however, prove a major advance in bomber design and it greatly influenced the Model 247, the first airliner produced in quantity by Boeing.

An unprecedented decision was made to completely re-equip the Boeing Air Transport System with the innovative new twelve-seater transport and an order for sixty Model 247s was placed while the design was still in the mock-up stage. The Model 247 was the first all-metal, streamlined monoplane transport. It was powered by two supercharged Pratt and Whitney 550hp S1D1 Wasps (the first time superchargers had been used on a transport type) and featured a retractable landing gear, an enclosed cabin, autopilot, trim tabs and de-icing equipment. In 1934 Congress passed legislation which forced aircraft and engine manufacturers to end all their links with airline operations.[1] In the 1930s it was accepted that a formation of unescorted bombers could

get through to their target if they were properly arranged and adequately armed. During air manoeuvres in 1933, pursuits repeatedly failed to intercept the bombers and there was even talk of eliminating pursuits altogether. Funds for new aircraft were very limited and mostly it was manufacturers who funded new developments which in turn might attract orders from the military.[2] Boeing's first bomber development, in 1934, was the massive Model 294, or the XBLR-1 (experimental bomber, long range), which became the XB-15. That same year the Air Corps issued a specification for a 'multi-engined' bomber, but manufacturers would have to build prototypes at their own expense. Although the term 'multi-engined' generally meant two engines, the four-engined Model 299 was already in the design stage and so on 16 September 1934, Boeing decided boldly to invest $275,000 in the Model 299. The new design, which was to become famous in World War II as the B-17, incorporated many lessons learned with the X-15, B-9 and Model 247. Powered by four 750hp Pratt and Whitney 'Hornet' radials, it would carry all bombs internally and accommodate a crew of eight. Thirteen service-test Y1B-17s went into service with the AAC and established many long-distance records, earning Boeing a well deserved reputation for rugged construction and reliable operation.

One of Boeing's biggest pre-war customers, who would prove fundamental to the success of Boeing

Early in 1936 the beautiful Model 314 was designed to meet a specification issued by Pan American Airways for a long-range, four-engined flying boat capable of carrying seventy-four passengers and a crew of six to ten. Boeing signed an agreement on 21 July 1936 for six 314s, or 'Clippers' as they were known and they were all delivered between January and June 1939. Six 314As followed for PAA, with more powerful engines and provision for three extra passengers and the first six 314s were brought up to the same standard. NC18602 42-88632 California Clipper (pictured) was operated by the US Army in World War II. The last flight of a Pacific Pan Am Clipper was on 8-9 April 1946 when NC-18606 American Clipper took off from Honolulu for Mills Field, San Francisco. The last Atlantic flight was on 24 December 1945. Post-war, the 'Clippers' were replaced by landplane types. (Boeing)

18

The Model 377 Stratocruiser was an airline development of the C-97 and 56 were built between 1947 and 1949. Pan American World Airways was the largest Stratocruiser operator, with twenty-nine Model 377s; Model 377-10-26 N1030V Clipper Southern Cross is pictured. Ten PM-26s were modified to Super Stratocruisers by adding an additional 450 gallons of fuel to permit non-stop flights between New York and London and Paris. Stratocruisers offered the last word in passenger comfort and fifty-five to a hundred-plus people could be accommodated according to the length of the route and the type of service. A complete galley for hot meal service was located near the tail and men's and women's washrooms separated the forward compartments from the main passenger cabin, where a spiral stairway led to a deck lounge on the lower deck behind the wing. When fitted out as a sleeper aircraft, the 377 was equipped with twenty-eight upper and lower berth units plus five seats. (Boeing)

airliners for decades to come was Pan American Airways, headed by Juan Terry Trippe, a wily, very clever businessman who had first learned to fly in World War I. Trippe followed a series of successful mergers by creating Pan Am in 1928, after winning highly profitable air-mail routes to the Caribbean. He then followed this with another merger in 1930, which led to Pan Am gaining lucrative contracts to carry air mail on his Fokker Tri-Motors and Sikorsky S-38 flying boats between the US and South America. In 1932 Pan American ordered its first four-engined flying boats when it took delivery of three Sikorsky S-42s and three Martin M-130s for forty-eight passengers. Soon, delivering air mail accounted for three-quarters of the company's revenues. In the mid-1930s Trippe expanded

Pan Am's operations to include the Pacific. Pan American Airways was the first big carrier to fly regular long-distance flights and quickly became the world's largest passenger airline as well as air-mail carrier. In 1936 Trippe ordered twelve Boeing B-314 flying boats, called 'Pullmans of the sky'. Each was capable of carrying seventy-four passengers and was fitted out with sleeping berths and dining areas. All twelve flying boats were called 'Clippers' and had romantic names such as *California Clipper* and *Pacific Clipper;* collectively they were known as 'China Clippers'. By the eve of World War II Pan Am World Airways were flying to London via Newfoundland and Lisbon and Marseilles via the Azores. During the war, Pan Am became the largest civilian troop carrier and almost all its energy was directed to assisting the war effort. Post-war, Trippe invested heavily in new aircraft and soon they were flying to every continent. As history was to show, Trippe, always committed to revolutionizing commercial aviation, would take every opportunity to invest in new aircraft and it was Boeing that would benefit most in the post-war years and beyond.

Following World War II, Boeing re-entered the commercial airliner market, starting in 1947 with the Model 377 Stratocruiser which was produced side by side with B-50s on the Seattle production lines until 1949. Throughout the late 1940s and 1950s, the Boeing Aircraft Company faced a challenge from other giants in the US aviation industry, notably Douglas, first with its DC-6, 6A and 6B designs and Lockheed, initially with its Constellation and then Super Constellation designs, for pre-eminence in the four-engined turboprop commercial transport market.

Boeing entered the jet age with the roll-out on 12 September 1947 of the XB-47 experimental pure-jet bomber prototype. It could be said that the first steps towards the 747 began with the B-47 Stratojet, with its podded engines and new thin wing, swept back at an angle of 35 degrees at the quarter-chord point, although the bomber was originally conceived by Boeing

engineers as a straight-wing design with buried engines. In part the swept-back wing shape owed much to the German jet designers in World War II.[3] Sweep angles as high as 45 degrees allowed a significant increase in speed by delaying the formation of shock waves as the wing approached the speed of sound. The buried engine layout of the XB-47 was also abandoned after objections from the US Army Air Force regarding its vulnerability and safety. Instead, the six 3,750lb thrust General Electric J-35 engines were hung under the wings in pods.

Whilst Boeing undoubtedly benefited from the German research into swept-wing design, the company had the added advantage of having its own high-speed wind tunnel which it had finished building in 1944 at a cost of $750,000. This enabled Boeing to test, remedy and perfect the B-47 swept-wing design and further exploit its lead in wing technology over other aircraft manufacturers. In appearance Boeing's final foray into the super bomber business - the B-52 Stratofortress - owed much to the B-47. Another feature of the B-47 which was later to be used on the 747 was the use of a multiple undercarriage layout, which on the B-47 was in tandem. Both the main two-wheel bogies, or trucks, were located on the centreline of the fuselage, ground

Boeing development of a jet bomber began in 1943 and the Model 450 was approved in April 1946. 46-065 being rolled out on 12 September 1947, was the first of the two XB-47 prototypes to fly, on 17 December 1947. The first steps towards the 747 began with the B-47 Stratojet with its podded engines and new thin wing, swept back at an angle of 35 degrees at the quarter-chord point. The second XB-47 flew in July 1948 with the more powerful General Electric J47 powerplant of 5,200lb of thrust in place of the earlier J35s of only 3,750lb of thrust. Altogether 2,032 B-47s were built, including 1.373 by Boeing. (Boeing)

stability being provided by outrigger wheels that retracted into the inboard nacelles, whilst the 747 was to have several sets of gear beneath the fuselage.[4]

Not for the first time in Boeing's illustrious history - and certainly not for the last - the company's next logical step up from the B-47 was to adapt its design to that of a new long-range jet-powered aircraft intended as a military tanker, but with clearly significant commercial possibilities. Of course, this source of development was nothing new in the aviation industry and, as has been seen, it was certainly not a new undertaking for Boeing. The company had long derived some very successful (and some less than successful) commercial designs from its corresponding military conversion programme. In this case though, Boeing would be gambling on a pure-jet airliner for the first time.

When Boeing engineer Wellwood Beall had

returned to Seattle from Britain in 1950, he brought news with him that the de Havilland Company had developed a medium-range jet airliner called the Comet. Though the British jet never realized its potential, Beall and the other Boeing engineers knew that jet transport would revolutionize air travel. Propeller-driven transports such as Boeing's C-97 Stratofreighter were approaching their performance limits and the combination of high speed and cost efficiency of the jet made long-distance air travel more practical.

Never afraid to take a gamble when the time was right (such a risk had paid off twenty years before with the B-17), in August 1952 Boeing announced that it was investing $16 million of its own money (two-thirds of the company's net profits from the post-war years) to build the prototype of an entirely new jet-powered transport. This was on the assumption that if Boeing did not build it, Douglas probably soon would and the

The Boeing Dash 80 - seen in the company colours of chocolate and yellow - passing over the Olympic Peninsula in Washington State.

aircraft was developed by Boeing in secrecy to protect its market. The prototype was designated Model 367-80, to disguise it as merely an improved version of the C-97. The Model 367 Stratofreighter was in production for the air force as the C-97, but the Model 367-80 was so far advanced that it bore no resemblance whatever to the cargo-transport; in fact, '80' referred to the number of study configurations that the Model 367 had finally arrived at. The 'Dash-Eighty', as the Boeing technicians called it, retained the B-47's 35-degree wing sweepback and its podded engine layout, although the latter were no longer hung in a two pairs and two singles arrangement: instead, the six GE turbojets had been replaced by four separately hung Pratt & Whitney JT3s, each capable of 10,000 lb of thrust.

Although for engineering and shop purposes the designation 367-80 was retained by Boeing, the number 707 which was later applied to the prototype came about as a result of Boeing's sequential model development numbering system that dates back to 1916. Seven has

always been a lucky number throughout the long and distinguished history of the Boeing Company, starting with the Model 247 and continuing to the B-47 jet bomber and the 707, 727 and 737 series commercial airliners. Each was an innovative and far-reaching design which met the technological demands of new and distant horizons and then surpassed them, setting the standard for others to follow. By 1951, the Boeing model numbers had been divided into large blocks among the company's various product lines, so the number assigned to the anticipated production versions of the 'Dash-Eighty' was in the 700 block (the 400, 500 and 600 series were already assigned to missiles and non-aircraft blocks). The number 707 chosen for the 367-80 thereby established the numbers for the 727, 737 and 747 series that would follow and become famous.

The 707's chief engineer was Maynard Pennell, a specialist in airframe structures, who after World War II had joined Boeing from Douglas, where he had formed an affinity for commercial airliners. Pennell was

The flightline at Boeing Renton during the heyday of the 727. Contracts for the Model 727-100 short-to-medium-range jet were signed in December 1960; this was to replace the many piston and turboprop aircraft in service. The first 727 designated 727-22. (N7001U for United Airlines), was rolled out at Renton on 27 November 1962. Some 408 727-100s were built. Originally Boeing planned to build 250 727s, but they proved so popular that a total of 1,832 aircraft - through -100, -100C and -200 - were produced at the Renton plant. The 737, which appeared in April 1967, proved another big money-spinner with no fewer than 1,114 -200s (which followed the thirty -100 models) being delivered by August 1988.

As first conceived, the 747 was seen only as a larger subsonic 'stop-gap' until in the late 1970s an anticipated 1,250 supersonic (SST) jets - such as the Boeing Model 733, 2707-200, seen here in mock-up form - took over the intercontinental passenger market completely; this left the 747s to be converted for use as large freighters. The US SST programme was abandoned in 1971.

determined to steer Boeing, which traditionally relied on producing bombers, towards becoming a prime supplier of jet airliners. He set out to bring together all that was best in Boeing's high-speed, sub-sonic jet development, gained from building bombers and to use it to help devise the company's first commercial jetliner. Pennell and colleague Jack Steiner, another advocate of jet airliners who went on to design the 727, had first evolved the 473-60C, a half-size airliner version of the B-47. This was never built.

When this failed to convince potential buyers, who preferred instead the propeller-driven Douglas DC-7C, Pennell knew that Boeing had to offer something more than adaptations of military designs. As in the case of the 747 a generation later, Pennell had to demonstrate that by using a combination of Boeing's unquestioned lead in swept-wing technology married to an aerodynamic body, he would produce an airliner so economical and so far ahead of anything else that no airline, no matter how radical the design, could ignore it. Backed by the president of the Boeing Airplane Company, William 'Bill' M. Allen, Pennell and his engineers did precisely that.

The American jet transport era can be said to have begun when the 367-80 first flew on 15 July 1954. From this date forward Boeing all but made the long-haul and the short-to-medium-range markets their very own, with a succession of hugely successful air transports. Douglas,

ever cautious, belatedly tried to catch up with its new rival, announcing in June 1955 that it was entering the long-range jet transport field with the not dissimilar DC-8; but it was too late to mount a serious challenge to the 707. By the end of 1961 just 176 DC-8s had been sold, while Boeing raced ahead, selling 320 707s and 720s (the 720 being a derivative design of the 707). The first customer was Pan American, a company which, under the steermanship of Juan Trippe, had never been afraid to buy and to buy big. The fact that no other airline in the US dared risk investment in the new jets - especially following the crashes, early in 1954, of two of the first BOAC Comet jet airliners to fly - seemed to spur Trippe on. In September 1955 he committed Pan Am to the purchase of twenty-five Douglas DC-8-31s (later reduced to nineteen) and on 13 October he placed an order with Boeing for six 707-121s. 'People thought we were crazy' said Trippe; in fact the airline became the first to place the 707 in service, on 26 October 1958. It is due to Trippe, first and foremost, that the commercial jet-airliner business really took off when it did.

Boeing's big gamble had paid off. Many of the design features - such as the Kreuger leading-edge flap, 14 feet x 12 feet installed inboard of the outboard engine pods to extend automatically when the main flaps were lowered 9.5 degrees - were adopted for use on later 700 series jetliners, right up to and including the 747.

Between 1957 and 1982 Boeing delivered 855

Model 707s in all three versions: the 707-120, the -320 and the -420 intercontinental airliners and no fewer than 725 of these aircraft, delivered between 1957 and 1978, were for commercial use. Boeing's smaller medium-range jet transports, the 727-100 and the -200, also out-performed their rivals in numbers built. Originally Boeing planned to build only 250 of the aircraft, but they proved so popular that a total of 1,832 were produced at the Renton plant. Only 153 720s were built, but the 737, which appeared in April 1967, proved to be another big money-spinner with no fewer than 1,114 -200s (which followed the thirty -100 models) being delivered by August 1988. Ultimately the 737 family (the 737-300 entered production in March 1981) out-stripped sales of the Douglas DC-9 and became the world's best-selling jet airliner.

If the introduction of the 707 had been innovative, the appearance of the 747, the first of the giant jetliners, had its inception in the early 1960s when market research indicated the need for a much larger capacity subsonic transport to cope with the growing passenger and cargo traffic of the 1970s. Boeing had always maintained its position as a leading supplier of commercial aircraft, backed by a safety net that if all else failed; its financial and managerial risk-taking initiative could always be vindicated by converting a design to meet a military requirement. The last time that risk-taking had occurred on this scale was when the company went out on a limb with its Model 299, which only eventually emerged as the famous wartime B-17 after a protracted and nerve-racking development phase when its competitors prospered for a while with less

innovative designs. Privately funded, the Flying Fortress, in turn, led to airliner derivatives. Now, thirty years on, the 747, like its famous forbear, was to be built using company funds - although there was no immediate prospect of a military derivative to placate the accountants if the figures did not break even. This at least had been an option with the ground-breaking 707, the last commercial design to break the mould in airline transportation.

By August 1965 a preliminary 747 design group had been formed, followed by project authorization in March 1966. A firm design proposal was offered to the airlines in early 1966. A logical outgrowth of the Boeing 707 series, the 747 not only built on the reputation of its forbears, but improved the breed to such a degree that a new name, 'Jumbo Jet', was coined by the press - and the name stuck. There had never been anything quite like the Jumbo Jet and even the nickname rang alarm bells in competitors' hearts - even though at Boeing the 747, as first conceived, was seen only as a larger subsonic 'stop-gap' until the Utopian daydream of the supersonic jet arrived on the horizon. Of course the Anglo-French Concorde carved a supersonic niche all of its own, but the 747 achieved what no other airliner, supersonic or otherwise, could ever have hoped to achieve: it opened up global air travel for the common man at prices undreamt of in the 1940s and 1950s, when transatlantic travel was the preserve of the rich and famous.

Everything about the 747 was larger than life, not least the development cost. The prize: untold riches and undreamt of capacity that no other plane maker could really challenge or meet, either technologically or

By August 1965 a preliminary 747 design group had been formed, followed by project authorization in March 1966. A firm design proposal was offered to the airlines in early 1966. The vast difference in size between the 707 and the 747 is never better illustrated than in this photo of the two famous airliners at Seattle. (Boeing)

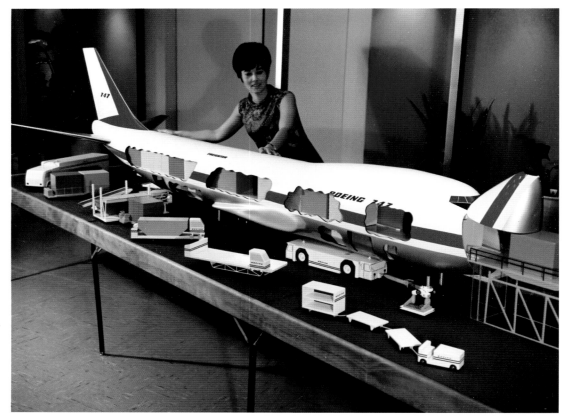

Boeing assumed that a large proportion of 747 sales would be for the cargo version which is why it was designed with the cockpit perched on top of the single deck so that that there would be room for a nose door big enough to load two 8 feet x 8 feet containers side by side into the cavernous cargo-hold, as this model shows. Pan Am argued repeatedly for the main deck to have a hinged nose section to permit straight-through cargo loading. (Boeing)

financially. Unhappily for them, if the new wide body succeeded, they would have to compete in an arena even more unfamiliar to them than the one that now confronted Boeing. As events were to prove, ultimately the only alternatives for Boeing's competitors were to merge and/or to diversify into other markets and leave the Seattle giant to make the gamble and the running.

Footnotes for Introduction

1   On 26 September, a government trust-busting suit, which divorced airplane and engine manufacturers from airline operations, had separated United Aircraft's airline and manufacturing activities and the Boeing Aircraft Company - renamed from the Boeing Airplane Company and a separate entity from Boeing Air Transport - had pulled out of United. The Boeing Aircraft Company resumed independent operation and moved into the bomber business.

2   By 1934 Model 247 production was winding down and the only business Boeing had was unfinished contracts for P-26A, and P-26C fighters. In August, 1,100 of its 1,700 workforce were laid off: cash on hand was barely $500,000.

3   Three of Boeing's leading engineers, Bert Kineman, George Martin and George Schairer, were part of Operation 'Seahorse', a US exploitation team led by Theodore van Karman, the renowned aeronautical engineer and physicist, which uncovered wind-tunnel data into swept wings at the German Aeronautical Research Institute near Brunswick at the end of April 1945.

4   The first of two prototype XB-47s flew from Boeing Field, Seattle, to nearby Moses Lake AFB on 17 December 1947. The second XB-47 flew in July 1948 with the more powerful General Electric J47 powerplant of 5,200lb of thrust in place of the earlier J35s of only 3,750lb of thrust. Major production began with the B-47B, which flew for the first time at Wichita on 26 April 1951.

Chapter 1

The Start Of it All

The 747 or something like it has to happen.

Joe Sutter, Boeing Chief of Technology.

Throughout aviation history some of those designs which failed to enter full-scale production, or which lost out to rival models, have been successfully reinvented to emerge as the format for a completely new type of aircraft. So it was with the 747, whose origins can be traced back to the early sixties when the US Air Force Military Air Transport Service sought an all-new high-capacity airlifter to increase significantly its airlift capacity in south-east Asia and throughout the world. In 1962 Project Forecast was established to gather data from academia and aerospace companies on the possibilities of giant airlifters and engine technologies to power them. At the same time the air travel industry was growing at a staggering 15 per cent per year and it was obvious to carriers such as Pan Am and to aircraft companies such as Boeing and Douglas that the 707 and DC-8 would have to be enlarged or even replaced by much larger commercial types.

The competition to build the all-new high-capacity airlifter, now named the CX-HLS, began in 1962. Established rivals Boeing, Douglas and Lockheed immediately announced their intention to enter designs, which had to be capable of carrying 750 fully equipped troops anywhere in the world. Equal emphasis was of course placed on engine manufacturers General Electric (GE) and Pratt & Whitney, who had to design and build

The 707 was a success, as can be seen here by the flightline at Renton. Boeing managed to stay ahead of its rivals Douglas and Convair with the 707, but the 747 would be a massive leap forward.

massive powerplants capable of around 40,000lb thrust per engine. The turbojet had been the main powerplant used to power airliners such as the first generation 707s and DC-8s and more recently the turbofan was being introduced on the 707 - but now, new engine concepts involving more powerful and quieter high-bypass-ratio engines would have to be perfected. Turbofans generate much more thrust by passing large volumes of air through a fan at the front of the engine. The fan is driven by the core of the engine and is basically similar to the original turbojet's core, but what was revolutionary was that a large amount of the fan-driven air 'bypassed' the core and went straight to the exhaust through an annular duct that enclosed the core. This results in greater thrust, while at the same time the bypass air wraps itself around the core, providing insulation to cushion the sound of the noisy jet blast. All in all, high-bypass-ratio engines produce a quieter, cleaner, more fuel-efficient and less smoky powerplant than the turbojet.

During the early 1960s Boeing stayed ahead of Douglas in the airline market by introducing short-haul and medium-range developments of the 707 series with models such as the 720 (165 seats), the 727- 100 (70-114 seats) and the 737 (88-113 seats), while the 707 (189 seats) maintained its unassailable position in the global arena by courtesy of a programme of continual improvement. This resulted in even bigger and better versions - but there comes a point when an aircraft design, even one as good as the 707, can go no further due to its structure and engine thrust limitations. So it proved ultimately with the 707, the 707-320 intercontinental proving the last of the famous breed. Compared to the DC-8's tall main landing gear, the 707's gear was lower off the ground, so the potential to 'stretch' the overall 707 design to increase passenger volume was immediately reduced. On the other hand, the Douglas airliner now enjoyed a decisive advantage over its more illustrious swept-wing rival because it was found that the DC-8-50 (117-173 seats) could be stretched more easily - by 36.9 feet - and so the famous

Before Sutter's appointment to head the 747 project it seemed that the new airliner would have a double-decker fuselage with six-abreast seating. However, this layout would have affected emergency evacuation procedures - it would have been extremely difficult to get passengers out, given the height of the upper deck from the ground. A mid-wing design meant that the main spar would run through the middle of the passenger cabin with all the attendant problems it caused, while the low-wing concept made the cabin look ungainly and top-heavy. Another model revealed three engines instead of four, mounted in the empennage topped by a high T-tail while yet another had the flight deck situated under the passenger cabin. Sutter completely disregarded the 'turkeys' as he called them.

The Pratt & Whitney JT9D engine (seen here on RA001 City of Everett) was characterized by the enormous front fan measuring 8 feet in diameter.

Super 60 series, capable of seating up to 251 passengers, was evolved almost effortlessly by comparison.

Restricted by limitations imposed by their model's shorter and stockier landing gear, Boeing struggled to make the figures work. At first they designed the 707-820 concept by 'stretching' the 707-320B by 40 feet and using a bigger wing, which would produce a higher gross weight of up to 400,000lb, seating for 230 passengers and a range of 5,000 miles. On a smaller scale, the 707-620 concept, seating about 200 passengers, was studied. The -620 concept was a non-starter, but the -820 concept could work if a suitable turbofan could be found to power it. Rolls-Royce, with its 17,500lb-thrust Conway Mk.508, was the first engine manufacturer to produce a conventional commercial turbofan. Pratt & Whitney followed with their 18,000lb-thrust JT3D-3, while General Electric weighed in with the CJ-805, which in its initial form powered the Convair CV-880 four-engined airliner. The CJ-805-21 derivative, which was based on the J79 engine used to power the Convair B-58 Hustler supersonic bomber and which produced more thrust when an 'aft fan' was introduced, was developed for the Convair CV-990.

While these turbofans produced enough thrust to power the DC-8-60 and Vickers VC-10 long-range airliners, they were not powerful enough for Boeing's stretched 707 concept airliners and nowhere near powerful enough for the CX-HLS (later the C-5A Galaxy). (For this project, General Electric abandoned development on the CJ-805 and proceeded with the 41,000lb-thrust TF-39-1 two-shaft turbofan, which ultimately proved successful.) A 22,500lb-thrust commercial version of the Pratt & Whitney JT3D-15 turbofan, developed for the Lockheed C-141 Starlifter, at last provided Boeing with new options. It would permit Boeing to stretch the 707-320B by 46 feet and so create the 707-820/505 and it allowed them to consider an even bigger version, the 820/506, which incredibly was 56 feet longer than the -320B and could carry up to 279 passengers. However, if these designs were to proceed successfully, then the bigger wing and longer fuselage would, in turn, mean a complete redesign of the

28

General Electric were so committed to perfecting their 41,000lb-thrust TF-39 engine to meet the performance requirements of the C-5A that they were unable to compete with Pratt & Whitney to provide the winning engine for the 747. However, from the start of the 747 project Boeing had wanted to use the GE engine and the CF6-50 was finally adopted for the 747-200B in 1972. (General Electric)

South African Airways maintenance on a RB211-524G. On 27 June 1975 British Airways ordered 747s powered by Rolls-Royce RB211-524 engines rated at 50,100lb; the third 747 engine-type option. The improvements to the 747-400 included more powerful engines with up to 58,000lb-thrust, with a choice of three power plants in four versions: the Pratt & Whitney PW4056, which utilizes single crystal turbine blades; the 58,000lb-thrust General Electric CF6-80C2B1F; or the 58,000lb-thrust Rolls-Royce RB211-524G/60,000lb-thrust -524H. (Rolls-Royce)

main landing gear and wing carry-through structure, while the tail would have to be extended upward as the ventral fin had to be deleted to avoid the danger of tail strikes. (By comparison, the more easily derived DC-8-61, with its simple stretch fuselage, could carry 251 economy class passengers, while the DC-8-62 and -62F, with nothing more dramatic than a shorter fuselage, 3 feet wing-tip extensions, new engine pylons and redesigned long-duct engine pods, could carry up to 189 passengers.) Not surprisingly, therefore, Boeing ultimately conceded that their stretched 707 concepts were unrealistic, even though they would have offered seat-mile costs (what it costs to carry a filled seat one

mile) 26 per cent lower than those enjoyed by the -320B.

With the prospect of ever more powerful turbofan engines brightening the horizon, the giants of the commercial aircraft industry could continue their studies of huge air-lifters and airliners with a degree of confidence, at least as far as jet propulsion was concerned. This confidence did not, however, extend to all parts of the CX-HLS project, which was consuming millions of dollars in development costs as design teams wrestled with the myriad problems associated with such a new and radical design. At stake was a $250 million development contract, but aerodynamic and structural problems had first to be overcome, while fatigue and structure weight considerations had to be confronted. The original requirement specified by MATS (Military Air Transport Service, later Military Airlift Command; MAC) was for the huge airlifter to haul 125,000lb for 8,000 miles and it had to be capable of operating at maximum weight from unpaved surfaces. A 'high flotation' landing gear with twenty-eight wheels solved the latter requirement but the original specification was never met. As it turned out, in some respects CX-HLS was to prove a role model for the Boeing 747, but in others its growth had to be carefully monitored and its growing pains avoided if price escalation was to be contained to acceptable limits.

By August 1965 Boeing, McDonnell Douglas and Lockheed were able to submit their final designs for the CX-HLS project. Although Boeing had estimated that the cost of developing and then building 115 C-5As (production models) would cost around $2,800 million, their bid was for $2,300 million, $500 million lower. McDonnell Douglas submitted a bid of $2,000 million and Lockheed undercut both of them to win the contract with a bid of $1,900 million, $300 million below the Pentagon estimate. In October the Georgia Company was selected prime contractor - but events were to make it almost a pyrrhic victory. Problems associated with the aircraft design, coupled with the attendant cost overrun and inflation, conspired against the aircraft and eventually production had to be reduced from one hundred and fifteen to eighty-one examples, equipping just four Wings. Furthermore, operational service resulted in wing fatigue which ultimately required a complete rebuild of the wing and inner sections at a cost approaching $1,000 million. What benefits could Boeing derive from the failure to win the CX-HLS contract? Obviously they could make excellent use of the development potential gained during the abortive airlifter project and if the company avoided the high cost overruns, there was no reason why an equally large airliner could not be successful.

Apart from anything else, the loss of the CX-HLS contract almost immediately strengthened Boeing's resolve, from chairman Bill Allen down, to start building huge new airliners (powered by high-bypass-ratio turbofans developed for the CX-HLS), especially since

KLM-Royal Dutch Airlines 747-200B crossing the Solent and passing the Isle of Wight en route from Amsterdam-Schiphol to the USA in April 1994. General Electric were so committed to perfecting their 41,000lb-thrust TF-39 engine to meet the performance requirements of the C-5A that they were unable to compete with Pratt & Whitney to provide the winning engine for the 747. However, from the start of the 747 project Boeing had wanted to use the GE engine and the CF6-50 was finally adopted for the 747-200B in 1972. The first 747 - re-engined with the 51,000lb-thrust CF6-50D - flew on 26 June 1973. KLM was the first airline to use GE CF6-50 engines (the 52.500lb-thrust -50E) on its 747-200s and ordered its first 747B powered by CF6-50E engines on 5 July 1974. The military F103-GE-100 version of the -50E also powered the USAF E-4s. (Author)

At the Renton plant on 4 January 1966 Boeing showed Pan Am representatives their designs for the seven 747 configurations. It was here that the airline executives saw the mock-up of the 747 double-decker for the first time. The outcome of the single- versus double-decker configuration was still in the balance but it was finally resolved in March 1966 when Juan Trippe flew to Renton to view the mock-up of the double-decker and the recently completed nose section of the single-decker. Much to the satisfaction of all concerned, Sutter included, the single-decker configuration won the day. (Boeing)

commercial carriers, led principally by Juan Trippe, chairman of the all-powerful Pan Am, were now 'threatening' to buy 'stretched' DC-8s which were still in the planning stage. Pan Am was seen as America's national carrier, so when Pan Am took a lead, the other carriers followed. When asked why Pan Am should order new jet airliners that were not yet off the drawing board, let alone tested, his answer was, in the light of his all-conquering pioneering spirit, predictable: 'We ordered big jets as soon and as quickly as we could; then asked our engineers and economists to prove that we had made the right decision.' He would adopt the same buccaneering business style when it came to buying Boeing's big jet airliner, the like of which had never been seen before.

Joe Sutter, then Boeing chief engineer, who had worked on the 737, was recalled from vacation by Bill Allen to head the studies on the 747. Sutter reported to the vice-president of engineering, George Snyder and was allowed to commandeer any particular engineers

that he wanted; however, he was expected to keep many already in place. (About a hundred engineers had crossed over to join the 747 project when the CX-HLS project had foundered, while others went over to the SST programme.) Among those who joined the 747 project was Rowland 'Row' E. Brown, head of the configuration group. It was Brown's group who would be responsible for sizing the 747 according to its intended passenger and cargo load. Brown was made aware that the new aircraft was first and foremost a large capacity airliner, both in terms of passenger and cargo, but supersonic transport (SST) aircraft designs were influencing thinking at the highest levels in the airline and aircraft industry and they led to a popular misconception that Boeing's new 'super-carrier' was but a 'stop-gap' until an anticipated 1,250 SSTs would take over the passenger routes by the late 1970s. When this happened, the 'super-carriers' would have to be converted for use as large freighters.

The Design Group therefore opted to design the new airliner as a cargo aircraft from the outset, making it 'big and wide', just like the C-5A Galaxy. It was not a view immediately shared by John Borger, Pan Am vice-president and chief engineer, who was a major influence on the final design of the 747 - among other things he wanted and got pod-mounted engines on a low wing - but ultimately it was the right one. In the final analysis, Borger and Boeing both recognized and agreed that speed and the attendant high cost of the SSTs could not hope to compete with the sub-sonic aircraft's lower operating costs, nor rival it in the mass transportation sector of the market.

When he arrived on the 747 project, Sutter was presented with something of a fait accompli for it seemed that the new airliner should have a double-decker fuselage (like two 707s stacked one above the other) with six-abreast seating. Indeed, a wooden mock-up and a brochure showing this arrangement were already being produced for the airlines and scale models had been constructed in just this configuration. While it

would be ideal for an aircraft carrying 1,000 passengers, to apply it to an aircraft carrying 500-600 seats would only result in a disproportioned airliner that was short and stubby with a huge wing. In turn this would create problems with cargo loading and the servicing of the aircraft. Above all, a double-deck arrangement would affect emergency evacuation procedures and the door arrangement: it would be a nightmare to get passengers out given the height (35-50 feet) of the upper deck from the ground.

Sutter disliked the double-deck design and he was equally disdainful of the high-wing, mid-wing and low-wing versions of the design study. A mid-wing design would mean that the main spar would run through the middle of the passenger cabin, with all the attendant problems it caused, while the low-wing concept made the cabin look ungainly and top heavy. Another model revealed three engines instead of four, mounted in the empennage topped by a high T-tail, while yet another had the flight deck situated under the passenger cabin. Sutter completely disregarded the 'turkeys', as he

After considering the use of two wing-mounted legs and one central leg, Sutter finally settled for a sixteen-wheel, four-main-truck landing gear, a configuration which would spread the 'footprint' and enable Boeing to use the same wheels, tyres and brakes used on the 707-320B. To save weight, body-gear steering was not installed at first and steering on taxiways and runways therefore had to be made using engine power for turns. This changed, after the early test flights, when the 747 blew into the mud a station wagon full of people watching from the side of the runway. A system slaved to the nose-wheel steering was installed, at a cost of $5 million! In keeping with the 747's multiple redundancy, in emergency, the main landing-gear strut was given its own extension system that unlocks the gear and the wheel-well doors to allow the gear to 'fall out' and lock in the 'down' position.

called them, but the last-named model, which was soon dubbed the 'anteater', did have merit if the flight-deck was moved upwards out of the way. Milt Heineman, who had previously worked on the 737 airliner, was responsible for working out ways of evacuating 350-400 passengers by the ninety-second rule laid down by the FAA; he shared Sutter's dislike of the double-decker configuration.

At Pan Am meanwhile, Juan Trippe enthused at the prospect of a single airliner carrying up to 500 passengers (but about 350 as a more typical load in mixed-class configuration) and a load of cargo, cruising as high as 35,000 feet. (In mid-November 1965, Pan Am tabled its passenger- and cargo-carrying requirements. The cargo-carrying version had to be capable of transporting 160,000lb 2,872 nautical miles - the distance between New York and London - at Mach 0.8.) Pan Am was sceptical of the 747's projected cruising speed and was not impressed with the range of 5,865 statute miles, which they thought a little short, bearing in mind that Pan Am's yardstick route for range was New York-Rome, which

was being flown by 707-320Bs. Trippe, however was more concerned with the delivery schedule and threw down the gauntlet to Boeing, insisting that any new airliner had to offer him a seat-mile cost some 30 per cent lower than the best achieved by the 707. It meant that the new 'super-carrier' had to be able to cruise at 100mph faster than the earlier airliner. The top men at Boeing were under no illusions either, knowing that if they proceeded with the 747 and their engineers and designers got the configuration wrong, the huge financial investment involved was such that there would not be a second chance to get it right: the company would simply go out of business and cease to exist. Thus the task which confronted Sutter and his colleagues in that summer of 1965, if Boeing was to build such a huge aircraft successfully, was phenomenal.

As in the early days of the evolution of the 707 a generation earlier, it was the cabin cross-section which ultimately decided the fate of the double-deck configuration and created the successful platform for the entire 747 project. The germ of an idea was sown by a

The interior of what is now called the 747-100 'Classic'. The average transport aircraft in the mid-1970s had more than one hundred analogue cockpit instruments and controls, and the primary flight instruments were already crowded with indicators, crossbars, and symbols, and the growing number of cockpit elements were competing for cockpit space and pilot attention. Later generations of aircraft were fitted with so-called 'glass' or digital flight displays. (Boeing)

Boeing president, William M. Allen [left] arm-in-arm with Juan T. Trippe, chairman of Pan Am. It is due to Trippe, first and foremost, that the commercial jet airliner business really took off when it did. He provided the impetus which enabled Boeing's big gamble to pay off. (Boeing)

new international standard for freight containers which decreed that although they could vary in length, to achieve commonality when carried by road, rail and ship, their cross-section should be no more than 8 feet x 8 feet. Row Brown, who had previously configured the fat body for the CX-HLS, took this into account and decided that if the 747 was to be used to carry cargo in the first instance and become a freighter later in its career, it would be quite sensible to apply the same dimensions to lightweight containers used to carry air cargo. This then posed questions of how to load the containers into the cargo hold of an aircraft and where to stow them. Brown arrived at an outline where first one and then two of the freight containers were placed side by side in the belly of the aircraft. This in turn determined the width of the cargo deck's floor. To finish, he drew a circle around the deck and the freight containers to create what was a very wide fuselage 20 feet across at the level of the passenger cabin - almost twice the width of a 707 - which was situated above the cargo deck.

Ed Wells was won over by Brown's wide-bodied single-decker configuration and at Pan Am Borger was of the same opinion since the greater cargo capacity appealed to him. Gradually Trippe would also be convinced, swayed by Heinemann's persuasive

arguments concerning payload, cabin layout and in particular safety, with the single-decker's two-aisle configuration uppermost. Two immediate problems for Sutter to resolve, however, were the question of the aircraft landing gear and the degree of wing sweep. The new aircraft was anticipated to weigh around 600,000lb but it would still be expected to use existing runways at airports and so the weight borne by each wheel was critical. Sutter considered several different landing gear configurations and dismissed the conventional two-legged layout because it would have been huge. Finally, after pondering the use of two wing-mounted legs and one central leg, he settled for a sixteen-wheel, four-main-truck landing gear, a configuration which would spread the 'footprint' and enable Boeing to use the same wheels, tyres and brakes used on the 707-320B. The layout found favour, especially with Ed Wells who generations before had designed the gear on the B-17 Flying Fortress.

Initially, wing size and structure appeared to pose few problems because of the experience gained on the C-54, although this was not the case later). While a straightforward wingspan of 200 feet plus would permit economical operation and keep fuel-burn within acceptable limits, thus keeping the airlines happy, the span had to be as short as technologically possible to

Pan Am's Juan Trippe decided that the upper deck would be used for passengers. The first 747-100s were built with six upper deck windows to accommodate upstairs lounge areas. Later, as airlines began to use the upper deck for premium passenger seating, Boeing offered a ten-window upper deck option, with some –l00s retrofitted. The upper deck created the problem of providing access. Straight stairs and one with an intermediate right-angled turn appeared cumbersome and took up too much space, so the spiral staircase, which had been used on the Stratocruiser, made a reappearance - it became one of the 747's famous features. Eventually the straight stair was adopted and used on all successive models of the 747. (Boeing)

permit acceptable operation on the ground. Maximum use was therefore made of such high-lift features as highly developed triple-slotted trailing-edge flaps and full-span leading-edge Krueger flaps. Sutter and his colleagues also wrestled with the problem of wing sweep, which was critical if they were to obtain the performance that Boeing promised to deliver. More wing sweep made the wing more prone to yaw (side to side oscillation) and yaw in turn caused 'Dutch roll' - a roll from which there is little chance of recovery.

The 707's wing was swept back by 35 degrees and Sutter wanted to go to 40 degrees (which had worked in the wind-tunnel model of the B-52) of wing sweep on the 747. Finally a compromise between all the interested parties at Boeing decided on 37.5 degrees, which lessened the risk of instability but permitted the higher speed. There was then the problem of the size of the wing. Ed Wells decided that the original wing area of 5,200 square feet was not big enough: he wanted it made bigger to lift a stretched fuselage in the future and so the 747's wing was enlarged to 5,500 square feet. The wing-flap system and the sixteen-wheel, four-main-truck landing gear would allow the 747 to operate from runways normally used by 707s.

All the major components were falling into place, but there was still the question of the engines to consider. At Pan Am, Trippe was in no doubt: right from the start he had wanted Gerhard Neumann's big General Electric 41,000lb-thrust TF-39 turbofan engine, designed for the C-5A. However, this engine was designed for the C-5A's lower cruising speed of Mach 0.78 and was therefore unsuitable for the 747. The GE engine had a very high bypass ratio (the amount of uncombusted cool air flowing round the hot engine core in relation to that passing through it) of 8:1. The early turbojets, like the de Havilland Ghost, four of which powered the Comet, were derivatives of military engines and had a bypass ratio of zero. (In a pure jet engine, air is drawn in at the intake in a steady stream; it is then compressed by a compressor, fed to a combustion chamber and heated by burning fuel and then passed as white-hot gas through a turbine which drives the compressor. The gas is then expelled backwards at hundreds of feet per second through a nozzle to provide thrust. This efflux converts the engine's heat and pressure into kinetic energy, driving the aircraft forwards.)

There then came the turbofan, pioneered by Rolls-Royce chief engineer, Adrian Lombard, with bypass ratios ranging from 0.5 to 1.5. Turbofans with high bypass ratios leading to maximum thrust are the most powerful engines. (Their larger compressor blades bypass additional air around the engine core, simultaneously increasing thrust and reducing noise and fuel consumption.) The first turbofan to enter service, in 1960, was the Rolls-Royce 17,500lb-thrust Conway Mk.508, powering the Boeing 707. Pratt & Whitney soon followed with their 18,000lb-thrust JT3D-3. In deciding the architecture and configuration of any engine, designers have to consider the critical questions of drag, weight, noise and emissions. John Cundy, head of Rolls-Royce propulsion systems engineering in the 1990s, explains:

'A major task is to improve the engine's fuel-burn by improving its propulsive and thermal efficiencies. Simply, better propulsive efficiency means getting more useful power to propel the aircraft from a given amount of energy in the engine exhaust. Thermal efficiency is improved by increasing the engine's overall pressure ratio and turbine entry temperature and using better, more advanced components. To get a higher propulsive efficiency you need lower waste energy in the engine's exhaust stream, which generally means lower jet velocity. Since thrust is the product of exhaust mass flow and velocity, if velocity has to be reduced then the mass flow needs to be increased to give a fixed level of thrust. This implies an increase in bypass ratio.'

Pratt & Whitney were convinced that it could build a more flexible turbofan engine, better suited to commercial, operation than the proposed GE CF6 engine, with a ratio of 5½:1. The larger diameter fans associated with higher bypass ratios, such as the ones proposed by GE and P&W for the 747; bring both benefits and penalties (as will be seen). The bare engine would have lower specific fuel consumption, but the larger fan - Pratt & Whitney's projected JT9D engine would be characterized by an enormous front fan measuring 8 feet in diameter - would require a large-diameter nacelle with consequent drag and weight penalties. In any event P&W, which at this time were responsible for 90 per cent of the world's jet engines, would virtually have the field to themselves. General Electric had their hands full trying to get their 41,000lb-thrust TF-39 engine to meet the performance requirements of the C-5A, let alone trying to use it to compete with the likes of Pratt & Whitney.[5]

Rolls-Royce, meanwhile, had staked the company's future on its RB.211 high-bypass-ratio engine (the 'R' is for 'Rolls' and the 'B' is for 'Barnoldswick', the town in Lancashire where much of the engine work is completed). Ever innovative, Rolls had come up with an engine that promised much, but it was still too early in the design stage and considered too complicated in its construction to interest Boeing and Joe Sutter in particular. The RB.211 was heavier than the GE and P&W engines - it was powered by three spools, or shafts, two more than the American engines - and Boeing was not impressed by the largest fan blades, called 'hyfil', which had a carbon-fibre core thinly coated with steel. Rolls claimed that these were lightweight but strong and therefore offered substantial

weight savings, but Boeing remained unconvinced. They no doubt felt vindicated some time later when the hyfil blades failed a vigorous engine field test after being bombarded by defrosted frozen chickens for forty hours![6]

An all-new Rolls-Royce company went on to produce the RB.211 after convincing the British government of the day to fund half the development of the more powerful -524 version of the engine. In 1973 the first static test runs were made, but it was not until mid-1975 when the British government at last provided the additional funding Rolls needed that the company could run the 50,000lb-thrust RB.211 into a production quality engine and further develop its full potential to 53,000lb of thrust. RB.211 engines (without the troubled hyfil blades) were finally fitted to the 747 when British Airways ordered its first four -524-engined 747-236Bs in June 1975. The first RB.211-powered 747-236B flew in 1976 and deliveries to British Airways began in 1977. The selection of the engine to power the 747 was due to be made by Boeing and Pan Am on 3 January 1966, but by the end of 1965 this looked untenable since no final design of the 747 had been arrived at and no engines chosen. Even so, on 22 December 1965, Juan Trippe signed a five-page letter of intent agreeing to buy twenty-five 747s, although this was only after first receiving a guarantee from Boeing that Pan Am would receive the first five aircraft built and then five of each of the first three batches of ten and five of the next

With a headline 'Pan Am's $23m flying penthouse', N735PA Clipper Constitution *was displayed to the press ayt London Heathrow. Top left: the spacious upper lounge, with seating for 16 passengers. Centre left: in addition to the First Class upstairs lounge, Pan Am offered First Class passengers a four-abreast seating arrangement on the main deck. Left: Six galleys were used by Pan Am's 747 flight personnel to servethe passengers. The double galley, seen here, provided a walk-through capability from isle to isle. Below:* Clipper Constitution *during turn-around at Heathrow.*

fifteen off the production line. Trippe obviously wanted to make the 747 market Pan Am's own for as long as possible in order to steal a march on his rivals; however, Boeing needed to sell at least fifty 747s just to recover its pre-production costs.

The aircraft was newly developed, untested and without engines and an entirely new aircraft plant would have to be built before production could begin. So in view of the enormous financial investment that Boeing was risking, the aircraft company stipulated that Pan Am pay a 2.5 per cent deposit on signature of the contract, then put up half the total price of each of the aircraft, paid in quarterly amounts, six months prior to delivery of the first 747. Each of twenty-five 747s would cost Pan Am $18 million - a $450 million investment - and the terms of the contract meant that the airline was paying a quarter of a billion dollars before the first aircraft flew. However, the future seemed rosy. In 1965, which had proved very profitable for Pan Am, it had been forecast that 35 million people would be flying the intercontinental routes and forecasters were predicting a 200 per cent increase by 1980.

At Renton on 4 January 1966 Boeing showed the six Pan Am representatives - General Larry S. Kuter, Sanford Kauffman, John Borger, test pilot Scott Flower and two senior captains - their designs for the seven final configurations. Four were single-deck designs (including one which was a fall-back, mid-wing, 'double-bubble' lay-out) with seating for eight, nine or ten abreast. (Sutter ultimately decided upon a low, swept-wing arrangement.) The other three were double-deck designs with a mid- or high wing. The double-deck designs had seating for six abreast on each deck in one configuration, seven in another and a third with seating for seven abreast on the top deck and eight across on the main deck. Pan Am's representatives could not fail to notice that the upper deck was more than 25 feet above the ground. This was brought home to them during their inspection of the mock-up where they had to make their way up to the upper deck by climbing unstable ladders, a tortuous and precarious route. By comparison, the drawing of the passenger deck on the wide-body configuration showed it to be a more manageable 16 feet from the ground, the cabin contained nine seats across and it had been given two aisles to make it easier for passengers to get to the exit doors in the event of an emergency.

John Borger in particular could not help but be impressed by the fact that in all of the single-deck designs, unlike the double-deck designs, there was room in the cavernous cargo hold for not one, but two 8 feet x 8 feet containers. So that it could be used more effectively in a freighter role, Borger had argued repeatedly for the main deck to have a hinged nose

section to permit straight-through cargo loading. Sutter's problem then had been to calculate where the flight deck was to go and ultimately he had moved the cockpit up and out of the way onto a small upper deck section, well above the 18 feet high ceiling of the forward cabin and more than 30 feet off the ground. This was to give the aircraft its distinctive 'hump', which became a classic feature of the 747 design. (The 747 was the only jet aircraft with passengers seated ahead of the pilots.) The top of the raised flight deck projected well above the top line of the fuselage, but rather than fairing it into the fuselage abruptly, the fairing was made long and formed the ceiling of an entire cabin.

The outcome of the single- versus double-decker configuration was still in the balance, but it was finally resolved in March 1966 when Trippe flew to Renton to view the plywood mock-up of the double-decker. First Bill Allen showed Trippe the lofty double-decker mock-up and then the single-decker, with all its innovative features such as the upward-opening nose door and the hump behind the flight deck, which Borger suggested could be used as a rest area for the crew. The Pan Am chief was having none of that, however, quickly realizing its revenue-earning potential and marking it out for passenger use - why, it could be used as a cocktail lounge. This in turn created the problem of providing access to the upper deck. Straight stairs with two right-angled turns appeared too cumbersome and consumed too much space, so the spiral staircase as had been used on the old Stratocruiser, made a successful reappearance; indeed, it became one of the 747's famous features. (Some airlines later used the upper deck cabin for a crew rest area or a first-class lounge, while others fitted seats and windows for nineteen passengers. As this feature gained in popularity, the cabin was progressively extended aft to accommodate as many as ninety-nine passengers.)

Trippe even went so far as to consider putting a few staterooms on the upper deck and asked if windows could be added to the front of the aircraft at the main-deck level (earmarked for the radar housing) so that passengers could see where they were going! All of this - and the fact that Boeing had deliberately placed a set of rickety steps up to the double-decker, but much firmer steps up to the nose section of the wide-body, thereby showing their preference for the latter design - carried the day and the single-deck arrangement was adopted as the winning design.

Despite the enormity of the project - no fewer than 75,000 engineering drawings would be used to produce the first 747 and more than 15,000 hours of wind-tunnel testing in eight locations in the US would be needed before the aircraft would fly - Boeing's designers did not envisage any dramatic technological problems. They

N7470, resplendent in its white livery with a red stripe down the window line, and the logos of its airline customers adorning the nose, was towed out. The run-up to the roll-out of the first 747 had been fraught with frenetic activity but roll-out day was a great success. (Boeing)

Delays were caused by engine problems, and by early 1970 a new 747 was coming off the production line once every three days with no upgraded engines for it. Instead, some thirty 747 airframes were parked on the Everett ramp with 9,600lb concrete blocks hanging off the wings where the engines should have been until enough JT9Ds could be delivered. Behind the 'gliders', or the 'aluminium avalanche' as Boeing engineers called this phenomenon, is the main assembly building, built at a cost of $200 million. The single roof reaches to a height often storeys, spans 63 acres and contains the largest volume of any building in the world, some 205 million cubic feet, 70 million cubic feet more than the Vertical Assembly Building at the Kennedy Space Center, previously the world's largest building. In 1980, the main assembly building was enlarged to 291 million cubic feet to further accommodate Boeing 767 production. (Boeing)

the huge airliner slowly forward into the crowded amphitheatre and magically the sun appeared, illuminating this white whale with a red stripe down its window line, logos of the twenty-six airline customers adorning its nose. Once the massive tail of the aircraft was clear of the doors, the tug came to a stop beside the reviewing stand. N7470 was then surrounded by the flock of stewardesses, each one carrying a bottle of champagne: at a signal from Stamper they approached the 747 and then waited to be counted before breaking their bottles of bubbly on pre-designated parts of the aircraft. This was meant to be a simultaneous action, but as some of the hostesses did not understand English, the bottles were actually smashed on the aircraft at random.

Overhead, a 707, a 707 and a 737, delayed by the weather, made low passes over the plant.

Once all the razzmatazz of the rollout had subsided there was a growing realization that, while there were still a myriad problems to rectify concerning the engines and the airframe, the 747 was now about to enter a crucial phase of its metamorphism. The P&W JT9Ds had not yet been run on the 747 and therefore the aircraft's hydraulic, electrical and fuel systems had not been tried either. Taxiing trials were now due to be completed and the first flight with all the attendant glare of publicity would be followed by extensive airframe testing in flight. Allen's and Trippe's combined dream was about to be realized.

Footnotes for Chapter 2

7   The 747 would remain the heaviest commercial aircraft in regular service until the debut of the Antonov An-124 Ruslan in 1982; variants of the 747-400 would surpass the An-124's weight in 2000. The Antonov An-225 cargo transport, which debuted in 1988, remains the world's largest aircraft by several measures (including the most accepted measures of maximum takeoff weight and length); one aircraft has been completed and is in service as of 2012. The Hughes H-4 Hercules or 'Spruce Goose' is the largest aircraft by wingspan, but it only completed a single flight. The 747 remained the largest passenger airliner in service until the Airbus A380 began airline service in 2007.

8   In 1980 the main assembly building was enlarged to 291 million cubic feet to further accommodate Boeing 767 production and today, major parts of the 747 and 767 manufacturing subassembly and final assembly functions are all housed under one roof.

9   See *Wide Body* by Cliff Irving.

Chapter 3

The Spacious Age

'Jack, I hope you understand the future of the company rides with you guys this morning'

Bill Allen speaking to test pilot Jack Waddell at Paine Field

The winter of 1968-9 was one of the worst in Washington State's history, with driving winds and snow squalls making work almost unbearable at Paine Field, where flight-testing of the first 747 would begin. Connie Smith, head of the pre-flight unit, was loath to release the aircraft to flight operations until he was satisfied that the untried JT9Ds could provide stable power: they were known to be extremely sensitive to wind effects which could cause 'flame out', or worse, they could stall. (An engine stall could be caused either by encountering a 10-knot crosswind, or if the wind blew directly into the JT9D's tailpipe.) The test-flight crew was led by chief test pilot Jack Waddell, who was a test pilot for North American before coming to Boeing in 1957. As well as being an experienced pilot (he had flown Navy fighters in World War II and latterly had been the project pilot on the C-5A), Waddell was also an accomplished aeronautical engineer, obtaining a masters degree from Cornell University in 1952. For the 747's test-flight programme he had selected as his co-pilot Brien Wygle, who had been chief test pilot on the 737 and Jess Wallick as his flight engineer. Both Waddell and Wallick had been involved from the outset with the 747 programme and had collaborated in parts of the design, especially the

Jess Wallick flight engineer (left) Jack Waddell, chief test pilot (centre) and Brien Wygle, co-pilot (right) (Boeing)

flight deck. They were understandably reticent to fly the aircraft until these problems were sorted out, but the flight-test programme was already nearly eight weeks behind schedule and the first 747 was due to be delivered to Pan Am by the end of December 1969.

It was not until the end of January 1969 that N7470 was passed for flight operations and could taxi out to the runway for the ground run-throughs. Sixty thousand pounds of test equipment and 1,000lb of water ballast in rows of 55-US gallon aluminium beer kegs had been loaded on board the 747. The 747's balance could be varied by pumping water from one group of beer kegs to another. More kegs were situated in the forward cargo hold, below the main deck and to bring the total weight up to just over 476,000lb, mailbags were loaded in the aft passenger cabin. Cameras were installed to monitor crucial areas such as the leading edge of the wing, the flight crew, instrument panels and the landing gear and to record the take-off.

By the end of the first week of February, Waddell had taken the N7470 to the brink of take-off, at 150 mph. At this time he was not enthused at the prospect of taking the aircraft off the tarmac with the P&W engines in their present state of development, but the only way of simulating the angle of attack (and the change of direction of the

Left: Waddell was concerned with having to judge the landing of the 747 from such a high flight deck, so he had Boeing engineers construct a mock-up of the flight deck and part of the nose. and mounted it 29ft (9m) up on top of a rig simulating the sixteen-wheel landing gear. Printed bright orange and with a grinning Halloween mask with black triangular eyes and toothy grin, the contraption was known as 'WaddeII's Wagon' and was towed around the airfield by a truck, with Waddell sitting in the 'cockpit' familiarizing himself with seeing the runway from on high. Boeing (Boeing)

The 747's 195ft 8in wide wings were designed to move up and down some 29ft at the tips to give the flexibility to cope with the effects of air turbulence on its surfaces. While the flight-test programme continued, a third airframe was deliberately tested to destruction by a combination of hydraulically actuated weights and pulleys. (Boeing)

air entering the engines in the nose-up attitude) was to take the 747 actually off the ground and into the air. His main concern was that all four engines would stall at the same time and without engine power he would lose his hydraulics and, consequently, all the controls. Joe Sutter therefore fitted the test aircraft with back-up electrical power provided by a bank of heavy-duty batteries to operate the hydraulics in the event of total engine failure. Waddell was also concerned with having to judge the

landing of the 747 from a flight deck that was so very much higher than anything he had flown before. He therefore had the Boeing engineers construct a mock-up of the flight deck and part of the nose and mount it 29 feet up on top of a rig simulating the sixteen-wheel landing gear. Painted bright orange with a grinning Halloween mask with black triangular eyes and toothy grin, the contraption became known as 'Waddell's Wagon' and was towed around the airfield by a truck with Waddell sitting

On Sunday 9 February 1969 Jack Waddell lifted N7470 into the air for the first time accompanied by the chase plane, an F-86 Sabre flown by Paul Bennett, seen here closing in so that Bennett can inspect the flying surfaces and the gear. He reported that the engines were burning clean and that there was no smoke. Waddell brought N7470 in over Everett and put the aircraft down safely, if a little faster than he wanted to, because of a fault with the flaps. In all other respects the 747, which had been airborne for an hour and sixteen minutes, flew exceptionally well. (Boeing)

in the 'cockpit' familiarizing himself with seeing the runway from on high. In fact he had no need to worry about the height of the flight deck from the tarmac and his fears regarding the quality of the 747's engines proved groundless: they behaved impeccably and by Sunday 9 February he was confident enough to try for the first flight, as soon as the weather lifted.

Bill Allen, informed that there was a possibility that the 747 would at last make its first flight, returned on the Saturday evening from visiting Juan Trippe at his retirement home in the Bahamas. By early Sunday morning the clouds had lifted slightly although the wind was gusting at between 10 and 15mph, from the south-east. A little after 9 am the pilot of a 707 that was being flight-tested from Boeing field called the flight operations centre at Everett and reported a clearance coming in from the west, toward the San Juan Islands. Waddell conferred with the 707 pilot and decided the conditions would be within bounds to enable him to take the 747 up for its first flight. Allen walked to the aircraft with Waddell, whose face betrayed a little anxiety - not surprising in view of the task ahead. His boss added unnecessarily to the pilot's already heavy responsibility by saying, 'Jack, I hope you understand that the future of the company rides with you guys this morning.'

Waddell climbed aboard and the crew took up their positions on the flight deck. The first engine was started at 11:07 hours and within four minutes all four were running. Waddell set the stabilizer at an angle of five degrees and called for the chase plane, an F-86 Sabre flown by Paul Bennett, to begin take off. By the time Waddell was ready to roll he could see buses moving on the runway and he had to call the tower to tell them to move further back before he could taxi out. There was still thick cloud cover at 1,500 feet but the wind had dropped slightly Waddell taxied out towards the northern end of the runway and held the brakes on while the JT9Ds reached take-off thrust. When Wallick announced that he had 'four stable engines', his pilot released the brakes and at just after 11:35 hours the 747 hurtled along the runway. Half way along, at 4,500 feet and at 150mph, Waddell felt the nose coming up and called 'Rotate'. Much to the excitement of everyone, the 747 lifted seemingly effortlessly into the air - though the efflux from the engines was too much for one photographer nearby who was promptly bowled over backwards by the blasts. Finally the gear unstuck and the turbines accelerated the aircraft up and away. There was no need for Waddell to put the nose down and carry out an emergency stop and the huge airliner sailed majestically away to altitude leaving those on the ground to wax lyrical and swell with pride. Joe Sutter's wife Nancy reportedly burst into tears with the emotion of it all.

747 chief pilot Jack Waddell, Jess Wallick, flight engineer and Brien Wygle, co-pilot walk triumpantly down the steps from N7470 after the first flight on 9 February 1969. (Boeing)

On 15 February, Waddell took N7470 up again, on a flight lasting two hours eighteen minutes, and this time the flaps were successfully retracted. Checks were carried out on the fuel-feed system, and the first full retraction and lowering of the landing gear in flight was made. (Boeing)

Waddell reported that the 747 was surprisingly light on the controls and felt good. He decided to carry out a shallow turn to port, all the way through 270 degrees, in order to bring the aircraft back over the field to give the assembled ranks of photographers an early opportunity to take more photos. Then the Sabre chase plane came in closer and Bennett inspected the flying surfaces and the gear: he reported that the engines were burning clean and that there was no smoke. Waddell playfully rolled the 747 30 degrees to the left and then to the right. So far so good, though Wallick reported that the number one engine was running 30 degrees hotter than the rest and that there was no sign of the temperature dropping. Undeterred at this news, Waddell continued climbing at 400 feet a minute until, just after 11:42 hours; they broke into clear, brilliant sky and smoother air.

With the airspeed now registering 160 knots, Waddell tried some fairly gentle pitch manoeuvres before climbing the aircraft through 12,000 feet to 15,000 feet and 280mph over the Strait of Juan de Fuca. Shortly before noon he initiated the part of the test plan designed to test the fail-safe systems. He shut down the

first independent hydraulic system and when the 747 handled as if nothing had happened, he shut down the second system; this effectively shut down the left outboard aileron, the left outboard elevator and the right inboard elevator and he had only half power to both inboard ailerons and to both rudders. Everything that the simulator had predicted would happen was thankfully coming true and Waddell was still able to fly the aircraft on the two remaining systems with no noticeable loss of control. (If anything really untoward went wrong during the test flight and the crew had to abandon the aircraft they were to leave via an emergency exit shaft with a pole running down from the upper deck to the floor of the cargo hold 20 feet below. Once there, the crew would have to pull a handle to activate a hydraulic ram to drive open the cargo door. Outside meanwhile, a retractable spoiler on the leading edge of the cargo compartment would open simultaneously, deflecting the air flow as the three men parachuted to safety.)

Waddell then restored all his hydraulic power and with the gear remaining in the 'down' position (gear and the flaps were to be raised and lowered again at least

N7470 taking off from Boeing Field during tests, which revealed wing flutter, or instability, problems. These led to the fuel-feed system having to be adjusted to alter the weight distribution to acceptable limits.(Boeing)

once during the flight), successfully put the aircraft through more tests. He checked on trim and stability, flew with unbalanced power settings and then tried to put the aircraft into a Dutch roll by kicking the rudder pedal - but the big tail did its job and the 747 refused. Unlike the 707 which had rolled so badly on a test flight that the aircraft had fatally discarded its engines, the 747, whose tail-fin area was 40 per cent greater than its predecessor, had no such vices. Everyone was elated.

Waddell now lowered the triple-slotted flaps from 25 to 30 degrees. Drag increased as the flaps extended back and downwards and then there was a disconcerting 'clunk' as they hit 30 degrees, followed by vibration. Waddell restored the flaps to 25 degrees and sent Wallick back to investigate. Wallick could see that a section of the right-hand flaps had shaken loose and wedged itself in a gap between the slots and it was this which was vibrating. (It was discovered later that a

Jack Waddell deliberately scraped the tail of N7470 along the runway to determine the lowest speed (VMU - 'velocity minimum unstick') at which the 747 will leave the ground safely. A wooden tail-skid was fitted to the underside of the rear fuselage to prevent damage. (Boeing)

Right: Boeing's newly-elected President, T. A. Wilson (seated, wearing jacket) accompanied Jack Waddell and his test flight crew for some of the VMU tests.

Below right: Boeing Flight-test engineers preparing the 747 on-board test equipment during the certification programme 'UI' the aircraft.

Below: Boeing engineers working flat out in the snow on the Pratt & Whitney JT9D engines. JT9Ds remained one of the maior troublesome factors in the 747 development. with no fewer than eighty-seven engines breaking down and fifty-five engine changes having to he made during the entire test programme.

Prototypes all! Boeing 747-100 N7470 behind the prototype 737-100 N73700 and the Dash 80, the latter two aircraft wearing the chocolate and yellow company colours. Even though the 747 is farthest from the camera, the size is most impressive.(Boeing)

747-121 N732PA, the third test aircraft. was delayed in production with the fitment of a 32 foot long aluminium pole to the nose for gust measurement testing; it was rolled out on 16 May 1969. N732PA (Clipper Storm King) finally flew on 10 July 1969, and was used mostly for flight~load survey testing before being cleared for airline service. On 13 December 1969 it crashed at the end of a short flight from Everett to Renton. It was repaired and delivered to Pan Am on 13 July 1970. (Boeing)

bearing housing under the canoes had failed.) Waddell prudently decided to terminate the flight with one hour still to run and return to Everett. By the time they were back over land and heading toward Lake Roesiger the 727, which had the press and Bill Allen on board, caught them up and came close enough for air-to-air photos to be taken of the 747 and the Sabre chase plane off its port wing. Waddell brought N7470 in over Everett and put the aircraft down safely, if a little faster than he wanted to, because of the faulty flaps. The 747 had been airborne for an hour and sixteen minutes.

Six days later, on 15 February, Waddell took N7470 up again, on a flight lasting two hours eighteen minutes and this time the flaps were successfully retracted. Checks were carried out on the fuel-feed system and the first full retraction and lowering of the landing gear in flight was made. The flaps were set at various angles and tested. On 17 February N7470 was flown on a twenty-three minute flight to retest flap handling at 25 degrees and checks were made on the main landing gear. Next day the 747 made two flights, totalling three hours six minutes, in which further approach and landing flaps tests were conducted, as well as the first checks on the nacelle cooling of the engines. In fact the JT9D1 powerplants remained one of the major troublesome factors in the 747 development, with no fewer than eighty-seven engines breaking down

and fifty-five engine changes having to be made during the test programme - that is, between February and December 1969.

After more flap-testing on 24 February the next day, Waddell flew N7470 on a static pressure and airspeed survey flight lasting just over two hours. Then Bill Allen joined him on the flight deck for the first time and he flew the aircraft on the short twenty-eight minute hop across Puget Sound to Seattle and into Boeing Field where the second phase of flight-testing was to take place. By the end of the first phase, speeds of up to 287mph had been achieved and altitudes of 20,000 feet had been reached. While everyone knew that this overall performance was well below what was expected of the airliner, the speed soon reached Mach 0.84, or 623mph, faster than any other airliner had ever done. However, Pan Am were still sticking to their expected specified speed of Mach 0.9, or 667mph, which was finally achieved. The higher speeds and adjustments to the fuel-feed system loadings, now presented Boeing with another, equally serious problem, one that would take six months to rectify.

Flutter, or instability, had begun to manifest itself at speeds of around Mach 0.86 and there was 'low damping' (wing shake) if the weight of the outer wing in particular was changed in any way. During flutter

Flight-testing included demonstrations of the 747's ability to carry a spare engine, complete in every way except for the fan blades and nose cowl, mounted under the left wing inboard of the number two engine. Fan blades were carried in shipping containers in the bulk cargo compartment. A nose cowl, fan cowl and forward strut fairing was provided as part of the spare engine kit. The kit also contained a plug to cover the exhaust nozzle. (Boeing)

testing between March and August 1969 - often delayed because of the severe wintry conditions - the flight crew had to continually juggle the weight of the fuel between tanks to keep the wing from oscillating. Finally the fuel-feed system had to be adjusted to alter the weight distribution to acceptable limits. Another way in which flutter could be contained was to increase the stiffness of the wing, but this would have involved further costly and time-consuming structural changes. One of the areas in which the oscillation was markedly bad was the engine struts and nacelles supporting the bulbous P&W powerplants. Sutter and Everette Webb therefore tried

to alleviate the flutter problem by actually reducing the stiffness in the struts, to give them more flexibility. This improvisation worked to a variable degree, but it was then found that more weight was needed in the outboard engine mountings (numbers one and four) so they could be used as counter-weights to the oscillating wing problems. To avoid any further redesign and because space inside the mountings was at a premium, bags containing 700lb of 'spent'- that is depleted of its fissionable isotope - uranium pellets (the heaviest metal available) were embedded in numbers one and four engine struts of the test aircraft (although wing stiffening

747-121 N732PA Clipper Storm King *(Clipper Ocean Telegraph from 1980) looking none the worse for wear for its accident at London Heathrow on 3 September 1980. (David Lee)*

Deliveries of 747-121 production models to Pan Am began on 12 December 1969. The airline flew over 300 employees from New York to London on 12 January 1970. Clipper Constitution, *which had been delivered just three days earlier, landed at Heathrow airport three hours late after one of its P&W JT9D fan-jet engines gave trouble and had to be changed. On 21 January 1970 Pan-American began a scheduled 747 commercial service with non-stop flights between New York and London when N736PA* Clipper Victor *completed the flight after N733PA* Clipper Young America *had suffered engine problems at JFK Airport. (Walt Truax)*

was used on the five aircraft used in the test programme).

Meanwhile N747PA, the second 747, destined to be Pan Am's first aircraft (*Clipper Young America*), was rolled out at Everett on 28 February 1969 - by which time twenty-seven airlines had ordered 160 aircraft. The aircraft flew for the first time on 11 April, more than a month later than scheduled. Before being issued to Pan Am it was assigned to test propulsion, fuel and electro-mechanical and avionics systems. On 23 April N731PA became the third 747 off the production line, even though it was actually designated as the fourth test aircraft. Later it was named *Clipper Bostonian* when in Pan Am service from 1970-81 and it became *Clipper Ocean Express* in 1981. It finally joined the test programme on 10 May and was used for functional and reliability testing, as well as some electro-mechanical system evaluations before being delivered to Pan Am on 11 July 1970. Meanwhile on 8 May 1969 N93101, the fifth aircraft and the first 747 for Trans World Airlines, had been rolled out. N93101 flew on 22 May and was assigned to test aerodynamics, stability and control before being delivered to TWA, on 18 August 1970. Finally on 16 May 1969, N732PA *Clipper Storm King*, the third test aircraft, which was delayed in production because of the need to fit a 32 feet-long aluminium pole to the nose for gust measurement testing, was also rolled out at Everett. It eventually flew on 10 July 1969 and was used mostly for flight-load survey testing before

being delivered to Pan Am on 13 July 1970.

Needing a boost, Boeing now sought to gain a quantum leap in publicity for the 747 programme. Bill Allen strongly suggested to 'T' Wilson that one of the test aircraft should be flown across the Atlantic to France early in June to take part in the 28th Paris Air Show. It would be especially satisfying for Boeing since Lockheed had considered and had then dropped the idea of flying the equally troubled C-5A to the show. Wilson conferred with Dix Loesch, head of flight-testing, to see if he had faith in the P&W powerplants powering the aircraft on a non-stop flight from Seattle to Paris, a distance of 5,160 miles. Loesch decided that only N731PA, the fourth 747 off the production line and which had ten hours' flying time, could make the long trip safely. Initially Loesch said that he first wanted a full check of the systems on the aircraft and wished to add another ten hours' flying time on the airframe and the engines, before it attempted a transatlantic flight, but after a few days and with the engines functioning reliably enough, he dropped his precautionary stance. The only additional flying hours would be the eighteen-plus hours gained on the return flight to Paris.

Although N731PA was due to be delivered to Pan Am, it was still painted in Boeing colours. When Pan Am found out about the Paris flight, Boeing refused the airline's insistent decree that it be repainted in the blue and white livery of American's premier airline for fear of affecting the sales potential of the other carriers. Because

Clipper Young America arrives in London on the first commercial flight by the new generation of wide-body jets, January 22, 1970. Boeing B747

Pan Am went to great lengths to mark and celebrate the introduction of the 747 on it's trans-Atlantic service, with a special business class menu along with a specially commissioned painting and explanation.

CLIPPER CLASS®

Welcome Aboard Pan Am's Special Business Class

Libations

Aperitifs   Cocktails   Spirits

Champagne   Premium Beer   Red and White Wines

Liqueurs and Cognac

Menu

Cocktail Nuts

Délice Fleurette Salad
Smoked Nova Scotia salmon with spring salad on a bed of fresh greens

Filet Mignon au Poivre
Select grilled tenderloin steak with a peppery brandy cream sauce. Served with Berny potatoes, buttered spinach leaves and glazed carrots

or

Sole Grimaldi
Filets of sole poached in white wine sauce. Served with parsley potatoes and sautéed green beans with tomatoes

Tart Bourdaloue
Ripe pear with caramel glazing nestled in a sweet pastry tart

Cold Collation

Plat Bellevue
A platter of select cold delicacies with vegetable salad and savoury relishes

Crusty Roll and Creamery Butter

Crisp Butter Cookies

Coffee   Taster's Choice Decaffeinated Coffee   Tea

Coca-Cola   Tab   Diet Coke   Canada Dry Beverages

Country Time® Lemonade Flavor Drink

choice of entree is not available.

Historic First Flights of Pan American Clippers

Clipper Young America arrives in London on the first commercial flight by the new generation of wide-body jets,

January 22, 1970

More than 350 tons of airplane, wide as a boulevard and longer by far than the Wright Brothers' first flight, a passenger capacity two and a half times that of a B707, more than 6,000 cubic feet of cargo capacity and a of 20 - the Boeing B747 that Pan Am conceived, helped design, and introduced goes into commercial ser-

Commanded by Captain Robert M. Weeks, the huge B747 (N736PA) made the crossing from New York in ours and 43 minutes. The B747 incorporates the most advanced technology, including an Inertial Navigation tem adapted from the Apollo Space Program that pinpoints the craft's position at all times without outside rences, and a fully automatic landing system.

About the Artist

In 1926, John T. McCoy became a working student for the Curtiss Flying Service, Curtiss Field, Long Island, New York.

When Charles A. Lindbergh arrived at Curtiss Field, his SPIRIT OF ST. LOUIS was housed in one of the Curtiss hangars. It was at this time that McCoy met Lindbergh, who was most cordial and friendly to those who worked on the flight line. In those days muscle power was the method used for starting engines, accomplished by swinging the propeller by hand. McCoy often pulled a prop through for Lindbergh.

Years later, when McCoy was commissioned to do paintings depicting the history of Pan American World Airways, Inc. - entitled HISTORIC FIRST FLIGHTS OF PAN AMERICAN CLIPPERS - he consulted with Lindbergh on the selection of aircraft and locations for the series.

This is one picture in a series of thirteen. If you would like to purchase 8½" x 11" or 16" x 20" limited edition prints, send your letter of inquiry to: Public Relations Department - Pan American World Airways, Inc., Pan Am Building, New York, New York 10166. Please include code number 304 in your letter.

Technical data (747 compared with 707) *The 747, built by Boeing of Seattle, is a sub-sonic jet aircraft following the same basic design as the well-proven 707 but offering roughly two and half times the 707's passenger capacity.*		**747**	**707**		**747**	**707**
	OVERALL LENGTH	231' 10"	152' 11"	ENGINES	4 PRATT & WHITNEY JT9D-3A	4 ROLLS-ROYCE CONWAY R.CO.1
	HEIGHT GROUND TO TOP TAIL FIN	63' 5"	42' 6"	THRUST	4 x 43,500 LB	4 x 17,500 LB
	WING SPAN	195' 8"	142' 5"	CRUISING SPEED	568 — 600 MPH	540 MPH
	MAXIMUM ALL-UP WEIGHT	316 TONS	140 TONS	RANGE*	5,000 STATUTE MILES	4,000 STATUTE MILES
	MAXIMUM CABIN WIDTH	21' 4"	12' 4"	CREW	18 OR 19	10 OR 11
	CABIN CEILING HEIGHT	8' 4"	7' 7"	TYPICAL PASSENGER CAPACITY	27F/335Y	16F/130Y

*with full fuel capacity, using maximum take-off weig[...]

At London (Heathrow), New York (JFK) and most other airports served by the BOAC 747, boarding and disembarkation is by means of telescopic weatherproof "fingers", involving no steps.

N731PA would be carrying the full weight of fuel it was decided that rather than leave from Everett or the 10,000 feet Boeing Field, the 747 would fly to Sea-Tac (Seattle-Tacoma) Airport and take off from the airport's longer, 12,000 feet runway. In the early evening of 2 June, senior engineering test pilots Don Knutson and Jess Wallick, assisted by chief experimental flight engineer, P. J. de Roberts, took the 747 off for Paris Le Bourget, the same airport where Lindbergh had landed at the end of his epic flight and set out across the north Atlantic for Europe. On board were Joe Sutter, Mal Stamper and 'Tex' Boullioun, head of the airliner division.

Nine hours and eighteen minutes later on the morning of 3 June the 747 arrived over Paris and touched down to share a hero's welcome with the first Anglo-French Concorde. VIPs, including Prince Philip and hundreds of airline chiefs, visited the 747 during its most memorable sojourn in Paris before it flew back to the north-west coast of the USA. All went well until it reached Moses Lake, just 140 miles from Boeing Field,

where one of the engines developed a power surge and had to be shut down. Untroubled, the flight crew landed the 747 at Boeing Field without further incident and having proved conclusively that the aircraft was more than capable of intercontinental airline operations, became once again, part of the 747's test programme.

So far during the test programme (which finally resulted in the five 747s flying 1,449 hours in 1,013 flights), there had been the usual problems associated with testing a new type of aircraft and several minor incidents had occurred, but nothing untoward had really befallen any of the test aircraft. On 13 December 1969 the first serious accident in the test programme occurred when test aircraft number three, N732PA flown by Ralph Cokely left Everett for Renton where all its test equipment was to be removed and airline seating installed prior to delivery to Pan Am (as *Clipper Storm King*). No 747 had landed on the 5,280 feet runway at Renton before, but N732PA weighed 390,000lb and at this weight it was calculated that the distance from a 50

BOAC published a lavish brochure for travel agents, extoling the virtues and comforts of their 747 fleet.

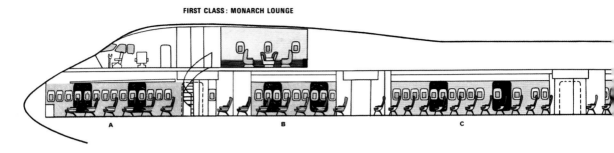

FIRST CLASS: MONARCH LOUNGE

A   B   C

'individual look' cabins create intimate atmosphere

BOAC HAS DIVIDED THE 747 INTERIOR INTO FIVE CABINS: two first class
and three economy class. In fact, in each of the economy class cabins
passengers will find themselves surrounded by *fewer* people than they do when
travelling by, say, the BOEING 707. Each cabin is furnished to look (and feel)
like a totally separate, self-contained entity. This has been achieved
by means of a different decor scheme for each one. Fabrics, fittings, sidewalls . . .
seats, head-rest covers, carpets, curtains . . . they all harmonise
in a series of restful colour combinations, one for each cabin. This way,
each projects its own 'personality' as a distinctive, luxurious sitting room.

6

FIRST CLASS *Monarch Lounge*   **A** *First Class Cabin*

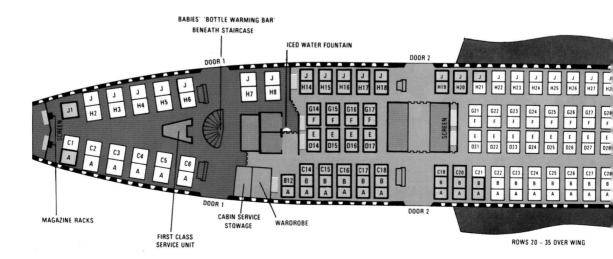

BABIES' 'BOTTLE WARMING BAR'
BENEATH STAIRCASE

ICED WATER FOUNTAIN

DOOR 1

DOOR 2

DOOR 1

DOOR 2

MAGAZINE RACKS

FIRST CLASS
SERVICE UNIT

CABIN SERVICE
STOWAGE

WARDROBE

ROWS 20 – 35 OVER WING

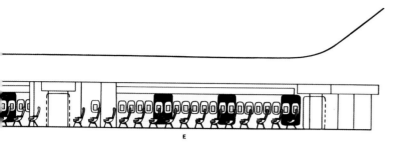

E

ss Cabin*
'conomy class cabin
gurations. See Pages 2 & 3.

C *Economy Class Cabin*

D *Economy Class Cabin*

E *Economy Class Cabin*

7

CARRYCOT POSITIONS

GALLEYS

TOILETS

SEATS FROM WHICH CINEMA SCREENS
CANNOT BE VIEWED
(THERE IS NO SCREEN IN THE ZONE
OCCUPIED BY SEAT ROWS 12-18)

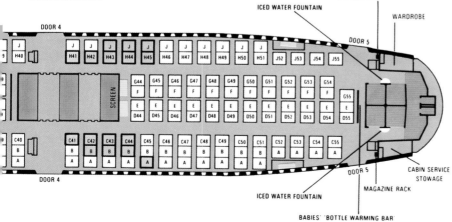

747s come together at Everett. Visible are aircraft allocated to Air France, Alitalia and Qantas.

feet altitude to a complete stop was 3,150 feet, without reverse thrust. At Renton a strong crosswind, gusting at times and intermittent rain did little to help matters, but everyone was still certain that even on a wet runway the 747 would still stop safely in the available distance.

Cokely brought the 747 in over Lake Washington where the runway runs to the edge of the water, but the aircraft was not high enough to miss an earth bank on the shoreline 20 feet short of the runway and 2 feet 6 inches below the runway threshold and the right-hand body gear and wing gear were buckled in the impact. Hitting the runway, the 747 careered along it, showering sparks from its numbers three and four engines as the wing settled. Cokely managed to keep to the runway centreline and the 747 came to a halt 3,500 feet down the tarmac. Cokely was sacked for this incident. *Clipper Storm King* was repaired and eventually delivered to Pan Am in July 1970. In 1980 it was renamed *Clipper Ocean Telegraph* and it served the airline until 1986 when it

was relegated to storage in the Arizona desert. In 1989 the 747 was taken out of storage and converted to a 747-121SCD cargo aircraft.

Behind the scenes there was added drama, even at this late stage. Formal FAA certification for the 747 had still not been issued - although the FAA had determined that the engine problems would not compromise safety and had passed these, it was not entirely satisfied with emergency passenger evacuation from the upper deck and wanted these doors redesigned. Pan Am, aggrieved at the lower level of performance on the 747 to that originally promised (it was still 7 per cent short on range), now threatened to withhold $4 million from the final payment of each aircraft until Boeing had corrected several problems. As December dawned, Boeing met brinkmanship with brinkmanship, even threatening to sell the first 747s to TWA instead of to Pan Am. By this time Boeing was in severe financial hardship - final 747 development costs were later put at $750 million - and the recession, which had begun towards the end of 1968, was really beginning to bite.

A compromise ensued whereby Pan Am would withhold $2 million from the final payment on each 747 delivered until the problems, mostly with the engines, were rectified, paying the remainder in instalments. Finally, on 13 December 1969 N733PA *Clipper Young America* became the first 747 to be delivered to Pan Am when it was flown from Everett non-stop to Nassau in the Bahamas with a cargo of freight and then on to the Pan Am complex at Kennedy Airport in New York. A week later, on 19 December, N734PA *Clipper Flying Cloud* - in 1980 it was renamed *Clipper Champion of the Seas* - followed. [10]

On 15 January 1970 First Lady of the United States Pat Nixon christened N733PA *Clipper Young America* at Dulles International Airport (later renamed Washington Dulles International Airport) in the presence of Pan Am chairman Najeeb Halaby. Instead of champagne, red, white and blue water was sprayed on the aircraft. Pan Am chose this aircraft to make the first flight across the Atlantic with paying passengers six days later. On a bleak, bitterly cold evening at Dulles on 21 January, 336 passengers - who had reserved their seats two years earlier at a cost of $375 for a first-class one-way ticket - three flight crew (headed by Captain Robert M. 'Bob' Weeks, New York chief pilot) and eighteen cabin attendants boarded *Clipper Young America* for the first commercial flight of the 747, to London- Heathrow. Delayed by problems with the doors and the cargo hold, there were further problems when

Weeks tried to start N733PA's engines. Gusting winds, which had been blowing off the mudflats of Jamaica Bay, blew into the JT9Ds' tailpipes, restricting the flow of compressed air and exhaust gas and causing the engines to surge and produce temperature rises. The crew finally managed to stabilize the engines for take-off and at 7.29 pm, N733PA taxied out for take-off; but almost immediately it had to return to the terminal again when the number four engine exhaust temperature ran too high. (Later the fault was traced to an insensitive barometric fuel-control system which finally failed due to the high crosswind.) All the passengers had to be disembarked and were bussed to the terminal for meals in the restaurants while Pan Am worked out what it could do to prevent the occasion turning into a public relations disaster.

Finally there was only one solution and that was to replace the ailing *Clipper Young America* with a substitute aircraft, N736PA *Clipper Victor,* which had been delivered to the airline only the day before and was to be used for training. Delayed by an air traffic controllers' dispute, *Clipper Victor* finally taxied out at around 1.30 in the morning and at 1.50 took off for the flight to London. Much to the relief of Pan Am and everyone else, no further serious problems were encountered and the flight was made without incident - and without the in-flight movies, since the reserve 747 was not equipped for showing them. *Clipper Victor* covered the route in just six hours 16 minutes and landed at London-Heathrow to a great reception.

The vast cost of developing the 747 and building the

In March 1970 Trans World Airlines began operating the 747-131 on its New York to Los Angeles service and in March 1973, on its New York to London route. Later that same year, TWA began 747 operations between the US and Paris and Rome. (Author's collection)

In 1970 United became the first airline to operate the 747 across the Pacific, on its San Francisco-Honolulu service. Pictured with a 1930s Boeing 247 airliner is 747-122 N4703U William M. Allen, *the fifty-second 747 built, delivered to the airline on 30 June 1970. The aircraft was later leased to Pan Am as* Clipper Nautilus *and in September 1988 was converted to a 122/SCD. This 747 is still in service, with Polar Air Cargo N853FT. Polar was established in June 1993 and began operations with five 747 freighters in July 1994. (Boeing)*

Everett plant resulted in Boeing having to borrow heavily from a banking syndicate. During the final months before delivery of the first aircraft, Boeing had to repeatedly request additional funding to complete the project. Had this been refused, the Company's survival would have been threatened. Ultimately, the gamble succeeded and Boeing held a monopoly in very large passenger aircraft production for many years. However, the 747's introduction into service coincided with a sharp downturn in international passenger air traffic. Originally, Juan Trippe at Pan Am had based his airline's 747 requirements on the prediction that this would grow by 15 per cent a year, but by 1970, due mainly to a worldwide recession, it was only growing by 1.5 per cent. In November 1970 the US Senate voted against the

expenditure of a further $290 million on the Boeing supersonic airliner. On 24 March 1971, when Boeing was more than $1 billion in debt, Congress voted to end the SST project. Thousands of engineers lost their jobs and further pruning at all levels finally reduced the Boeing workforce by two-thirds, from 150,000 to 50,000. Fortunately the US government refunded the $31.6 million development costs Boeing had already paid out on the SST. The sale of the SST mock-up, which had been built at a cost of $12 million, to a Florida promoter, raised another $43,000!

Despite the gloomy outlook, one by one many of the national airlines began operation of the 747 on the world's routes. In March 1970, when Boeing production of the 747 peaked at seven aircraft a month, TWA began

Braniff International's N610BN 'Big Orange' seen at London Gatwick. On 15 January 1971 Braniff introduced the 100th 747 into service, on its Dallas-Fort Worth to Honolulu, Hawaii, route. For a two-year period this single -127 was accumulating flying time faster than any aircraft in the world, with a daily round-trip flight of 7,500 miles) between Dallas, Texas and Honolulu. Daily utilization was fourteen hours, a figure never before attained by the airline industry. (G M Simons Collection)

operating 747-131 (N93102 *City of Paris*, which had been delivered on 31 December 1969) on its New York to Los Angeles service; three years later, in March 1973, it was operating on its New York to London route. Later that same year, TWA began 747-131 operations between the US and Paris and Rome. Also in March 1970 American Airlines began 747 operations on its New York to Los Angeles route using two 747-121 aircraft - *Clipper Rival* and *Clipper Derby* - leased from Pan Am pending delivery of its own aircraft. The first overseas airline to buy the 747 was Lufthansa, whose first aircraft, 747-130 D-ABYA *Nordrhein-Westfalen* (the twelfth 747 built), first flew on 18 February 1970 and

was received on 10 March. The following month D-ABYA entered service on the German national carrier's Frankfurt-New York route, where it replaced 707s. In June 1970 Continental Airlines introduced the 747-124 on its Los Angeles to Honolulu route and JAL began operations between Tokyo, Hong Kong and Los Angeles. In July 1970 Northwest Orient began 747-151 flights between New York, Chicago, Seattle and Tokyo. United Air Lines became the first to operate the 747-122 over the Pacific, on its San Francisco-Honolulu service. By the end of 1970 a dozen airlines were operating 747s: Pan Am, American, Continental, Northwest Orient, United, National and Delta in the US (the last two on

By the end of 1970, three other European airlines were operating 747-100s: Air France was flying -128 F-BPVB, one of sixteen -128s for the airline, pictured, which was delivered on 25 March 1970; Alitalia; and Iberia. Japan Air lines (JAL) was the first airline in Asia to take delivery of the 747, with eight -146s. (Boeing)

El Al 747-256B 4X-AXA taxiing at LHR. This aircraft first flew on 15 May 1971 and was delivered to the airline eleven days' later.

By the end of 1970, seven US airlines were operating Boeing 747-100s: Pan Am, American, Continental, Northwest Orient, United, National and Delta (the last two on domestic routes only). Pictured is a Northwest Orient 747-151 (nine of which were ordered).

domestic routes only) and Lufthansa, Air France, Alitalia and Iberia in Europe and Japan Air Lines OAL) in Asia. On 15 January 1971 Braniff introduced the 100th 747 (-127 N601BN) into service, on its Dallas-Fort Worth to Honolulu route. In November 1970 Eastern Airlines had begun 747 services using *Clipper Constitution* on lease from Pan Am and in January 1971 also leased this airline's *Clipper Bostonian* and *Clipper*

Red Jacket. By the end of 1971 these operators were joined by other, European 747 customers, by Aer Lingus, the Irish national carrier, BOAC and the Belgian airline SABENA. BOAC had ordered six 747-136s as early as 1966 and the first began scheduled services in April 1971. Five years later BOAC (since 1974, British Airways) had increased its 747-136 fleet to eighteen.

The 'Spacious Age' had indeed arrived.

Footnotes for Chapter 3

10 Full FAA 747 Type Approval was obtained on 31 December 1969 with the issuing of Approved Type Certificate A20WE.

Chapter 4

Pilot Error

Flights involving 747-100 aircraft rarely had any serious incidents. In the five years after the first aircraft went into service in January 1970, the 747 had already established itself as probably the safest and most dependable aircraft in airline history. In service with a dozen airlines and with a total of over two million hours in the air, its safety record remained 100 per cent intact. Before the 747, no new aircraft flew as many as 500,000 hours without a fatal accident. Insurance companies, assuming that there would be a crash of some description for every half a million hours of operation, had predicted that 747s would suffer three fatal crashes in the first eighteen months of operation. During the first ten years of service, there were five fatal 747 crashes, three of which were pilot error. Besides these, on 6 September 1970, 747-121 N752PA Clipper Fortune *of Pan Am, en route from Amsterdam to New York, was hijacked by Palestinian terrorists and flown to Cairo where it was blown up on the ground after the passengers and crew had been released. The aircraft had only been delivered to the airline just four months earlier.* [11]

At 1501 Pacific daylight time on the afternoon of 30 July 1971 747-121 N747PA *Clipper America* with 199 passengers and nineteen crew on board departed from the gate at San Francisco International Airport for the second leg of Pan Am Flight 845 to Tokyo.[12] The flight had originated in Los Angeles at 1311 and forty-seven minutes' later had arrived at San Francisco International where the crew changed before continuing on to Japan. The crew consisted of 57-year old Captain Calvin Y. Dyer of Redwood City, California who had been a pilot with Pan Am for thirty-two years, First Officer 41-year old Paul E. Oakes of Reno, Nevada, Second Officer 34-year old Wayne E. Sager of Arvada, Colorado, First Flight Engineer 57-year old Winfree A. Horne of Los Altos, California, Second Flight Engineer Roderic E. Proctor of Palo Alto, California who was also 57 years' old; and fourteen stewardesses. Captain Dyer began flying as a pilot with Pan American in 1939. He was in the first class of Pan American pilots to check out in the 747. He attended and satisfactorily completed ground school in San Francisco during December 1969 and then began his flight training on the 747 at Roswell, New Mexico on 7 February 1970. Paul Oakes was employed by Pan American in November 1955. He began his 747 ground school training in December 1969 and his flight training in March 1970. He received his rating on the 747 on 14 March 1970 after nine hours of flight training and received above average grades on both his rating and right seat qualification rides.

Captain Dyer and Paul Oakes had already calculated the three critical take-off speeds - V1, VR and V2 - for a departure from runway 28L.[13] To arrive at these calculations the first officer would have checked the maximum permitted take-off weight of the 747 in the conditions prevailing and using the table for runway 28L with runway length and gradient in mind and also wind components and temperature.

Having calculated the take-off speeds for 28L, the airport's recorded information service then announced that this runway was unavailable. With runway 28L denied them, Captain Dyer asked for another runway and after some heated discussion, was given 01R. This runway ends on the bay shoreline and built out into the water is a long pier with handrails and tall angle-iron gantries, carrying the runway approach lights. The Pan Am dispatcher advised Captain Dyer to 'start at the painted line' and told him that he would have '9,500 feet plus clearway ahead of you'.[15] However, the start line of 01R had been moved 1,000 feet so that jet blast did not affect traffic on a freeway nearby, so only 8,500 feet was usable; shorter compared to 28L, with less favourable wind conditions. (The 747 needs about 1½ miles of runway to accelerate to its take-off speed.) Despite the shorter length, it was later determined that the aircraft could have taken off safely, had the proper procedures been followed. On the assumption that they would have 10,600 feet available for departure on runway 28L, Captain Dyer and his crew had decided to use 10 degrees of flap. This would not be quite enough for a 747 departure from runway 01R. The 'bug' markers on the airspeed indicator (ASI) for the V1, VR and V2 speeds had previously been calculated for runway 28L. The 747 took off at 15:29 PDT. Oakes watched his ASI and dutifully called out to the captain as the aircraft went through the V1 and VR speeds. With 10 degrees flap and the power settings employed, the 316 tons of aircraft and payload should have seen the nose-wheel lift off at 157 knots (VR). Oakes actually called VR at around 160 knots instead of the planned 164 knots, because by now the crew could see that they were fast running out of runway. As the ASI registered 165 knots the 747 began ripping through 300 feet of the pier-like structure extending out from the runway over the bay.

A smaller aircraft would not have survived the impact. *Clipper America,* however, was able to climb away even though three lengths of angle iron 17 feet long and 2 inches' square penetrated the cabin floor, destroyed the wing flaps, bent the landing gear and shattered the fuselage bulkheads. The right main under-body landing gear was forced up and into the fuselage

and the left under-body landing gear was ripped loose and remained dangling beneath the aircraft. Other systems damaged in the impact included Numbers 1, 3 and 4 hydraulic systems, several wing and empennage control surfaces and their mechanisms, electrical systems including the anti skid control and three of the evacuation slides. Wreckage too was embedded in the tail-plane and elevator system. Incredibly no one was killed, mainly because there were few people sitting in the cabin above the wing where the impact occurred. However, one of the light gantries which penetrated the cabin, severely injured two passengers; one in seat 47G (near amputation of left leg below the knee) and the other in 48G (severe laceration and crushing of left upper arm) before exiting through the roof and lodging in the vertical fin. Another piece ripped through three toilets before exiting through the rear of the cabin.

'It didn't get up in the air fast enough and hit something at the end of the runway' said Mrs. Teresa Galloway, a passenger, 'Part of the inside seat sections were pushed up and that's how people got hurt.'

Crucially, the 747's quadruple redundancy prevented total catastrophe. Although three of the hydraulic systems were severed in the impact, the fourth escaped when a 'missile' of angle iron missed it by just four inches. Captain Dyer was thus able to circle the area for an hour and forty-two minutes while the crew dumped fuel prior to landing on runway 28L where emergency services were deployed. During this time damage to the aircraft was assessed and the injured treated by doctors on the passenger list. During landing, six tyres on the under-wing landing gear failed but fortunately, enough of the undercarriage remained to be able to use the wheels, but the damaged elevators did not work properly and the reverse thrust on three of the engines failed. (Reverse thrust functioned only on engine 4), causing the 747 to veer off the runway on its damaged landing gear and came to a halt. Evacuation commenced from the front due to a failure to broadcast the evacuation

N736PA Clipper Victor *comes in to land at London Heathrow The aircraft was destroyed in what was to become known as the Tenerife air disaster on 27 March 1977..*

order over the cabin address system (it was erroneously broadcast over the radio), the order being given by one of the flight crew exiting the cockpit and noticing that evacuation had not commenced. During this time, the aircraft settled aft, resting on its tail in a nose-up attitude.[16]

The four forward slides were unsafe for use due to the greater elevation and high winds. Most passengers evacuated from the rear six slides. Eight passengers using the forward slides sustained serious back injuries and were hospitalised. Other passengers suffered minor injuries such as abrasions and sprains. During the subsequent emergency evacuation twenty-seven more passengers sustained injuries, eight of them serious.

The accident was investigated by the National Transportation Safety Board (NTSB), which issued its final report on 24 May 1972. According to the NTSB, the Probable Cause of the accident was: ... the pilot's use of incorrect takeoff reference speeds. This resulted from a series of irregularities involving: (1) the collection and dissemination of airport information; (2) aircraft dispatching; and (3) crew management and discipline; which collectively rendered ineffective the air carrier's operational control system.[17]

Pan Am still had a safety record that was the envy of the airline industry and the 747 was the safest airliner ever operated by the carrier but in the late 1970s, 747s hit the headlines for all the wrong reasons. Once again in the long history of aviation, it was human error that was to blame but in neither of two fatal 747 disasters - the 747-121 ground collision with a KLM 747-206B at Tenerife in March 1977 and the terrorist bombing of Flight 103 in December 1988 - was the 747 or the Pan Am crew held to blame.

On Sunday 27 March 1977 N736PA *Clipper Victor* (the same 747-121 that had made the inaugural flight from New York to London-Heathrow on 22 January 1970) and 747-206B PH-BUF *Rijn* [Rhine] on KLM charter Flight 4805 from Amsterdam were among the airliners en route to Las Palmas Airport on the east coast of the Spanish island of Gran Canaria just off the west coast of North Africa. *Clipper Victor* was on charter to Royal Cruise Lines and making Pan Am Flight 1736 from Los Angeles and New York mostly carrying a group of elderly tourists, but also including two children to join a cruise ship. N736PA had departed Los Angeles on the evening of 26 March local date (01.29 hours GMT, 27 March) with 275 passengers for New York and Las Palmas. On the stop-over at JFK a further 103 passengers boarded, bringing the total to 378. The crew of 16 was changed. At 07.42 hours GMT Flight PA1736, call sign Clipper 1736, departed Kennedy for Las Palmas under the command of Captain Victor Grubbs with First Officer Robert Bragg and Flight Engineer George Warns. Also on board were thirteen flight attendants.

About 1¼ hours after *Clipper Victor's* take-off from New York, KLM Flight KL4805 left Schiphol Airport in Amsterdam at 09.00 hours also en route to Las Palmas. The KLM 747-206B was operated by KLM on behalf of Holland International travel group. On board were 234 tourists bound for the Canary Islands, plus a Dutch tour guide named Robina van Lanschot, who lived on the island in the town of Puerto de la Cruz. After disembarking the passengers, PH-BUF was scheduled as Flight KL4806 to fly back to Amsterdam with an equally large group of returning holidaymakers. The pilot was Captain Jacob Veldhuyzen van Zanten, a senior KLM training captain. He had given Klass Meurs the First Officer his Boeing 747 qualification check about two months before. The third member of the flight crew was the Flight Engineer William Schreuder. Also on board were eleven cabin staff to look after the charter passengers.

As both 747s converged on Las Palmas, at 1.15pm a bomb planted by the separatist organisation Fuerzas Armadas Guanches [18] was detonated in the passenger terminal at Las Palmas Airport about one hour before the arrival of the KLM 747, damaging the check-in area and injuring a number of people. The explosion was followed by a warning of the possibility of a second bomb. As a precaution the authorities declared the airport closed and all flights were diverted to Los Rodeos Airport on Tenerife located just 50 miles from Gran Canaria in the northern part of the island and surrounded by mountains ranging from 6,600 feet to 14,500 feet. The Las Palmas blast killed no one but it directly set in motion a sequence of events which ultimately would lead to a catastrophe of horrific proportions.

Captain van Zanten diverted to Los Rodeos airport and that same afternoon landed at 13.38 hours GMT, the same time as local, on Runway 30. Grubbs had asked permission to hold until Las Palmas was available again, but this request was denied and he too made for Los Rodeos, his alternative destination and *Clipper Victor* touched down thirty-seven minutes after the KLM jet. By now the apron was crowded with diverted airliners and some were parked on the taxiways. At first van Zanten was reluctant to disembark his passengers because Las Palmas might suddenly reopen, but after twenty minutes of waiting he changed his mind and the passengers were disembarked and bussed to the terminal while Pan Am's passengers remained on board.

The weather was clear and sunny. Many aircraft were diverted from Las Palmas that day and, with Tenerife's own weekend traffic, Los Rodeos was becoming overcrowded. When Las Palmas reopened, at about 14.30 hours Tenerife air traffic control released the Pan Am 747 to continue its journey. Two Pan Am staff joined the flight for the short hop to Las Palmas and they were placed in the jump seats on the flight deck, bringing the total on board to 396; 380 passengers and 16 crew. The KLM passengers were called from the terminal building, but it took time to bus them back to their 747 and re-board the flight. Of those who landed in Tenerife only Robina van Lanschot, who wanted to see her boyfriend that night, chose not to re-board the 747, giving a total on board PH-BUF of 248; 234 passengers and fourteen crew.

Clipper Victor's path to the take-off runway was blocked because it was parked behind four other airliners on the Runway 12 holding area only a short distance from the main apron on the northern side of the runway, with the KLM 747 nearest of these, next to the threshold of Runway 12. The other three airliners were a DC-8, a Boeing 737 and a Boeing 727 and being smaller than a 747 they managed to ease past the KLM -206B; but Captain Grubbs and Robert Bragg had to leave the flight deck and measure the distance between the two 747s to see if they could pass safely. They saw that they could not, so reluctantly they agreed that they would have to wait until the KLM 747 taxied out and took off first. This procedure was delayed by an hour and a half because the KLM 747's passengers had to be bussed back out from the terminal and later, Captain van Zanten decided that he needed to refuel, presumably to save time at Las Palmas before the return flight to Amsterdam.[19] It was therefore evening before the KLM 747 was finally ready for departure. [20]

The time was now about 16.30 hours and the Pan Am crew had been on duty for $10^{3}/_{4}$ hours. They were beginning to feel the strain and were looking forward to their rest after the short 25 minute hop to Las Palmas. The KLM crew had been on duty for $8^{3}/_{4}$ hours, but they still had to complete the round trip back to Amsterdam. Three hours remained to the deadline for departure from Las Palmas, but the weather, which had been fine when the aircraft had first landed, was now turning quite bad, with cloud and fog reducing visibility dramatically and the KLM time limit could easily be compromised if the Dutch flight crew had to wait for the clouds to clear. As it was, the duty limit had not yet been confirmed and even with fuel on board the transit through Las Palmas could be slow in the overcrowded airport. If the KLM crew ran out of hours and PH-BUF was grounded in Las Palmas, there would be insurmountable problems finding 250 beds at such short notice and they and the joining passengers would no doubt have to spend the night in the airport. The crew would also be late back to Amsterdam and the aircraft would miss the next day's schedules so it was hardly surprising that van Zanten was anxious to leave Los Rodeos. Grubbs and his crew, too, more than a little irritated at being held back by KLM, would also be happy to get moving.

Permission for KLM to depart did not come through until refuelling was almost finished and vindicated Captain van Zanten's decision to complete the process in Tenerife. As the Clipper crew waited, the American passengers were invited to view the flight deck and questions about the flight were answered. At 16.45 hours Captain van Zanten signed the fuel log and at 16.51 hours, with pre-start checks completed, KLM requested start-up. Alert to the situation Pan Am heard KLM's radio call. 'Aha,' said Captain Grubbs, 'he's ready!'

The Clipper also received start clearance as KLM was starting engines and the two crews prepared to taxi but by now clouds of varying density from light to dark were blowing down the departure runway 30 with the north-westerly 12 to 15 knot wind. At times the runway visibility increased to two or three kilometres and at other times dropped to 300 metres. The runway centre line lights were inoperative making judgement on take-off more difficult. There was also heavy moisture in the air with the passage of the clouds and aircraft were frequently required to use their windscreen wipers to clear the view when taxiing.[21] Both the Pan and KLM flight crews had to rely exclusively on radio communication for their instructions. In the tower two controllers were on duty and they were using one radio frequency for taxi instructions and the approach frequency for both take-off and approach communications.[22]

The KLM 747 received permission to backtrack along the full length of Runway 12 and carry out a 180-degree turn into wind to face the take-off direction. In the meantime, Pan Am 1736 received clearance to backtrack also and to exit at the third taxi-way. The very poor visibility, the radio communication difficulties, as well as fatigue and mounting frustration, all combined to cause confusion, as a result of which the Pan Am crew missed the third exit in the fog bank and carried on to the next exit before leaving the runway.

At 17.05:28 Captain van Zanten stopped the aircraft at the end of the runway. Highly impatient, he immediately opened up the throttles much to the consternation of Klass Meurs the first officer and William Schreuder the flight engineer, and was already rolling down the runway even though he had not received clearance to take off. Meurs said 'Wait a minute, we don't have an ATC clearance' but at 17.06:11 van Zanten released the brakes and a second later said, 'Let's go, check thrust' without taking his hands off the throttles. Meurs heard the Pan Am 747 communicate with the tower saying that they would confirm when N736PA was clear of the runway, meaning that at this stage it was not. The KLM 747 was now on a collision course with the Pan Am 747 which was still turning towards the exit and had not yet cleared the runway!

The Pan Am flight crew were not as yet aware that the KLM had started his take-off run. Grubbs said, 'Let's get the hell out of here.' Robert Bragg agreed. ''Yeh, he's anxious, isn't he.' George Warns said, 'Yeh, after he held us up for an 'hour and a half ... now he's in a rush.' Warns had no sooner finished speaking when Grubbs saw KLM's landing lights appear, coming straight at them through the cloud bank.

Pandemonium broke out. Grubbs exclaimed, 'There he is ... look at him ... that ... that son-of-a-bitch is coming.'

Bragg shouted: 'Get off! Get off! Get off!'

When the Pan Am crew saw the KLM 747 bearing down on them out of the fog with its landing lights on, Victor Grubbs opened the throttles and tried desperately to swing his aircraft to the left and off the runway in an attempt to run clear. At about the same time Klass Meurs the Dutch first officer, still unaware of Pan Am's presence, called 'Vee one', the go or no go decision speed. Four seconds later the Dutch crew spotted the Pan Am 747 trying to scramble clear. By this time, however, the KLM 747 had reached V1 and was committed to take off. Then Captain van Zanten saw the Pan Am 747 in front of him. The Dutch captain exclaimed 'Oh...' At this point the KLM 747 was doing 150mph so it was too late for any evasive action - all van Zanten could do was pull back sharply on the control column and hope that he had enough height to miss the top of the Pan Am jet. The Dutch jet's tail struck the ground in the high nose up angle leaving a twenty metre long streak of metal on the runway before becoming airborne about 1,300 metres down the runway, near the Charlie 4 turn-off. The nose wheel of the Dutch aircraft skidded over the top of the Pan Am 747 and the KLM left outboard number one engine just grazed the side of the American jet. The main landing gear smashed into the American 747 about the position of Clipper's number three engine and sheared off its tail. The collision was not excessively violent and many passengers thought that a small bomb had

exploded. Pan Am's first-class upstairs lounge disappeared on impact, as did most of the top of the fuselage. Openings appeared on the left side of the fuselage and some passengers were able to escape by these routes. The Pan Am jet had its nose sticking off the edge of the runway and survivors simply jumped down on to the grass. The first-class lounge floor had collapsed, but the flight crew, plus the two employees in the jump seats, managed to leap below into what was left of the first-class section and make their escape. On the left side the engines were still turning and there was a fire under the wing with explosions taking place. In all, 326 people died instantly in the Pan Am 747. Only seventy people escaped from the wreckage and nine died in hospital later from their injuries. Amazingly, fifty-two passengers and nine crew had survived. John Coombs of Haleiwa, Hawaii said that sitting in the nose of the Clipper probably saved his life: We all settled back and the next thing an explosion took place and the whole port side, left side of the plane, was just torn wide open. The main landing gear of the KLM 747 sheared off on impact. The jet remained airborne briefly before hitting the runway about 500 feet further on. It slid for a further 1,000 feet and veered to the right, rotating clockwise through a 90-degree turn before coming to a halt and PH-BUF then exploded.

The controllers in the tower heard the explosions and at first thought that a fuel tank had been blown up by terrorists, but reports of a fire were soon received. The fire services were alerted and news of the emergency was transmitted to all aircraft. Both 747s on the runway were called in turn without success. The fire tenders had difficulty getting to the scene of the carnage in the misty and congested conditions but eventually the conflagration was seen through the fog. On closer inspection the KLM jet was found completely ablaze. Then another fire was seen further down the runway and

KLM's 747-206B PH-BUF Rijn *seen undergoing routine servicing during a turn-around at Amsterdam.*

was assumed to be a part of the same aircraft. Then it was evident that it was a second aircraft. Since the KLM jet was already beyond saving, all efforts for the time being were concentrated on the Pan Am aircraft. Airport staff and individuals bravely ran to help the survivors but all 248 passengers and crew on board the KLM aircraft were dead. In all 583 people had perished aboard the two jets. As the survivors were being tended in Santa Cruz, firemen at the airport continued to fight the conflagrations on the runway. Fire crews succeeded in saving the left side of the Pan Am jet and the wing, from which 15,000-20,000 kilogrammes of fuel were later recovered. It was not until the afternoon of the following day that both fires were extinguished.

Captain van Zanten was KLM's preferred pilot for publicity such as magazine advertisements. As such, the airline attempted to contact him to give public statements regarding the disaster, before learning that he was the captain involved. About 70 crash investigators - or 'tin-kickers' as they are called in America - from Spain, the Netherlands, the United States and the two airline companies were involved in the investigation. Facts showed that there had been misinterpretations and false assumptions. Analysis of the CVR transcript showed that the KLM pilot was convinced that he had been cleared for takeoff, while the Tenerife control tower was certain that the KLM 747 was stationary at the end of the runway and awaiting takeoff clearance. It appears Meurs was not as certain about take-off clearance as the captain.

In 1978 a second airport was inaugurated on Tenerife: the new Tenerife South Airport (TFS). This airport now serves the majority of international tourist flights. Los Rodeos, renamed to Tenerife North Airport (TFN), was not used by the major airlines after April 1980 when a Dan Air 727 crashed on approach to the airport, killing all 146 passengers and crew. It was then used only for domestic and inter-island flights, but in 2002 a new terminal was opened and it carries international traffic once again, including budget airlines. Los Rodeos has since been replaced by a new airport constructed at Reina Sofia on the southern and much lower reaches of Tenerife.

The first loss of passengers in a 747 accident had occurred on 20 November 1974 when Flight 540 flown by D-ABYB *Hessen,* a Lufthansa 747-130, which was carrying 157 people (140 passengers and 17 crew members) crashed shortly after take-off at Embakasi Airport, Nairobi. The flight was operating the final segment of its Frankfurt-Nairobi-Johannesburg route. As the aircraft was making its takeoff from runway 24 the pilots felt a buffeting vibration. The captain continued the ascent and retracted the landing gear. However, as this was being done, the aircraft started to descend and the stall warning system light came on. The aircraft continued to descend and approximately 3,700 feet from the end of the runway, the 747 grazed bushes and grass. It then struck an elevated access road and broke up. The left wing exploded and fire spread to the fuselage. Fifty-five passengers and four crew died. [23]

The cause of the crash was determined to be a stall caused by the leading edge flaps having been left in retracted position. Without leading edge flaps deployed, the 747-130's stalling angle of attack was much lower, especially at a hot and high airport like Nairobi's with its airport elevation of 5,327 feet. The thinner air at higher altitudes generates less lift and further degrades the aircraft's ability to handle high angles of attack, as well as reducing the thrust provided by the 747's four turbofan engines. The elevation and temperature at the airport were within the capability of the 747, but only with leading and trailing edge flaps extended. With the leading edge flaps retracted, the aircraft lacked sufficient lift and thrust to continue climbing once out of the ground effect found near the surface. The flight engineer was found to have failed to open the engine bleed air valves as required on the pre-flight checklist. This prevented bleed air from flowing to the 747's pneumatic system and since the leading edge flaps on the 747 are pneumatically driven, kept it from deploying the leading edge flaps for takeoff.

Prior to this, no fewer than eight previous take-offs by 747s of other airlines had resulted in problems with the leading-edge flaps. Each of these incidents was reported to the FAA, who did nothing; neither did the CAA. Fortunately, thanks to the safety margins built into the 747 and to the fact that none of the airports involved was at extreme height above sea level, the lack of leading-edge flaps on take-off was not as critical as it should have been and all the aircraft involved still managed to get off safely.

D-ABYB's flight crew was blamed for not performing a satisfactory pre-take-off checklist, but the accident report also faulted the lack of adequate warning systems which could have alerted the crew to the problem. Two previous occurrences of this error had been reported, but in those cases the pilots had been able to recover the aircraft in time. After this third deadly incident, Boeing added systems to warn pilots if such conditions existed prior to takeoff.

In 1972 an incident involving BOAC had resulted in only half the leading-edge flaps on each wing being extended before take-off. Fortunately the 747 had taken off safely and the fault was later found to be an electric circuit breaker which had been left in the tripped (or off) position after an engineering maintenance check.

However, there had been no TOCW ('take-off configuration warning' system) alert and on further investigation it was found that there was a simple reason for this: incredibly, there was no connection fitted between the TOCW warning device and the leading-edge (LE) flap system. Also, it was found that it was possible for pilots to take off without any of the LE flaps extended and to receive no warning of this at all because of the way the green warning-light circuits were wired. BOAC warned all its 747 pilots of the need to double-check the flap settings and the company dutifully notified Boeing, who issued a maintenance service bulletin giving the necessary changes in the LE flap circuit wiring. Unfortunately the bulletin was only ever issued for BOAC and Aer Lingus 747s.

Because the 747's wings, like most large airliners, are slender and lean and provide sufficient lift for optimum cruising speeds of over 500mph, they will not normally provide enough speed in the 150mph region - that is during take-off and landing - when lift and low approach speeds, respectively, leave little margin for error. The 747 therefore employs triple-slotted, trailing-edge (TE) flaps on the rear of the wings, while three conventional Krueger flaps are hinged to the leading edge inboard of the inner engine pylon, to provide a total twenty-six LE flaps thirteen on each side) arranged in sections along the front of the wings. The variable-camber LE flaps fold flat under the wing when not in use, but for landing and take-off they are extended by a clever linkage mechanism which simultaneously 'bends' the fibreglass panels into a curved aerodynamic contour.

Prior to take-off, the TE flaps that extend from the rear of the wings in a downward curve and the LE flaps, are let out to provide the additional lift that the 747 needs to clear the runway safely. (Used in conjunction, the flaps increase the wing area by as much as 21 per cent and lift by almost 90 per cent.) When a safe flying speed is attained, the flaps are returned to the inside of the wings and the aircraft can proceed on its way without incurring any further aerodynamic drag penalty. Pilots have the choice of settings so they can vary the total amount extended; this is so that they can select the correct degree of flap in relation to the weight of the aircraft, the length of runway being used, the weather and altitude conditions and engine power required for take-off.

On the 747 the TE flaps are driven hydraulically, each of the four systems being pressurized separately to 3,000 psi by a pump mounted on each engine. The LE flaps, on the other hand, are powered by five pneumatic motors driven by bleed air from the engines at up to 45 psi and operated via torque tubes. (Both the TE and the LE flaps can be actuated by back-up electrical motors if required.) Just one lever mounted on the flight deck of 747 s controls and harmonizes groupings of both the TE and LE flaps. As soon as the TE flaps are selected and move through 5 degrees, the LE flaps will deploy automatically. (This sequence was adopted to reduce wing loading and prevent excessive asymmetry in the event of a control-system failure.) If the flaps were not selected for take-off, a green light would illuminate on each pilot's instrument panel, while a separate green light for each of the twenty-six sections on the wings would light up on the flight engineer's panel. In retrospect, mounting the pilots' green light very near the three green lights that confirm that the gear is down and locked, could probably cause the pilot to miss the fact that a light was out. Judging by the number of 747 take-off incidents prior to the Nairobi crash where the aircraft got off the ground without extending the flaps, this must have happened on more than one occasion.

Just before the Nairobi crash, Lufthansa and some other European airlines changed their engine start-up procedures, Previously, Lufthansa required pilots to start their engines while the air valves to the five pneumatic motors were open. Pilots could now start their engines

D-ABYB, Lufthansa's 747-130 Hessen.

with the LE pneumatic valves closed, their pre-take-off checklist reminding them to turn the valves on again before the flaps were selected. (The TOCW klaxon, which blares out on the flight deck if any item has not been set prior to take-off, was wired to sound as the third engine thrust lever was advanced beyond 50 per cent of its travel.) Because both the TE and LE flaps were activated simultaneously by just the one lever, the TOCW klaxon alert would only sound if the TE flaps were not correctly set - as the LE flaps are set in the same action that sets the TE flaps, there seemed no reason to fit a separate warning device for the LE flaps. However, if the pneumatic valves had not been opened after engine start-up, the LE flaps would not have been extended - and because there was no TOCW device linked directly to the LE flaps, no audible warning would have alerted the flight crew to this fact.

So, early in the morning of 20 November, Lufthansa flight 540/19 from Frankfurt taxied out at Nairobi after its short refuelling stop and prepared to take off for Johannesburg. At the controls for take-off in the right-hand seat was the 35-year-old first officer, Hans-Joachim Schacke. His captain, 53-year-old Christian Krack, would fly the 747 on the last leg of the flight to South Africa. Everything seemed normal on take-off, but as the 747 reached 145 knots (165mph) the aircraft began to buffet and shake. It lost acceleration and passed only 100 feet above the airport perimeter before it plummeted earthward. D-ABYB's tail struck the ground 3,674 feet from the end of the runway and the 747 bounced and impacted on the ground. Fifty-five passengers and four cabin crew died in the resulting inferno and another fifty-four people were injured before they could be rescued. Fortunately, eighty-five passengers and thirteen crew survived. This time the failure to extend the leading-edge flaps on take-off had proved critical because without them the 747 simply could not obtain maximum lift in the thin air at Nairobi Airport (which is 5,327 feet above sea level) to become airborne.

The last of 167 standard 747-100s was delivered on 12 July 1976 but ever since 1968 Boeing had been developing plans for a heavier and more powerful version known initially as the '747B'. A two-phase programme was created for the 747B, whereby Phase A looked to an improved 747-100 weighing 733,000lb and Phase B, where the weight would rise to 795,000lb. The first phase idea was essential if Boeing were to maintain its 747 momentum with the airlines, although the changes were not as great as those involved in the second phase; in this wholesale structural changes would be made to the aircraft and more powerful engines would be required than were then available. In Phase B, Boeing would have to increase the span by 24 feet to 219 feet 8 inches and re-engineer the outboard wing structure to move the number one and number four engines further outboard. The bigger wing would deliver greater performance with shorter take-off and better initial cruise altitude and noise on take-off would be noticeable reduced. Although Phase B represented a major departure from the 747 as first conceived, the incentives were vastly increased passenger and cargo loads on the transatlantic and polar routes.

Phase B relied heavily on a suitable powerplant becoming available and the Pratt & Whitney JT9D problems which continued to manifest themselves during development of the 747-100 hardly inspired confidence. The 43,500lb-thrust JT9D- 3A engine which powered the initial production versions of the 747 was simply not powerful enough to lift the heavier versions planned for the 747. By using water-injection, Pratt & Whitney were able to offer a quick-fix solution to the problem of increasing the available thrust on the JT9D-7. This innovation, which had been introduced successfully on piston-engined aircraft in World War II and more recently on military jets, involved squirting distilled water into the turbines to make the air-fuel mixture expand faster and lower the operating temperatures.

Used in short bursts, the JT9D-3AW produced an additional 1,500lb of thrust to increase maximum take-off thrust to 45,000lb per engine. Static 747 tests carried out in February 1970 proved that not only could Phase A still take place, but the possibility of developing the 747B further came with the news that the aircraft weight could in fact be upped to 755,000lb. (This was just as well because amongst other things the static tests revealed that the increased weights meant that the side-of-body wing ribs needed to be strengthened.) Starting in November 1970, all Pan Am's twenty-four remaining 747-121s were returned to Everett to have the new water-injected engines installed. The re-engined aircraft, which during the upgrade also received improved fuel system, flaps, landing gear and doors, were classified as 747-100A by Boeing. Their take-off weight was increased to 755,000lb, as anticipated, which gave an additional 460 miles in range, or a 15 per cent greater payload.

Boeing, meanwhile, planned to complete the first bigger-winged Phase B passenger version by June 1971 and the first 'super-freighter' version was planned to follow it by February 1972. However, problems with the JT9D became too great and Phase B never materialized. In April 1973 Boeing looked again at ideas to stretch the baseline -100 series for the short- and long-range routes. Having leapfrogged ahead of the competition and created a completely new market, Boeing had been even more far-sighted when it came to future development of the aircraft. Even with the same basic 747 wing, Boeing were of the opinion that the aircraft could be stretched or expanded to carry up to 1,000 passengers if need be.

Ironically, when they were first offered the huge 747 some airlines had stated that the aircraft was too big for their needs and had wanted it down-sized before they would buy it; but from the outset, the -100 series was planned to be stretched as and when the passenger market demanded it. Convenient 'break'-points at certain sections in the fuselage had been designed in before -100 construction, whereby two fuselage 'plugs', one forward of the wing and one aft, could be inserted in section 42 and between sections 44 and 46, respectively, to lengthen the baseline fuselage by up to as much as fifty feet. In all, Boeing came up with four potential growth proposals, of which two involved stretching the fuselage, one was a double-deck version and another was a double-deck and stretched configuration. The potential extent of the 'stretch' or enlargement to a double-deck configuration varied depending on whether the aircraft would be used for short-range or long-range operation. The smallest of the stretch options was to insert a 60 inch fuselage plug ahead of the wing and a 140 inch plug aft of it: on the short-range version this would allow 666 passengers to be carried and on the long-range version it would permit seating for 472 people. At the same time, Boeing

examined the possibility of extending the upper deck in preference to stretching the single-deck areas or adopting a double-deck arrangement. A second stretch option was to insert a 300 inch plug ahead of the wing and a 140 inch plug aft of it. This combined extension would increase the overall length of the 747 to more than 280 feet, allowing 716 passengers to be carried on the short-range version and up to 544 passengers on the long-range version. Of the two double-deck designs, one involved extending the upper-deck area to the tail, while the other, much more ambitious proposal, was to employ the same upper-deck stretch and also insert a 160 inch plug forward of the wing and a 140 inch plug aft of it. The first of these proposals would allow 624 passengers to be carried on the long-range version and 847 passengers on the short-range version. Stretching the upper deck and adding the two fuselage plugs would create cabin areas on the long-range version for the seating of 732 passengers and up to 1,000 passengers on the short-range version. The perennial problem of whether engines powerful enough to fly them could be developed successfully also had to be considered.

The timing of all these proposals could not have been worse, coinciding as they did with the 1973

747-237B VT-EBD Emperor Ashoka *first flew on 8 March 1971 and was delivered to Air India on 22 March. On 1 January 1978 the aircraft crashed into the Arabian Sea after take-off from Bombay. (Boeing)*

747-3B3 HL-7468 of Korean Air. This aircraft crashed in hills on approach to Antonio B. Won Pat International Airport, Guam on 6 August 1997. Altogether, 228 of the 254 persons on board died. (Boeing)

international oil crisis which resulted in a reduction of passenger traffic and several airlines did not have enough passengers to fly the 747 economically. They replaced them with the smaller and recently introduced McDonnell Douglas DC-10 and Lockheed L-1011 (and later the 767 and A300 twinjets). Having tried replacing coach seats on its 747s with piano bars in an attempt to attract more customers, American Airlines eventually relegated its 747s to cargo service and in 1983 exchanged them with Pan Am for smaller aircraft; Delta Air Lines also removed its 747s from service after several years.[24] Although none of the four potential growth proposals actually left the drawing board, they did serve to encourage the later development in stretched upper-deck philosophies and they also provided added impetus to engine manufacturers in the USA and the United Kingdom.

In September 1977 Boeing announced an improved 747-100 with reinforced structure, greater gross weight (753,000lb), later series Pratt & Whitney JT9D-7 engines and options for other series of General Electric CF6 and Rolls-Royce RB.211 engines, features already available in the pre-existing Model 747-200B. Pratt & Whitney now offered three new engine options; the 45,500lb-thrust JT9D-7, the 46,950lb-thrust JT9D-7 A and the 47,900lb-thrust 9D-7W. Rolls-Royce countered with the 51,000lb-thrust RB.211-524C fan engine. The first -100B customer was Iran Air, which originally placed an order for four 186B versions, powered by 48,000lb-thrust JT9D- 7F engines, but three were later cancelled by the airline. The only other customer was Saudi Arabian Airlines, which bought eight 747-168B/146Bs powered by the Rolls-Royce RB.211 fan engine. In addition to these -100B versions, a further twenty-eight SR versions

of the standard -100B, with a strengthened structure, were built for the Japanese home market.

United Airlines' Flight 811 - 747-122 N4713U - experienced a cargo door failure in flight on Friday 24 February 1989 after its stopover at Honolulu International Airport, Hawaii.[25] The resulting decompression blew out several rows of seats, resulting in the deaths of nine passengers. Flight 811 took off from Honolulu International Airport bound for Auckland, New Zealand with three flight crew, fifteen flight attendants and 337 passengers at approximately 01:52 HST. Its flight crew consisted of Captain David Cronin, First Officer Al Slader and Flight Engineer Randal Thomas. During the climb, the crew made preparations to detour around thunderstorms along the aircraft's track; anticipating turbulence, the captain kept the seatbelt sign lit. After N4713U had been flying for approximately sixteen minutes and was passing between 22,000 and 23,000 feet, a grinding noise was suddenly heard in the business-class section, followed by a loud thud which rattled the whole aircraft. One and a half seconds later, the forward cargo door blew out abruptly. The pressure differential caved in the main cabin floor above the door, causing ten seats as well as an individual seated in 9F, to be ejected from the cabin and leaving a gaping hole in the aircraft. Nine fatalities resulted and Mae Sapolu, a flight attendant in the Business Class cabin, was almost pulled out of the aircraft and was seen by passengers and fellow crew members clinging to a seat leg; they were able to pull her to safety inside the cabin, although she was severely injured. Laura Brentlinger, the Chief Purser and also a flight attendant in the Business Class Cabin, hung on to the steps leading to the upper deck and was dangling from them when the decompression occurred. The pilots began an emergency descent to rapidly get the aircraft down into breathable air while performing a 180-degree left turn to fly back to Honolulu. The decompression damaged components of the on-board emergency oxygen supply system, which was primarily located in the forward cargo sidewall area, just aft of the cargo door.

The debris ejected from the aircraft during the explosive decompression caused severe damage to the Number 3 and 4 engines, causing visible fires in both. The crew did not get fire warnings from either of them, although engine No. 3 was experiencing heavy vibration, no NI reading and a low EGT and EPR. This led the crew to deactivate Engine 3. At 02:10 an emergency was declared and the crew began dumping fuel to get the aircraft's weight down to an acceptable landing weight. Initially, they pushed the Number 4

engine slightly to help force the 747 down faster; once they noticed that its NI reading was almost zero and its EGT reading was high and that it was emitting flames, they shut it down also. Some of the explosively ejected debris damaged the right wing's LEDs (Leading Edge Devices), dented the horizontal stabilizer on that side and even struck the tailfin. NTSB reports found human remains in the fan blades of the Number 3 engine, suggesting that some of the victims died almost instantly as they were pulled out of the aircraft. During the descent, Captain Cronin ordered Flight Engineer Thomas to tell the flight attendants to prepare for an emergency landing, but Thomas was unable to contact them. He asked the captain for permission to go down to find out what was happening. Cronin agreed. Thomas saw severe damage immediately upon leaving the cockpit: the aircraft's skin was peeled off in some areas

On February 24, 1989 United Airlines Flight 811, a Boeing 747-122, N4713U, took off from Honolulu (HNL) at 0133 local time, bound for Sydney, Australia, with an intermediate stop at Auckland, New Zealand. The initial climb passed through an area of thunderstorms, so the captain elected to keep the seat belt sign on. As the aircraft was climbing, between 22,000 and 23,000 feet, explosive decompression was experienced. An emergency was declared at approximately 0220 HST. The forward lower lobe cargo door had opened in flight, taking with it a large portion of the forward right side of the cabin fuselage. The starboard side engines were damaged and had to be shut down. Parts of the leading and trailing edge flaps where also damaged resulting in the crew electing to use only 10-degrees trailing edge flaps for landing (a non-normal configuration). This resulted in the aircraft having to land at a higher speed than it would under normal conditions. The aircraft was cleared to land at HNL runway 8L. At 0234 HST, Honolulu tower was notified by the flight crew that the airplane was stopped and an emergency evacuation had commenced on the runway.

on the upper deck, revealing the frames and stringers. As he went down to the lower deck, the magnitude of the damage became obvious to him as he saw the gigantic hole in the side of the jet. Thomas came back to the cockpit, visibly pale and reported that a large section of fuselage aft of the Number 1 exit door was open. He concluded that it was probably a bomb and that considering the condition of the aircraft, it would be unwise to exceed 250 knots. The stall speed was around 240 knots, producing a narrow operating envelope.

As the 747 neared the airport the landing gear was extended. The flaps were only partially deployed, as a result of damage sustained following the decompression. This resulted in a landing speed between 190-200 knots. Regardless, Captain Cronin was able to get the jet to a halt without going off the end of the runway. Fourteen minutes had elapsed since the emergency was declared. Evacuation was carried out and all passengers and flight attendants were off in less than 45 seconds. Every flight attendant suffered some injury during the evacuation, however, ranging from scratches to a dislocated shoulder. The accident was most likely caused by improper wiring and deficiencies in the door's design. Unlike a plug door which opens inwards and essentially jams against its frame as the pressure outside drops, the 747 was designed with an outward-hinging door which, while increasing capacity, required a locking mechanism to keep the door closed. Deficiencies in the design of wide-body aircraft cargo doors were already known since the early 1970s from flaws in the DC-10 cargo door. Despite the warnings and deaths from the DC-10 incidents and early Boeing attempts to solve the problems in the 1970s, the problems were not seriously addressed by the aircraft industry and the National Transportation Safety Board until much later.

The 747's cargo door utilized a series of electrically-operated latch cams that the door-edge latch-pins close into, the cam then rotates into the closed position holding the door closed. A series of L-shaped arms, called locking sectors, actuated by the final manual moving of a lever to close the door, are designed to reinforce the now unpowered latch cams and prevent them from rotating into the unlocked position. The locking sectors were made out of aluminium and of too thin a gauge to be able to keep the latch cams from moving into the unlocked position against the power of the door motors. If an electrical switch designed to cut electrical power to the cargo door when the outer handle was closed was faulty the motors could still draw power and rotate the latch cam to the open position. The same could happen if frayed wires were able to power the cam-motor even if the circuit power was cut by the safety switch. It appeared in this case that a short circuit in the aging jet caused an uncommanded rotation of the latch cams, which forced the weak locking sectors to distort and allow the rotation, thus the pressure differential and aerodynamic forces to blow the door off the fuselage, ripping away the hinge fixing structure, the cabin floor and side fuselage skin, causing the massive decompression.

Lee Campbell, a native New Zealander returning home, was one of the casualties on Flight 811. After his death his parents, Kevin and Susan Campbell, investigated the cause of the decompression independently of the National Transportation Safety Board. The Campbells' investigation led them to conclude that the design of the aircraft's cargo door latching mechanism was flawed. As early as 1975 Boeing realized that the aluminium locking sectors were of too thin a gauge to be effective and recommended the airlines add doublers to the locking sectors. In 1987 Pan Am Flight 125 outbound from London Heathrow Airport encountered pressurization problems at 20,000 feet, causing the crew to abort the flight and return to the airport. After the safe landing, the aircraft's cargo door was found to be ajar by about 1.5 inches along its

N605FF of Tower Air - the aircraft came to rest at the end of a runway at JFK with a collapsed nosewheel.

ventral edge. When the aircraft was examined in a maintenance hangar, all of the locking arms were found to be either damaged or sheared off entirely. Boeing initially attributed this to mishandling by ground crew. To test this concern, Boeing instructed 747 operators to shut and lock the cargo door with the external handle and then activate the door-open switch with the handle still in the locked position. Since the S-2 switch was designed to deactivate the door motors if the handle was locked, nothing should have happened. Some of the airlines reported the door motors did indeed begin running, attempting to force the door open against the locking sectors and causing damage to the mechanism. Soon after the Pan Am incident in 1987 Boeing had issued a Service Bulletin notifying operators to replace the aluminium locking sectors with steel locking sectors and carry out various inspections. In the United States, the FAA mandated this service by means of an Airworthiness Directive (AD) and gave US-flag airlines 18 months to comply with the AD. After the Flight 811 incident, the FAA shortened the time to 30 days.

In 1991 an incident occurred at New York's John F. Kennedy International Airport involving the malfunction of a United Airlines Boeing 747 cargo door. At the time, United Airlines' maintenance staff were investigating the cause of a circuit breaker trip. In the process of diagnosing the cause, an inadvertent operation of the electric door latch mechanism caused the cargo door to open spontaneously. This incident led to latch damage similar to that observed on the cargo door of Flight 811. Two pieces of the Flight 811 cargo door were recovered from the Pacific Ocean on 26 September 1990 and 1 October 1990. [26]

On 20 December 1995 747-136 N605FF of Tower Air - Flight 41, bound for Miami with 451 passengers and seventeen crew - was pushed back from the gate at JFK at 10:36. At 11:00 de-icing procedures using both Type I and Type II fluids were started. The crew received clearance for runway 04L at 11:16 and began taxiing slowly towards the assigned runway. Flight 41 was stopped on the taxiway to clear the engines of any ice by increasing power to 45% for ten seconds before continuing and the flight was cleared to taxi in position and hold at 11:32. The flight crew received take-off clearance at 11:36. The take-off was normal, until shortly before 80 knots when the 747 started to move to the left, corrections by the crew proving ineffective. The captain then aborted the takeoff by retarding power levers to idle and by applying maximum braking. He did not use reverse thrust because of the slow speed, long runway and the possibility that it could worsen directional control. At 2,100 feet past the threshold, the 747 departed the left side of the runway. The aircraft finally struck a transformer, causing the no.4 engine to separate. The 747 came to rest at 4,800 feet past the threshold and 600 feet to the left of the runway centreline with the nose gear collapsed.

On 17 July 1996 TWA 747-131 N93119 departed Athens, Greece as Flight 881 and arrived at the gate at John F. Kennedy International Airport in New York at about 16:38. Because of technical problems with the thrust reverser sensors during the landing ground-maintenance crew locked-out the thrust reverser for the No. 3 engine and severed cables for the engine thrust reverser were replaced. [27] N93119 was scheduled to depart for Leonardo da Vinci International Airport, Rome with a stopover at Paris-Charles de Gaulle Airport at around 19:00, but the flight was delayed until 20:02

The re-assembled wreckage of Flight 800. The four-year NTSB investigation concluded with the approval of the Aircraft Accident Report on August 23, 2000, ending the most extensive, complex, and costly air disaster investigation in United States history. The report's conclusion was that the probable cause of the accident was an explosion of flammable fuel/air vapours in a fuel tank, and, although it could not be determined with certainty, the most likely cause of the explosion was a short circuit. As a result of the investigation, new requirements were developed for aircraft to prevent future fuel tank explosions.

United Airlines' 747-122 N4723U seen during pushback before the in-flight incident.

by a disabled piece of ground equipment and a passenger/baggage mismatch. Some of the notable passengers on the flight included Pam Lychner, American crime victims' rights advocate and former TWA flight attendant; Jack O'Hara, executive producer of ABC Sports and sixteen members of the French club at Montoursville High School in Montoursville, Pennsylvania and their five chaperones. After the owner of the baggage in question was confirmed to be on board, the flight crew prepared for departure. On the flight deck were Captain Ralph G. Kevorkian, Captain/Check Airman Steven E. Snyder and Flight Engineer/Check Airman Richard G. Campbell (all with more than 30 years employment at TWA) and Flight Engineer Trainee Oliver Krick, who was starting the sixth leg of his initial operating experience training.

The 747 pushed back from gate 27 at the TWA Flight Centre and took off but at about 20:31 EDT, 12 minutes after takeoff, N93119 disappeared from radar screens. The last radio transmission occurred at 20:30 when the flight crew received and then acknowledged instructions from Boston Air Route Traffic Control Centre (ARTCC) to climb to 15,000 feet. The captain of an Eastwind Airlines 737 reported to Boston ARTCC that he 'just saw an explosion out here,' adding, 'we just saw an explosion up ahead of us here...about 16,000 feet or something like that, it just went down into the water.' Subsequently, many air traffic control facilities in the New York-Long Island area received reports of an explosion from other pilots operating in the area. Many witnesses in the vicinity of the crash stated that they saw or heard explosions, accompanied by a large fireball or fireballs over the ocean and observed debris, some of which was burning, falling into the water. N93119 had exploded and crashed into the Atlantic near East Moriches, New York, killing all 230 people on board.

After the biggest salvage operation ever mounted to retrieve the wreckage it was established that there had been an explosion in the centre fuel tank. [28] This had happened before. On 11 May 1990 a Philippine Airlines'

737 suffered an explosion as it was being pushed back from a gate at Manila airport. Eight people were killed and 30 injured. The National Transportation Board (NTSB) investigated and discovered that the cause was an explosion in the centre fuel tank, which had not been filled for over two months. The NTSB also discovered that the flashpoint of the vapour was between 112 and 117 degrees Fahrenheit; only 20 degrees above the ambient temperature outside the aircraft (95°F). When the TWA 747 had been stationary on the ground for some time at JFK air conditioning heat exchangers sited directly under the fuel tank would have heated them to the correct (or incorrect) temperature. [29] The NTSB investigation's final report on 23 August 2000 determined that the probable cause of the TWA 800 accident was: An explosion of the centre wing fuel tank, resulting from ignition of the inflammable fuel/air mixture in the tank. The source of ignition energy for the explosion could not be determined with certainty, but, of the sources evaluated by the investigation, the most likely was a short circuit outside of the CWT that allowed excessive voltage to enter it through electrical wiring associated with the fuel quantity indication system.'

When on 28 December 1997 United Airlines' 747-122 N4723U took off from Tokyo-Narita Airport on Flight 826 for Honolulu, the departure and climb out were uneventful but about one hour and forty minutes into the flight the jet encountered 'wave action' and the captain turned the seatbelt sign on as a precaution. He also radioed Northwest flight 90 ahead of him requesting a ride report. NW 90 reported that the ride was smooth with an occasional ripple of light turbulence at their altitude. The first turbulence encounter happened no more than one to two minutes later. Seconds later, Flight 826 experienced another turbulence episode. The captain made a PA announcement for the flight attendants to sit down and then he made a PA announcement to the passengers telling them not to be alarmed. The captain ordered the first officer to reduce speed and he complied by reducing the indicated airspeed to approximately 330-340 knots IAS. At the point the captain requested permission from ATC to climb to FL330 and he asked the purser to provide him with information about the conditions in the cabin following the turbulence. The purser told him that a flight attendant was in the aisle, the cabin was 'a mess' and there were several injuries. The captain then asked the purser to see if a doctor was on board. Two doctors were found who asked for and were given the jet's medical kit, oxygen bottles and first aid kits. One doctor stayed with the flight attendants in the back of the cabin who were performing CPR on an unconscious passenger. The other doctor assisted the flight attendants who were providing first aid to other passengers. Upon making an assessment of the injuries and determining that the aircraft had not sustained structural damage, the captain made the decision to return to Narita for medical assistance. The 747 was declared damaged beyond repair because the 747 would have been taken out of service early 1998 in any event.

Following the accident, United Airlines issued Flight Safety Information Bulletin 98-1, titled *'Turbulence Encounter and Passenger Fatality.'* This bulletin described the circumstances of the accident, commended the crew for conscientiously discharging its duties and also reiterated the importance of effective communication between pilots and flight attendants. Shortly after the accident, United Airlines took measures to reinforce its policy of encouraging passengers to wear seat belts whenever seated and regardless of whether the seat belt sign is illuminated.

Footnotes for Chapter 4

11 A JAL-246B was also destroyed on the ground at Benghazi by terrorist activity in 1973 at the end of a hijack. United Airlines Flight 811, which suffered an explosive decompression mid-flight on 24 February 1989, led the National Transportation Safety Board (NTSB) to issue a recommendation that 747-200 cargo doors similar to those on the Flight 811 aircraft be modified. Korean Air Lines Flight 007 was shot down by the Soviets in 1983 after it had strayed into Soviet territory, causing US President Ronald Reagan to authorize the then-strictly military Global Positioning System (GPS) for civilian use. TWA Flight 800, a 747-100 that exploded in mid-air on 17 July 1996 led the FAA to propose a rule requiring installation of an inerting system in the centre fuel tank of most large aircraft that was adopted in July 2008, after years of research into solutions. It was expected that the new safety system will cost US$100,000 to $450,000 per aircraft and weigh approximately 200lbs. As of September 2010 the 747 had been involved in 124 accidents or incidents, including 49 hull-loss accidents, resulting in 2,852 fatalities. The 747 had been in 31 hijackings, which caused 25 fatalities..

12 747-121 N747PA c/n 19639 was manufactured on 29 January 1970 and delivered to Pan Am on 3 October 1970 as the first 747 in its fleet and the third 747 off Boeing's production line. It had logged 2,900 hours of operation at the time of the accident.

13 V is for 'velocity. These speeds are used on every aircraft take-off. 'V1 is the 'go' or 'no-go' decision speed. This means that in the event of an emergency occurring before V1, sufficient runway is available for stopping, but after V1 the aircraft is committed to take-off. 'VR' is 'rotation' or lift-off speed and 'V2' is the safe climb-out speed at which the aircraft can remain airborne and controllable even in the event of an engine failure at V1.) For a takeoff at 708,002lbs with a 10° flap setting, those speeds were V1; 156 knots, VR; 164 knots and V2, 171 knots. These calculations were made while the crew was in the dispatch office and were based on a wind from 300° at 15 knots, a temperature of 19°C and a barometric altimeter setting of 29.99 QNH. (The value of pressure for a particular airport and time, which when set on the sub-scale of a statistical altimeter will cause the altimeter to read the height of the airport when the aircraft is at rest on the airport).

14 Flight 845's crew had planned and calculated their takeoff for runway 28L, but discovered only after pushback that this runway had been closed hours earlier for maintenance and that the first 1,000 feet of runway 01R, the preferential runway at that time, had also been closed. After consulting with Pan Am flight controllers and the control tower, the crew decided to take off from runway 01R.

15 In the *New York Times'* on 22 August 1971 Calvin Dyer told the NTSB 'that his information had come from the Pan American flight dispatcher, F. R. Keithley who testified at the Federal hearing that he got his information from the San Francisco International Airport Tower. Tower personnel denied it. Frank Coil, assistant chief in the control tower, testified he had not discussed runway lengths with the dispatcher before take-off'. 53-year old Francis R. Keithley had been a dispatcher for 28 years and he had been hired by Pan Am on 3 May 1943.

16 There was no fire, though video tape of the landing showed brief flames from the area of the left under-wing landing gear. After stopping, the aircraft slowly tilted backwards due to the missing body gear, which had been ripped off or disabled on takeoff. The aircraft came to rest on its tail with its nose elevated. Until this accident it was not known that the 747 would tilt backwards without the support of the main body gear.

17 Subsequent to the accident, the aircraft was repaired and returned to service. N747PA was re-registered and leased to Air Zaire as N747QC from 1973 until March 1975, when returned to Pan Am, where it was renamed *Clipper Sea Lark* and then *Clipper Juan T. Trippe* in honour of the airline's founder. It remained with Pan Am until the airline ceased operations in 1991 and was transferred to Aerolineas Argentinas and then briefly to Kabo Air of Nigeria, back to Aerolineas

and was finally scrapped in 1999 in San Bernardino, California. The aircraft served as a restaurant in Hopyeong, Namyangju, South Korea for some time, until the restaurant closed down. The aircraft was scrapped for good in 2010.

18 The Movement for the Independence and Autonomy of the Canaries Archipelago.

19 Van Zanten, concerned that there might be insufficient time to complete the round trip back-to Holland, contacted Amsterdam on high frequency long-range radio. A few years before, a KLM captain was able to extend the crew's duty day at his own discretion according to a number of factors which could be readily assessed on the flight deck. The situation was now infinitely more complex and crews were advised to liaise with Amsterdam in order to establish a limit to their duty day. Captains were bound by this limit and could be prosecuted under the law for exceeding their duty time; Amsterdam replied that if the KLM flight could depart Las Palmas by 19.00 hours at the latest they would not exceed their flight time limitation. This would be confirmed by a message in writing in Las Palmas. *Air Disasters* by Stanley Stewart (Ian Allan Ltd 1986; Arrow 1988).

20 Grubbs had been listening in on KLM's radio conversation with the tower and knew of the Dutch captain's desire to leave as early as possible but; unaware of KLM's tight schedule, he felt the Dutch were further delaying both their departures unnecessarily. Clearance for Captain van Zanten to start could come through at any moment but would now have to wait completion of KLM's refuelling. *Air Disasters* by Stanley Stewart (Ian Allan Ltd 1986; Arrow 1988).

21 Owing to the prevailing north-westerly wind, both aircraft had to enter the runway from the holding area for runway 12 and taxi right to the far end of the 11,150 feet runway, a distance of over two miles, for take-off in the opposite direction on runway 30. *Air Disasters* by Stanley Stewart (Ian Allan Ltd 1986; Arrow 1988).

22 The control tower had three radio frequencies available of 121.7MHz, 118.7MHz and 119.7MHz. Only two controllers were on duty, however and 118.7MHz was used for ground taxi instruction and 119.7MHz, the approach frequency, for both take-off and approach communication. KLM was cleared to taxi at 16.56 hours but was instructed to hold short of the runway 12 threshold and to contact approach on 119.7MHz. On establishing contact, Flight KL4805 requested permission to enter and backtrack on runway 12. Clearance was received to taxi back down the runway and to exit at the third turn-off, then to continue on the parallel taxiway to the runway 30 threshold. The first officer misheard and read back 'first exit' but almost immediately the controller amended the taxi instruction. KLM was directed to backtrack the runway all the way, then to complete an 180 degree turn at the end and face into the take-off direction. The first officer acknowledged the instruction but the captain, now concentrating on more pressing matters, was beginning to overlook radio calls. The visibility was changing rapidly from good to very poor as they taxied along the runway and it was proving difficult to ascertain position. The approach controller issuing taxi instructions could see nothing from the control tower so was unable to offer any help. One minute later van Zanten radioed the approach controller asking if they were to leave the runway at taxiway Charlie I. Once more KLM were instructed to continue straight down the runway. *Air Disasters* by Stanley Stewart (Ian Allan Ltd 1986; Arrow 1988).

23 This was the first fatal accident and third hull loss of a Boeing 747. This was also the third fatal accident involving a wide-body aircraft, after Eastern Air Lines Flight 401 and Turkish Airlines Flight 981.

24 Delta would later merge with Northwest Airlines.

25 The aircraft was delivered to United Airlines on 20 October 1970.

26 The NTSB issued a recommendation for all 747-100s in service at the time to replace their cargo door latching mechanisms with new, redesigned locks. A sub-recommendation suggested replacing all outward-opening doors with inward-opening doors, which cannot open in flight due to the pressure differential. No similar fatality-causing accidents have officially occurred on this aircraft type, although other investigations indicate the possibility that other old 747s were afflicted. In 1989 the flight crew received the Secretary's Award for Heroism for their actions. United Airlines ran a simulation through a flight simulator and were, despite many attempts and various tweaks, unable to successfully land a plane after losing the forward cargo door. The aircraft was successfully repaired, re-registered as N4724U in 1989 and returned to service with United Airlines in 1990. In 1997 the aircraft was registered with Air Dabia as C5-FBS and abandoned in 2001 during overhaul maintenance at Plattsburgh International Airport.

27 During refuelling of the aircraft, the volumetric shutoff (VSO) control was believed to have been triggered before the tanks were full. To continue the pressure fuelling, a TWA mechanic overrode the automatic VSO by pulling the volumetric fuse and an overflow circuit breaker. Maintenance records indicate that the 747 had numerous VSO-related maintenance

28 The Centre Wing Tank fuel quantity gauge was recovered and indicated 640 lbs instead of the 300 lbs that had been loaded into that tank. Experiments showed that applying power to a wire leading to the fuel quantity gauge can cause the digital display to change by several hundred pounds before the circuit breaker trips. Thus the gauge anomaly could have been caused by a short to the Fuel Quantity Indication System (FQIS) wiring. The NTSB concluded that the most likely source of sufficient voltage to cause ignition was a short from damaged wiring, or within electrical components of the FQIS. As not all components and wiring were recovered, it was not possible to pin-point the source of the necessary voltage.

29 See *Black Box: Inside the World's Worst Air Crashes* by Nicholas Faith (Boxtree 1996).

Chapter 5

Continuing the Classic Line

Cruising at 35,000 feet in a 747 over the South Pacific to Australia is a most pleasurable experience. It is even more so (?) when your fellow George Pick Aerotours' passengers are aviation enthusiasts or knowledgeable types who have worked in the industry and are prepared to share their aeronautical experiences with you. It is only when boys of all ages in the seats next to you turn out to be fanatical number-crunchers, armed to the teeth with notebooks, spotters' books, binoculars and telescopes, that the journey resembles a scene from Airplane. You know the one; where the Japanese soldier with the bifocals commits hari-kari rather than listen to the ex-pilot's war experiences in the Pacific. Lunch can be completely ruined when the 'twit(cher)' in the next seat who has been known to use a telescope through the cabin window to read serial numbers of airliners below and whose faithful companion carefully records each number twice (because he was collecting some for a friend)' says, 'Do you know what 'plane this is?' SPAM responds with, 'It's a 747.'

Smiling benignly, 'twitcher' responds with, 'Yes, but which one?'

'I don't know - a 747-400? suggests SPAM.

'No, no, no'

'I give up....'

'- its City of Edinburgh.'

SPAM always wanted to know this!

'You know.... the same Jumbo that lost all four engines after flying through the volcanic cloud of ash off Indonesia six years ago and almost fell out of the sky.

SPAM's house red suddenly tastes worse than that Court Line plonk he had had twenty years ago.

'Number Crunching For Beginners' or 'How I Learned To Stop Twitching And Love The Aplomb' by SPAM

A second variant of the 747, the 747B, later the -200, was announced on 25 November 1967; this was designed to provide greater range. The dimensions of the - 200 were similar to the 747-100 and it had the same passenger capacity, but structurally it was strengthened with thicker wing skin and stronger wing stringers, spars, landing gear, beam, flaps and a stronger rib-and-wing-panel splice. The fuselage was made stronger also, with strengthened gear supports, keel beam, section 44 bulkheads, skins, stringers and some door frames. There were changes in the undercarriage design, with all major parts of the landing gear being individually strengthened and fitted with 49X 17 inch, 30-ply main and nose-wheel tyres. Brake capacity was increased, too. In the empennage, a strengthened horizontal stabilizer torque box and centre section replaced the earlier tail unit and the trailing-edge flap actuation system and leading-edge flaps were also improved. Additional fuel was carried in the wing centre section to bring total capacity up to 51,430 US gallons. All these improvements and upgrades increased the 747- 200B's maximum gross take-off weight to 775,000lb.

Originally, power was provided by the Pratt & Whitney JT9D-3AW (water injection) engine, with the water running from tanks at the wing leading-edge root. Later - 200Bs were powered by the JT9D-7R4-62 and -7W engines of 54,750lb thrust, later gross take-off weight increased to 785,000lb when the 47,670lb-thrust JT9D-7A became available in 1973. However, two alternative

The first 747-300 in Boeing's house colours.

powerplants were also soon available - the General Electric CF6-50E of 50,100lb thrust and the Rolls-Royce RB.211-524-02 of 51,600lb thrust. The installation of the CF6 engine was tested in the Boeing-owned developmental 747-100, N7470, before being incorporated into production aeroplanes. During testing of the first RB.211 installation a 747-283B set a new weight record on 1 November 1976, at a gross weight of 840,500lb.

The first 747-200B, a -251B for Northwest Airlines (N611US), the eighty-eighth 747 on the production line, was rolled out at Everett on 30 September 1970. The aircraft flew for the first time on 11 October when it was test-flown to Edwards AFB, in the Mojave Desert of California. There, a series of test flights was conducted with the aircraft being loaded with more and more weight, until on 12 November it took off at a maximum take-off weight of 820,700lb. This was ten tons heavier than the previous unofficial record take-off weight established by a USAF Lockheed C-5A Galaxy. The 747-200B received FAA certification on 23 December 1970. The first carrier to take delivery of the new model was KLM, which flew the initial -200B (PH-BUA) *Mississippi* to Amsterdam's Schiphol airport on 16 January 1971, entering service the following month. (Northwest received N611US on 26 March 1971).

The first 200Bs were fitted with three windows on each side of the upper deck as on the -100 series, but the extra weight capacity of the -200 meant that more seating could be installed in this area for first-class passengers, something the airlines were quick to capitalize on. (Most -200Bs had an internally stretched upper deck, allowing for up to 16 passenger seats). The normal range of a 747-200B with 442 passengers and baggage at a gross weight of 820,000lb is 6,440 miles; ferry range is 7,710 miles. 747-238B VH-EBA *City of Canberra* for QANTAS, the 147th 747 built and which first flew on 8 July 1971, became the first 747 to have the internally extended upper deck. Although the characteristic 'hump' was externally no different from the -100 series, internally it was extended by 6 feet to 25 feet in length to seat sixteen people. This 747, delivered to the Australian carrier in July 1971, was also the first to feature a lower-deck galley, reached by an internal elevator system.

In order to meet the insatiable appetite of the airlines for a 747 with extra payload and range, Boeing carried out a long study of possible stretches to increase the passenger capacity of the 747-200 series. By 1976 they were actively looking to stretch the -200B fuselage by 25 feet to extend the overall length to about 256 feet. At the same time they looked to lengthen the upper deck to station 1000 over the wing, the hump being faired into the body of the main deck almost back to station 1241, or almost as far back as the wing trailing edge (this was a much longer extension than on any previous upper deck design studies). The proposed

SP-68 HZ-AIF first flew on 4 June 1981 and was delivered to Saudia Airlines on 23 June. (Boeing)

Condor 747-230B D-ABYF Fritz, *the 128th 747 built, first flew on 17 March 1971 and was delivered on 2 April. It was leased to several carriers and was then put into storage in the Mojave Desert of California. It was finally broken up in July 1996. (Boeing)*

fuselage extension would mean inserting a 140 inch plug at fuselage station 741.10 ahead of the wing root (but would not have extended into the upper deck) and one 160 inch plug aft of the wing root. The proposed 25 feet fuselage extension never left the drawing board, but the proposal to extend the upper deck did at least offer some possibilities in the development of the -300 series. On 11 June 1980 Boeing finally came up with the stretched upper deck (SUD) version of the 747. Swissair's interest at the drawing-board stage in July that year was the driving force behind Boeing's decision to go ahead with production of the new -300 series. By giving the all-important launch order for four (later five) 747-357s - two all-passenger versions and three Combis - Swissair played a crucial role in getting the new aircraft series off the ground. These -300s were used on Swissair's North Atlantic and Far East routes and on services to other long-haul destinations at certain times of the year.

Boeing engineers extended the hump further aft by 23 feet 4 inches to seat about forty-four more passengers than the standard -200B. This new arrangement would provide for up to ninety-one tourist-class passengers or thirty-eight business-class passengers in the upper deck; the latter was also given two larger exits and additional windows. Changes were made to the main cabin, too: by placing five pairs of wider Type A exits on the main deck and replacing the mid-stairway with a new straight stairway that led upwards to the aft section of the upper deck, passenger seating could be increased to 550. Swissair's –357s can accommodate eighteen passengers in both standard and Combi versions in all-slumberette layout. Business-class seating is provided to the rear of first class and on the upper deck, offering a total of sixty-six seats. It is in economy class that the two versions differ: the economy class of the all-passenger version has 304 seats, giving a total capacity

of 388 passengers. The Combi version seats 181 in economy, for a total capacity of 265.

The increased length of the upper deck upped the empty weight of the -300 by about 10,000lb compared with the -200B, limiting range to 6,440 statute miles with 452 passengers and luggage. This was largely offset by the aerodynamically refined contouring of the upper deck extension which reduced drag and increased the typical top cruise speed from Mach 0.84 to 0.85. Swissair's -357s can land in category 3A conditions of minimum visibility, a decision height of just 20 feet and runway visual range of a mere 500 feet. At first the new aircraft was offered as a SUD, or extended upper deck (EUD), version of the - 200B and was launched with an order for four from Swissair. The airline already had a 747 on order - HB-IGC - and this was to be stretched on the production line. It finally emerged as a 357M, the SUD/EUD being re-designated the 747-300 series. On 5 March 1983 Swissair took delivery of HB-IGD Basel-Stadt, a -357 Combi and HB-IGC *Bern* followed, on 19 March. Swissair began 747-300 services on 28 March.

The first 747-300, a 3B3 version[30] for French airline UTA (Union de Transportes Aeriens), was rolled out on 15 September 1982 and made its first flight on 5 October. Flight-testing began with two different engines, the JT9D-7R462 on 5 October 1982 and the CF6-50E2 on 10 December. F-GDUA flew for the first time on 10 December 1982 and was delivered on 1 March 1983. [31]

Altogether, twenty-one Combi versions of the -300 were sold; however, no freighter versions were ordered. Sales of the -300 series generally were disappointing, with sixty all-passenger versions bought by Air France, Cathay Pacific, Egyptair, KLM, Korean Air, Malaysian, QANTAS, SAA, SABENA, Saudia and Singapore (the first of fourteen was delivered to the latter in April 1983 and all have been dubbed 'Big Tops'). Production of the -300 series

Above: SX-OAD Olympic Flame of Olympic Airways. This aircraft was delivered to Singapore Airlines as 9V-SQI on 2 August 1979 and one of three -2128s bought from Singapore Airlines by Olympic in 1984-85.

Middle: 747-2B5B N1798B first flew on 16 April 1973 and was delivered to Korean Air Lines (as HL-7410), on 1 May 1973. This aircraft is still in service with this airline, registered HL-7463. (Boeing)

Bottom: 747s on the line at Everett in 1970. Nearest aircraft is 747-131 N93104, fleet number 17104, of TWA which received this aircraft on 20 February 1970. (Boeing)

Top: Boeing 747-270C (SCD) YI-AGN of Iraqi Airways.

Middle: Air Canada 747 taxies out at LHR on 10 June 1978. (Graham Dinsdale)

Bottom: 747-341 PP-VNH, one of five -341s for Varig (Viarao Aerea Rio-Grandense), which first flew on 22 November 1985; it was delivered to the Brazilian airline on 10 December that year. (Boeing)

ended in 1990, the last aircraft being delivered to SABENA. With eighty-one -300 series being sold, the situation was disconcerting for Boeing, to say the least, because sales of the 747 had entered a downward trend for the previous eight years in succession. In September 1982, when the first -300 was rolled out, the 747 production rate at Everett had slowed to less than two a month, down from seven 747s a month just two years before. The order book for 1983 was even worse, with production dropping to an all-time low of just one 747 per month. However the work force could still be kept relatively busy, as existing 747-200 models could undergo the extended upper deck modification. In October 1983, not only did KLM agree to buy its second -306, it also placed a contract with Boeing to have ten of its GE CF6-50E2-powered -206B Combis converted to SUDs. This work was extensive and involved removing half of the upper fuselage as far back as the leading edge of the wing and replacing it by three new upper fuselage sections. It also added two emergency escape doors and slides. The first KLM -206B - PH-BUP *Ganges*, a Combi - arrived back at Everett late in 1984 and was completed in December that year. The other nine KLM -206s - one -206B and eight Combis - returned to Everett during 1985; the last of these (PH-BUT *Admiral Richard E Byrd*) was flown back to the Netherlands in March 1986.

In 1986 Boeing also modified two GE-powered -2B3B Combis with upper decks for UTA of France and built two new short-range 146 SUD versions for JAL. The first of these was JA8190 (designated 747-100B SR/SUD), which first flew on 26 February 1986 and was delivered on 24 March that year. The second, JA8176, made its delivery flight on 29 August 1986. These brought the number of SUD versions build to ninety-five. This total includes four 747-346SR short-range derivatives of the 747-300 for JAL, powered by P&W 54,000lb-thrust JT9D-7RG2 engines, capable of carrying 563 passengers. JA8183, JA8184, JA8186 and JA8187 were delivered to JAL in 1987-88. The first aircraft (JA8183) flew on 24 November 1987 and was delivered to JAL on 10 December.

Multiple redundancy incorporated into aircraft design has proved the difference between safety and catastrophe and in the very few occasions that the 747 has called on it, rarely have the systems been found wanting. The obvious advantage of a four-engined jet over a two-engined aircraft is, of course, that if one powerplant should fail, then there are three remaining engines to power the aircraft. The statistical chances of two of the engines failing in flight must be remote, for three to fail, even more unlikely and the eventuality of all four failing - when, if they were not restarted, the aircraft would stay airborne for only about twenty minutes - must be virtually non-existent.

On the night of 24 June 1982 the crew of British Airways' 747-236B G-BDXH *City of Edinburgh*, under the command of Captain Eric Moody, expected an uneventful flight scheduled from London Heathrow to Auckland, with stops at Santacruz International Airport, Bombay, Meenambakkam Airport, Madras, Sultan Abdul Aziz Shah Airport, Kuala Lumpur and Perth and Melbourne, Australia. G-BDXH, or Speedbird 9, to give its call-sign, had taken off laden with 247 passengers and 200,620lb of fuel for the flight. The night was moonless but clear, the flying conditions were smooth and the en route weather forecast was good. The flight crew sat down to a meal after settling into the cruise at 37,000 feet. In the right-hand seat beside Moody was his senior first officer, Roger Greaves and behind sat Senior Engineering Officer Barry Townley-Freeman. The crew had finished their meal by the time the 747 was south of Jakarta on Airway B69. Moody had a quick look at the area ahead of the aircraft with the weather radar and picked up nothing more interesting than returns from the surface of the sea. He made his way aft and descended the stairs to the first class area; he had just started a conversion with the forward purser Sarah de Lane Lea when he was called back to the flight deck by Fiona Wright, the first stewardess. As he climbed the stairs he noticed puffs of 'smoke' billowing out from the vents at floor level and a smell which he described as 'acrid, or ionized electrical', such as one finds near sparks from electrical

Several airlines, such as Highland Express, snapped up second-hand 747-100s and -200s. Pictured is 747-123 G-HIHO Highlander, *which was operated by this airline for a few months in 1987. G-HIHO was repossessed in January 1988 and later leased to QANTAS, Air Pacific, Aer Lingus and Virgin Atlantic, as* Miami Maiden *and, from 1992,* Spirit of Sir Freddie. *This 747-123 first flew on 28 October 1970 (N9669). (GMS)*

747-270C VI-AGO Euphrates *of Iraqi Airways at Frankfurt on 6 February 1989. This aircraft was delivered to Iraqi Airways on 17 August 1986. It was put into storage at Tunis, Algeria, in February 1991. (Graham Dinsdale)*

machinery. He entered the flight deck to find the windscreens ablaze with what appeared to be the most intense display of St Elmo's fire he had ever experienced. Moody strapped himself into his seat and again looked at the weather radar. Nothing of significance was in view, but he was pleased that in his absence, the other two crew members had put on the seat-belt signs and the engine igniters.

Roger Greaves then pointed out of the side windows at the engine intakes, which were glowing as if lit from within. Passengers who had a view out the aircraft windows noted that the engines were unusually bright, with light shining forward through the fan blades. The electrical discharges had a stroboscopic effect and this gave the illusion that the fans were moving slowly backwards. At the same time the St. Elmo's fire on the windscreen had given way to a display of what looked like tracer bullets. All this happened so quickly that there was little time for discussion, besides which Moody had his attention on what he considered to be the most important problem, the smoke which appeared to have got into the air-conditioning. It was first assumed to be cigarette smoke. However, it soon began to grow thicker and had an ominous odour of sulphur. At approximately 13:42 UTC (20:42 Jakarta time) engine number four began surging and soon flamed out. Before Moody could speak, Barry Townley-Freeman called out, 'Engine failure number four!' Moody immediately asked for the Engine Fire Drill and the other two crew members carried it out. The flight crew immediately performed the engine shutdown drill, quickly cutting off fuel supply and arming the fire extinguishers. Greaves believes the crew were helped by the fact that the

problem compounded itself gradually, the feeling of the danger they were all in building up only slowly so they avoided the trauma of being plunged all at once into an extreme situation. They became more alert and concentrated as the incident became more complex and at no time lost control of their reasoning processes. However, they were soon forced to face the full consequences of their problem by the voice of the flight engineer:

'Engine failure number two...2'

'Three's gone!'

'They've all gone!'

Engine two had surged and flamed out less than a minute after number four. Within seconds and almost simultaneously, engines one and three had flamed out. Moody stared at the instrumentation in front of him and refused to accept the full impact of what had been said. He had practised a four-engine failure drill on the simulator some months earlier, but then the assumption had been that all the generators would fail, leaving the aircraft on standby electrical power, fed from the aircraft batteries. This would have caused a failure of the co-pilot's instrumentation and much of the cockpit lighting - yet the former all appeared to work and the autopilot remained in control. The display on the engine instruments was also very confusing as these were a mixture of Smiths and General Electric, some of which froze under the power loss and some whose needles dropped off the scale. There were also some amber lights indicating that the engines had exceeded their maximum gas temperatures. (Without engine thrust, a 747-200 has a glide ratio of approximately 15:1, meaning it can glide forward 15 kilometres for every kilometre it drops. The flight crew quickly determined that the aircraft was capable

Top: 747-130 N1800B of Aerolineas Argentinas in flight. This aircraft, the twelfth 747 built, first flew on 18 February 1970 and was delivered as D-ABYA Nordrhein-Westfalen to Lufthansa; the first overseas airline to buy the 747 on 10 March. In April 1970 D-ABYA entered Lufthansa service on the Frankfurt-New York route, where it replaced 707s. It is still in service with Tower Air, registered N603FF Suzie. (Boeing)

Middle: Delta Airlines 747-100 N9897 Fitzgerald.

Bottom: Kuwait Airways 747-200 Wallner.

747-2B3BC F-BTDG, the 518th 747 built first flew on 1 April 1981 and was accepted by French carrier UTA (Union de Transports Ariens) on 23 April, this aircraft was converted to 2B3M/EUD in March 1986 for Air France. (Boeing)

Right: 747-124 HK-2000 (N747AV) Eldorado on lease to Avianca (Aerovias Nacionales de Colombia), 1976-82. This aircraft first flew on 2 July 1970 and was delivered to Continental Air lines on 13 July. It is currently operated by Tower Air. (Boeing)

Below: 747-243BC Combi I-DEMC Taormina first flew on 14 November 1980 and was delivered to Alitalia on 26 November 1980. (Boeing)

Mount Galunggung erupting. It was into this ash cloud that Speedbird 9 flew. (L. J. R. Allen ANZ)

of gliding for 23 minutes and covering 91 nautical miles (169 kilometres) from its flight level of 37,000 feet).

While he studied this confusion, Moody heard Townley-Freeman suggest that he shut the engines down; at the same time he noticed that the airspeed was decreasing. He put the autopilot into a gentle descent and turned to his co-pilot with the instruction:

'OK Roger; put out a Mayday.'

At 13:44 UTC (20:44 Jakarta time), Greaves declared an emergency to the local air traffic control authority: 'Jakarta, Jakarta, Mayday, Mayday, Speedbird 9. We've lost all four engines. We're leaving 370 [37,000 feet].'

However, Jakarta Area Control misunderstood the message, interpreting the call as meaning that only engine number four had shut down. It was only after a nearby

Garuda Indonesia flight relayed the message to Air Traffic Control that it was correctly understood. Despite the crew 'squawking' the emergency transponder setting of 7700, the aeroplane could not be located by Air Traffic Control on their radar screens.

Owing to the high Indonesian mountains on the south coast of the island of Java, an altitude of at least 11,500 feet was required to cross the coast safely. The crew decided that if the aircraft was unable to maintain altitude by the time they reached 12,000 feet they would turn back out to sea and attempt to ditch into the Indian Ocean. Moody controlled the aircraft using the autopilot, while the other two carried out appropriate emergency drills. Both pilots shared the task of moving the engine start-levers on different occasions. Because the autopilot remained in

Samples of volcanic ash taken from number three engine. (Eric and Pat Moody Collection)

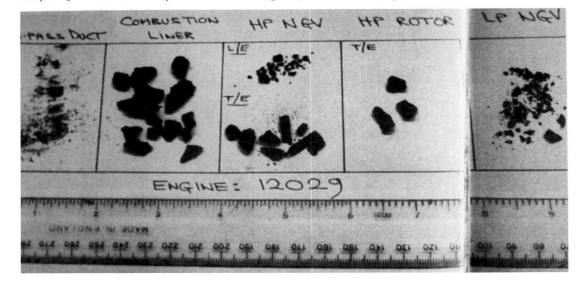

control Moody had time to consider me likely cause of such a multiple failure and what he might do about it: electrical? (Check all circuit breakers); fuel? (Turn on all pumps and cross-feed cocks); icing? (Turn on the engine anti-icing). The crew began engine restart drills, despite being well above the recommended maximum engine in-flight start envelope altitude of 28,000 feet. The first relights were attempted on engines one, two and three, but Moody decided, with the agreement of the crew, to attempt relights on the number four engine along with the others. (The number four engine fire-handle had been pulled when the fire drill had been carried out.)

At 26,000 feet the cabin pressure warning horn sounded as the cabin climbed through 10,000 feet. The crew started to don their oxygen masks - although when Greaves removed his mask from the stowage it fell to pieces in his hand: the bayonet fitting came out of the supply pipe and the tubing disengaged itself from the mask. As a result, Moody was presented with an unenviable choice. Should he continue to descend as slowly as possible and have his co-pilot suffer the effects of anoxia, or should he increase the rate of descent until the aircraft was at a more survivable altitude? He chose the latter and began an emergency descent.

He decided not to extend the gear as instructed in the flying manual, however, because he knew he might have to ditch the aircraft with gear extended, should it prove impossible to retract them. With hindsight it is now obvious that during gear extension, the hydraulic power from

windmilling engines might not be powerful enough to move the gear and the flying controls at the same time. They had previously turned the aircraft on a northerly heading back towards Jakarta and they decided that with a safety height of 10,500 feet in that area, they would turn back out to sea when the aircraft reached 12,000 feet. At this time the inertial navigation systems were giving a display of gibberish and were no use in fixing their exact position. When they reached 20,000 feet Moody retracted the flight spoilers and reduced the rate of descent. He noticed that Roger Greaves ironically had by then managed to fit his oxygen mask together.

At this point Greaves noticed that his airspeed indication showed 320 knots whilst Moody's showed 270 knots. Moody thought that it was worth assuming that the higher figure was correct in case they had been attempting to start the engines while outside the relight envelope. Again they had no luck - although the fuel had been igniting behind the engines and treating those passengers with window seats a view of what appeared to be four engines on fire. At about that time the cabin reached 14,000 feet and the passenger oxygen masks were deployed. Moody decided it was time to have a word with them. In what has been described as 'a masterpiece of understatement', he told them: 'Good evening, ladies and gentlemen: this is your captain speaking. We have a small problem. All four engines have stopped. We are doing our damnedest to get them going again. I trust you are not in too much distress.' Many passengers, fearing for their lives,

The flight crew of City of Edinburgh, *24 June 1982: (left to right) SFO Roger Greaves, Capt Eric Moody and SEO Barry Townley-Freeman. (Eric and Pat Moody Collection)*

wrote notes to relatives. One such passenger was Charles Capewell, who scrawled: Ma. In trouble. Plane going down. Will do best for boys. We love you. Sorry. Pa XXX on the cover of his ticket wallet.

Moody asked the Cabin Service Director to come to the flight deck and attempted to explain the problem to him while wearing his oxygen mask. Graham Skinner could not understand Moody's words, but he realized that his presence on the flight deck was not helping matters, so he nodded and returned to his job of helping the passengers.

It was at about this point that Moody started to consider the awesome consequence of attempting a dead-stick touchdown on the sea at night. His father had taken him, as a child, to Hythe pier to watch the flying boats land and had learned that flying boats did not fly at night because of the difficulty in judging height above water. He remembered, with some amusement, a training film made by British Airways which simulated a ditching at sea. The captain playing the role - and he was an authentic captain,

not an actor - had used the phrase: 'it's not our day!' in passing the bad news to the cabin crew. This reverie was interrupted by sounds of jubilation from the other two crew members as number four engine started. (This was the engine which had first run down and the success amply repaid Moody's gamble in trying to start it.) The other three engines started, an almost interminable ninety seconds later. They were at 12,000 feet.

'13.57 'Speedbird 9: we're back in business! All four running; level 12,000.'

They immediately requested a climb to a height which gave them more clearance over the high ground ahead of them and asked for clearance to Halim Perdanakusurna Airport in Jakarta. They climbed to 15,000 feet - and at about this height ran into St Elmo's fire again. When the throttles were pulled back to level out, the number two engine surged continually. It felt as though it would shake the aircraft apart, so it was shut down, but not without great reluctance. At this point Moody suspected that St Elmo's fire, above 15,000 feet was somehow connected with the engine problems and concluded that the engines themselves were severely damaged. He decided to descend to get away from the strange atmospheric effects, although he resolved to leave the throttles in their present position and to control the aircraft speed and descent by the use of speed-brakes, flaps and undercarriage. This required a leap of the imagination, because up until then they

Above: fused volcanic ash on the high-pressure nozzle guide vane of No.2 engine.

Right: The effect of volcanic ash erosion on lP, numbers 1, 2, 3 and 4 rotor blades. (both Eric and Pat Moody Collection)

had all had strong suspicions that the engines had failed because of an oversight or an error by the crew. They were cleared to Jakarta airport where the weather was fine, with calm wind and good visibility. The only added complication was that glide-path information was not available for Runway 24.

'14.21. 'This is Speedbird 9; could you turn runway lights fully up please.'

While the aircraft was on the base leg for Runway 24 the crew had great difficulty in picking up any lights on the ground and in particular in picking out the runway lights. Eventually the runway was spotted to the right of the aircraft, out of the co-pilot's side window. When they lined up with the runway the lights disappeared immediately the crew realized that their front windows were almost opaque. The final descent to touchdown was made using the localizer to stay on the centre-line and by peering through the outer edge of the left-hand front window, which was still clear. Moody was just able to make out the lights of the visual approach slope indicators (VASIs) on the left of the runway. The other two crew members called out the radio altitude and DMF distance to help in judging the descent. When they were over the runway the entire front window area was filled with a diffused glare of light. This was comforting in that it proclaimed the general proximity of the runway, but the delay before the wheels touched down felt like minutes rather than seconds. The landing itself was smooth. Moody felt that the earth seemed to gather them up: downstairs in the cabin spontaneous cheers and clapping broke out from the passengers.

The crew taxied the aircraft off the runway towards the terminal building. The glare of light from the parking area again filled the front windows with a blinding glare. They decided to call it a day and parked the aircraft.

'14.31. 'Speedbird 9. I can't see with the light in my eyes. I'll hold it.'

It was two days before the crew received any explanation of the incident. Barry Townley-Freeman was convinced that it was caused by an encounter with volcanic ash when he found his hands and clothes covered in a fine black dust as they waited for the steps to be brought to the aircraft. And indeed, he was right, because when they got inside they found that all the leading edges, engine nacelles and nose-cone were stripped of paint as if the aircraft had been sandblasted - as in one sense it had: it transpired that they had flown into the dust cloud from a volcanic eruption from Mount Galunggung, on the west of the island of Java and 110 miles south-east of Jakarta. (While cumulo-nimbus thunder-clouds and the like show up on aircraft weather radar screens, volcanic dust does not because the radar will only register echoes from water droplets contained in thick cloud, rain, snow and hail. The plume of ash started to become visible on satellite weather photographs, after the event.)

The engines were the worst affected parts of the aircraft, with the turbine blades having sustained the most

British Airways' 747-236B G-BOXH City of Edinburgh *at London-Heathrow in October 1988 prior to its departure to Sydney and Brisbane, Australia. On the night of 24 June 1982, BOXH - or 'Speedbird 9' as it was coded - under the command of Captain Eric Moody, experienced an eventful flight from Kuala Lumpur to Perth, western Australia, when it lost all four engines while overflying Java. (Author)*

The flight deck and cabin crew of City of Edinburgh *following their ordeal.(Eric and Pat Moody Collection)*

damage; the tips of the blades were ground away where they had been blasted by me ash at high speed. The material of the ash was mostly silicate particles, with a mean diameter of .075mm. Quite apart from wearing away the high-speed parts of the engine, the 'salicacious refractory material sintered in contact with the hot metal, fusing itself to the blades'. This is what happens inside steel furnaces. The changes in blade shape and size had serious effects on the efficiency of the engines, with the number four engine (significantly the engine which ran down first) being the least damaged. Ash was also found in the pitot tubes which had caused the differing airspeed readings. [32]

In October 1984 ICAO issued a special report on the dangers of volcanic ash to aircraft, where it was pointed out that the incident on 24 June 1982 was the ninth eruption of Mount Galunggung that year.[33] The report found that prevention was better than cure, but suggested that any pilot who encountered such a problem should, altitude permitting, reduce thrust to zero, descend and leave the area as soon as possible. Consideration should be given to turning off engines and restarting them when clear of the ash and inside the relight envelope of the aircraft. No warning about the danger from volcanic eruption had been issued to the crew at the pre-flight weather briefing before their departure from Kuala Lumpur - and information about the eruption in the 'Notices to Airmen' (or NOTAMS) was conspicuous by its absence or had air traffic alerted the crew by radio, while they were en route, of any significant or hazardous changes in the weather (SIGMETS). In fact volcanic hazard was only entered into the NOTAM network the following afternoon, long after Speedbird 9 had landed and even then it was not timed or dated, which makes the information suspect at worst! Although the airspace around Mount Galunggung was closed temporarily after the incident, it was reopened days later. In view of the lack of ready data, it is probably not surprising that nineteen days later (13 July) a Singapore Airlines 747 was allowed to fly into the same area and the volcano was still active. This time the dust cloud put three of the engines out of action, but the captain managed to land safely at Jakarta. Indonesian authorities closed the airspace permanently and rerouted airways to avoid the area; a watch was set up to monitor clouds of ash.

The crew of *City of Edinburgh* were feted by the world's press and the television media and Moody in particular was praised for his coolness and professionalism in averting a near-disaster. One Australian passenger, a young lady, kissed the tarmac after landing and promised not to chastise any 'Poms' ever again. None of the worlds' press quoted Moody's vivid description of the blind landing which he described - in a rich Somersetshire accent - as '...like flying up a badger's arse'! [34]

A nearly identical incident occurred on 15 December 1989 when KLM Flight 867, a Boeing 747-400 from Amsterdam to Anchorage, Alaska, flew into the plume of the erupting Mount Redoubt, causing all four engines to fail due to compressor stall. Once the flight cleared the ash cloud, the crew was able to restart each engine and then make a safe landing at Anchorage.

The Mount Galunggung incident featured in an episode of the Mayday documentary TV series *Air Crash Investigation* titled *Falling From the Sky*. This episode was repeated a number of times when in April 2010 the Eyjafjallajökull volcano in Iceland erupted and most of the ash was carried by westerly winds causing a large-scale shutdown of European airspace and severe disruption for several weeks as hundreds of flights were cancelled. Captain Eric Moody gave an interview to the July 2010 edition of *Flaps Podcast,* where he recounted his experience.

Another way of getting sand-blasted was by landing a 747 at Princess Juliana International Airport. Here Corsair 747-300 F-GSKY is seen approaching Juliana Airport on the Caribbean Island of St. Maarten in the Dutch West Indies where final approach is conducted 40 feet above Maho Beach to make the most of the short runway! (Boeing)

Just how close it gets to the public can be guaged by this picture of a KLM 747 just about to touch down at Princess Juliana International Airport.

Above: Virgin Atlantic 747-238B G-VLAX California Girl *which was leased from 1 May 1991 having formerly been operated by QANTAS as* City of Darwin, *which was delivered to the Australian airline on 10 October 1974 and operated until April 1991.*

Middle: SAS 747-283B Huge Viking *SE-DDL which first flew on 26 February 1971, pictured at Stockholm Arlander.*

Bottom: Nationair 747-124 C-FFUN at Orly on 31 May 1990. This aircraft was delivered to Continental Air Lines on 25 June 1971 and operated as Robert F Six. *After conversion to 747-101 it was operated from December 1974 by Wardair, Canada as* Romeo Vachon. *Nationair leased the aircraft from 17 May 1990 to June 1992 when Garuda Indonesian Airways sub-leased the airliner. (Graham Dinsdale)*

Top: 747-273C N747WA, the 209th 747 built, first flew on 23 March 1973 and was delivered to World Airways on 27 April 1973; a second -273C, N748WA, was delivered on 25 May 1973 and the third, N749WA, was delivered on 10 June 1974. N747WA was leased to Pan Am, 1974-79, where it was named Clipper Mercury. World Airways owned the aircraft until 15 October 1983, leasing it out to several airlines. N747WA was bought by Overseas National Airways in November 1983 and it is currently in storage at Evergreen International Airlines at Marana, Arizona. Evergreen still operates N749WA (as N470EV). (Boeing)

Bottom: At Everett the completed 747s are taxied across the highway bridge at night (so as not to distract drivers) to the paint shop for painting in their respective airline liveries. Typically it takes up to four days and 560 man hours to paint a 747. These freshly painted 747-200s and -300s were pictured at Seattle in 1989. (Author)

747-400s being prepared for delivery in April 1994. Since 1990 Boeing had spent more than $1 billion on the 777 Working Together Celebration project, which included expanding the size of the Everett final assembly building (lower centre) from 63.3 acres to 98.36 acres. In addition, two office buildings (top) had been built to house engineering and administrative personnel and a third paint hangar (bottom, far right) had been added to paint 777s, as well as 747s and 767s. (Boeing)

Footnotes for Chapter 5

30   Line No.573/F-GDUA.

31   F-GDUA was badly damaged by fire during maintenance at Paris-Charles de Gaulle Airport on 16 March 1985 and had to be scrapped.

32   Post-flight investigation revealed that *City of Edinburgh's* problems had been caused by flying through a cloud of volcanic ash from the eruption of Mount Galunggung. Because the ash cloud was dry, it did not appear on the weather radar, which was designed to detect the moisture in clouds. The cloud sandblasted the windscreen and landing light covers and clogged the engines. As the ash entered the engines, it melted in the combustion chambers and adhered to the inside of the power-plant. As the engine cooled from inactivity, and as the aircraft descended out of the ash cloud, the molten ash solidified and enough broke off for air to again flow smoothly through the engine, allowing a successful restart. The engines had enough electrical power to restart because one generator and the onboard batteries were still operating; electrical power was required for ignition of the engines. Engines one, two and three were replaced at Jakarta, as well as the windscreen, and the fuel tanks were cleared of the ash that had entered them through the pressurisation ducts, contaminating the fuel and requiring that it be disposed of. After being ferried back to London, engine number four was replaced and major work was undertaken to return the aircraft to service.

33   Flight 9 was not the first encounter with this eruption - a Garuda DC-9 had encountered ash on 5 April 1982.

34   The crew received various awards, including the Queen's Commendation for Valuable Service in the Air and medals from the British Air Line Pilots Association. Following the incident, the crew and passengers formed the Galunggung Gliding Club as a means to keep in contact. G-BDXH's engineless flight entered the Guinness Book of Records as the longest glide in a non-purpose-built aircraft. One of the passengers, Betty Tootell, wrote a book about the incident, *All Four Engines Have Failed.* She managed to trace some 200 of the 247 passengers on the flight and went on to marry a fellow survivor, James Ferguson, who had been seated in the row in front of her. British Airways continued to operate the Flight 9 route from London Heathrow to Sydney; in March 2012 the route was curtailed to Bangkok. *City of Edinburgh,* - which was renamed *City of Elgin* in July 1989 -, continued to fly for British Airways after the incident, before being sold to European Aviation Air Charter. The aircraft was taken out of service in February 2004; in 2009 the then 30-year-old aircraft was scrapped. In September 2009 the environmental group 10:10 bought the fuselage of *City Of Edinburgh* to be made into tags. The tags, bearing the campaign's logo, were worn as necklaces or bracelets and used to raise awareness of 10:10's work: the organisation aimed to persuade individuals, organizations and businesses to reduce their carbon emissions by 10% in 2010.

Chapter 6

Off Course to Disaster

18.21':35: '805, the target's light is blinking. I have approached the target to a distance of about two kilometres.'
18.22:02: '805, the target is decreasing speed.'
18.22:17: '805, I am going around it. I'm already moving in front of the target.'
18.22:23: '805, I have increased speed.'
18.22:29: '805, no. It is decreasing speed.'
18.22:42: '805, it should have been earlier. How can I chase it? I am already abeam of the target.'
18.22:55: '805, now I have to fall back a bit from the target.'
18.23:18: '805, from me it is located 70° to the left.'
18.23:37: '805, I am dropping back. Now I will try rockets.'
18.24:22: '805, Roger. I am in lock-on.'
18.25:11: '805, I am closing on the target. Am in lock-on. Distance to target is eight kilometres.'
18.25:46: '805, ZG.'
18.26:20: '805, I have executed the launch.'
18.26:22: '805, the target is destroyed.'

Tuesday 30th August 1983 was a wet and windy evening at JFK Airport in New York as passengers began checking in at the American Airlines' terminal building for the scheduled midnight departure of Korean Air Lines' flight KE007 for the seven-hour flight to Anchorage. After a short transit HL-7442, a -230B formerly D-ABYH owned by German carrier Condor, would then proceed to the South Korean capital of Seoul, arriving at Kimpo Airport after an eight-hour journey, on the following morning. This routeing, which crossed many time zones, resulting in both sectors being flown through the hours of darkness with each long leg beginning late at night, avoided over-flying the airspace of the USSR, although it lay very close to its eastern border.

HL-7442 lifted off from JFK at about 00.20 hours local New York time after a thirty-minute delay and arrived at Anchorage at 03.30 hours local Alaskan time. Scheduled departure for Seoul was 04.20 hours local, which allowed just enough time for the 246 passengers, mostly Korean, Taiwanese and Japanese, to stretch their legs and visit the airport transit lounge. Almost all the

passengers had commenced their journey in New York. Among them were a few Korean Air Lines crew returning to base, some Americans including Congressman Lawrence 'Larry' McDonald, national chairman of the right wing conservative John Birch Society, and a few Canadian and British. The 747 was cleaned, replenished and refuelled for the onward flight to Seoul. The crew which had flown the jet from JFK disembarked and a fresh crew of 45-year old Captain Chun Byung In, First Officer Sohn Dong Hui (47) and Flight Engineer Kim Eui Dong and 20 cabin staff - seven stewards and 13 stewardesses - prepared to board the flight. Captain Chun Byung was one of Korean Air Lines' most highly experienced and respected pilots. He had joined KAL in 1972 after serving for several years in the South Korean Air Force where he had acquired a reputation for boldness and aggressiveness. Sohn Dong Hui was also a South Korean Air Force veteran, who had had left the service in 1977 with the rank of Lieutenant Colonel. [35]

Continental Airlines prepared the flight plan, which had been telexed earlier from Los Angeles. The flight

747-230B HL-7442 of Korean Airlines at Los Angeles in October 1979. HL-7442 was shot down over the Sea of Japan by a Soviet Sukhoi Su-15 Flagon interceptor on 30 August 1983 with the loss of all on board. (Gerry Manning)

crew carefully read all the information, noting that the VOR radio beacon at Anchorage was unserviceable and that the Anchorage to Kimpo journey time had been shortened a little from 8 hours 20 minutes to only seven hours 35 minutes because of favourable forecast winds. Kimpo airport was not due to open until 06.00 hours local, so Captain In simply delayed departure by thirty minutes.

Captain Chun Byung In and his crew would have begun their checks, including programming the three inertial navigation systems (INS) (the multiple redundancy used on the 747 means that if a fault develops in one of the INS systems, another takes over). INS provides an exact position for the aircraft by detecting the rotation of the earth from a gyroscopically stabilized platform and permits a crew to read their exact position in degrees and minutes of latitude and longitude throughout a flight. After the INS is switched on, the aircraft must remain stationary for twenty minutes to allow the gyros to stabilize. The INS can also be connected to the autopilot to create a completely automated navigation system which forms the integral part of the flight management system (FMS).

Before departure from Anchorage at 05:00 hour's local time KE007 was cleared to push back and taxi to runway 32 and, with the start checks completed, the aircraft was soon on its way. The INS would have been programmed to follow Route R20 out over the Bering Sea and north Pacific and all the waypoints (INS locations) along the route entered in. It could be that the INS had been incorrectly programmed. Alternatively, after take-off and the direct clearance to Bethel on the Alaskan coast, the captain may have turned the aircraft using the auto-pilot control heading knob and forgotten to switch it back

to INS later, an oversight which would leave the 747 to continue flying on a magnetic compass heading (when the INS is not connected the aircraft is guided by its magnetic compass). The magnetic compass setting overrides the instructions from the INS, but the crew would be warned of this - the three green lights showing that the INS was connected would simply not have been lit. Also, the distance-to-go meter would not have counted down to zero as the 747 passed each waypoint and instead would have registered many miles north of track. (Just before each waypoint an amber light shows on the INS to warn the crew and so they can send a time and position on VHF). The automatic direction finder (ADF) would also show the anomaly. If left unchecked, with the INS unconnected and the magnetic compass affected by wind drift and magnetic variations, the 747 would simply be led away from its intended course. Whatever the reasons, before KA007 had left Alaskan airspace it was already twelve miles north of its intended course and by the time they were well into the flight they were 150 miles north of their correct course: on this heading, the 747 would end up flying over highly sensitive Soviet territory on the Kamchatka peninsula.

Around the same time that HL-7442 overflew the Kamchatka peninsula, a USAF RC-135 intelligence-gathering aircraft was in the same general area and Soviet radar operators picked up an unidentified target on their screens about 75 miles ahead of the Korean 747. The RC-135's presence in the area was not unexpected as such aircraft patrolled the region on up to 20 days per month and sometimes a relay of aircraft remained on station for 24 hours a day. Soviet thinking was that it was probably a RC-135, although its speed seemed too fast. Perhaps it was a converted Boeing 747 - an E-4A or E-4B intelligence gathering aircraft? The behaviour of the RC-135 did not give cause for concern to the Soviets, but by now they were becoming extremely disturbed by the approach of the unidentified Korean 747. As the airliner approached the Kamchatka Peninsula with its early warning radar systems, missile testing sites and the port facilities at Petropavlovsk, a base for nuclear armed submarines, the Soviets scrambled six MiG-23 all-weather fighters on the Kuril Islands whose pilots were ordered to intercept the airliner. On Sakhalin Island at the Dolinsk-Sokol air base crews were briefed and more fighters were placed on alert. As the 747 continued on its course, they too were scrambled to intercept. KE007 passed abeam Nippi at 17.07 hours and should at that moment have been entering Japanese controlled airspace but the airliner was in fact 185 miles off track. At 17.09 First Officer Sohn Dong Hui radioed: 'Korean Air 007 over Nippi one seven zero seven, level three three zero, estimate Nokka (another imaginary reporting point lying 660 miles away, about 100 miles south of the Kuril Islands) at one eight two six.' The 747 cruised over the Sea of Okhotsk, now back in international airspace and continued on a heading towards the southern tip of Sakhalin Island, which controlled the approach to the Sea of Japan and the important naval base of Vladivostok. On the south coast of Sakhalin, by the Soya or La Perouse Strait, is situated the strategic naval establishment of Koraskov, surrounded by a number of air force bomber and fighter stations and a major missile site. It was a highly sensitive area, second only to the submarine base at Petropavlovsk.

The south of Sakhalin Island is at its widest only 80 miles across and the 747 would traverse Soviet airspace in less than ten minutes. Just a few miles southwest of the island at the far side of the Soya Strait, lay the northern Japanese island of Hokkaido and the forbidden area of Japanese airspace. If KE007 was allowed to proceed beyond the shores of Sakhalin Island it could not be followed. It had to be intercepted before that point. The Soviet fighters climbed rapidly from their Sakhalin base to 33,000 feet and under radar control flew out across the Sea of Okhotsk to meet the transgressor. With radar guidance the interceptors turned behind the approaching airliner and took up positions on its tail. Japanese military radar stations observed the scene and saw what appeared to be a Soviet transport aircraft being escorted by some fighters. Air-to-ground transmissions between the fighters and their control centres that were picked up indicated that three Soviet interceptors with call-signs 805, 163 and 121 were conducting communications between control stations codenamed Deputat, Kamaval and Trikotazh. 805 was

identified as a Sukhoi Su-15 Flagon and it was in contact with ground control centre Deputat.

Captain Chun and his crew carried on towards Sakhalin Island unaware of the danger they were in. After being radar vectored on to the intruder's tail, 805 piloted by Major Gennadi Osipovich picked up the intruder on his radar' and moved in for a closer look. KE007 was flying on course 2400 at 33,000 feet and at a ground speed of about 500 knots. At just before 18.06 hours, as the Su-15 closed the gap on the 747, the Soviet pilot could see his target's navigation lights and he jubilantly called Deputat: '18.05:56 805 R/T: 'I see it!' There was no attempt made to call the airliner. The Su-15 turned slightly right and Osipovich pulled almost abreast of the 747's starboard side, but remained some way off. Mistakenly KE007 was reported as changing course. At 18.12:10 Osipovich radioed that he could see it visually and on radar. The moon was still visible, although less than half full, but should have given sufficient light to identify the airliner in the clear sky. It must have been obvious by now that the aircraft was not an RC-135, but could perhaps be an E-4B. Osipovich's responsibility was not to identify the target; he was simply obeying instructions. He then activated identification procedure 'IFF - identification friend or foe – but Soviet systems were not compatible with other equipment because he stated that the target was not responding to IFF.

On the flight deck of the Korean 747 the crew seemed oblivious to all this activity and were more interested in climbing to the next suitable flight level. First Officer Sohn Dong Hui radioed Tokyo on HF for approval: 'Korean Air 007, requesting three-five-zero.' 'Tokyo HF R/T: 'Roger, standby. Call back.'

At 18:20 Osipovich confirmed that his ZG indicator was illuminated, which confirmed his radar guided missiles were locked on target. He remained at lock-on for only a short while before he announced that he was turning lock-on off and approaching the target.' At about this moment KE007 received a call from Tokyo with approval to climb and maintain level three five zero. The 747 was 365 miles off track. Chun selected vertical speed mode on the autopilot and began the ascent to 35,000 feet. Osipovich fired 120 rounds from his cannons in four bursts; possibly as a warning but airline crew does not appear to have seen any tracers.

Finally, at 18.25:46 and from a range of eight kilometres, Osipovich fired two AA-3 Anab radar-guided missiles, which seconds later destroyed the tail and knocked off one of the inboard engines. The Soviet pilot watched as the 747 exploded in the darkness and spiralled down to the Okhotsk Sea near Sakhalin Island. Calmly Osipovich called ground control at 18.26:22, announcing that the target was destroyed, followed by

'I am breaking off the attack.'

The 747 flight crew, surviving the initial strike, were taken completely by surprise. Desperately Sohn Dong Hui transmitted a few garbled words to Tokyo Control: 'Korean Air 007...all engines...rapid decompression... one zero one... two delta'. Nothing more was heard from KE007. The time was 18.28 hours GMT on 31 August, 03.28 hours local Japanese and Korean time on 1 September. Japanese military radar operators witnessed the 747 spiralling from the sky and at about 18.30 hours saw the wreckage strike the sea off the west coast of Sakhalin Island, just outside Soviet territorial waters. All 269 passengers and crew perished.

Once the misguided theory that the Korean Air 747 was on a spying mission over Soviet territory had been quashed, the more logical and probable reasons for the aircraft straying from its intended flight plan were put forward. The most likely cause for this centred on the 747's navigation system.

This was not the first time that the Soviets had shot down a Korean airliner. On 20 April 1978 a Korean Air Lines 707 1,000 miles off course was intercepted over the heavily fortified Kola Peninsula south of Murmansk by a Soviet fighter whose pilot took aim and fired a burst from his cannons at the airliner. The shells sheared off the outer 15 feet of the left wingtip of the 707 and shrapnel from the blast tore a hole in the forward fuselage. Two passengers were killed and 13 others injured. The cabin instantly depressurised and Captain Kim Chang Kyu had to make an emergency descent from the 35,000 feet cruising level to a lower altitude. Kim somehow managed make a wheels-up forced landing on a frozen lake near the town of Kern, 300 miles south of Murmansk. His amazing piece of airmanship ensured that all but the two passengers killed by cannon fire survived.

In an unprecedented move, the Soviets laid on a press conference in Moscow. A large chart displayed how, in the Soviet opinion, the Korean 747 had rendezvoused with the US RC-135 before proceeding deliberately to violate Russian airspace. Marshal Nikolai Ogarkov, Chief of the Soviet general staff, gave almost a repeat account of the shooting down of the Korean 707 south of Murmansk in 1978. Ogarkov claimed that the 747 had been tracked by military radar for several hours; that the aircraft was flying without lights; that the crew did not respond to attempts to contact and that warning shots were ignored. 'There was no doubt that it was a reconnaissance plane' and 'the aircraft's destruction and the loss of life should be blamed on the US'. In the words of the *New York Times* Ogarkov gave a 'spellbinding performance'. US-Soviet relations suffered and detente soured but a year later Washington no longer maintained that the shooting was a deliberate and callous act and

Moscow openly admitted that the shooting was a grave error.[36]

In October 1985, the captain of a JAL 747 flying from Tokyo to Paris strayed over Soviet territory after flying around some turbulence and forgetting to re-engage the NAV mode of the INS. Fortunately, this time the Soviets did not send up their fighters to shoot down the airliner: contact was eventually established between the 747 and the ground and the airliner was allowed to continue. Five years' earlier, on 18 November 1980 a Korean Air -2B5B crashed at Seoul airport on approach.

On 23 June 1985 Air-India 747-237 *Emperor Kanishka* cruised over the mid-Atlantic at 31,600 feet as it flew towards Heathrow Airport towards the end of its eastbound journey of a round trip between India and Canada. The Flight from New Delhi and Bombay had transited Frankfurt when travelling westbound to Toronto and had flown to Montreal for the 6¼ hour return trip to Heathrow as Flight 181. A large expatriate Indian community had emigrated to Canada and the Air-India Canadian weekly service was usually full. Flight 182 was over three-quarters full with 307 passengers who were mostly returning on a visit to India from their adopted country. Captain Hanse Singh Narendra and the crew of 22 had enjoyed a six-day stop-over in Toronto before taking over *Emperor Kanishka*, named after the Emperor who ruled an Indian State in the second century. Sitting in the right-hand seat was Captain Satninder Singh Bhinder and the flight engineer was Dara Dumasia, about to retire and completing his last trip. The 19 flight attendants of Captain Narendra's crew were under the charge of Sampath Lazer.

At 06.00 hours GMT on Sunday 23 June, about 2½ hours from landing, Kanishka was estimated to arrive at Heathrow at 08.33 hours as the flight was running about 1¾ hours late because of the time taken in Toronto to fit a 'fifth pod' or spare engine. On 8 June an Air-India aircraft had an engine failure after take-off and had landed back at Toronto where an Air Canada engine had been borrowed for the homeward journey. The engine had been returned one week later and Kanishka now flew back with the broken engine fitted below the port wing between the inboard engine and the fuselage for repair in India. Captain Narendra had requested a reduced cruising Mach 0.81 on the North Atlantic track instead of the normal 0.84 Mach cruise to comply with the restricted speed. Apart from the delay over the fitting of the 'fifth pod' all was normal and routine.

At 07.05 hours GMT Flight 182 passed track position 510N 15°W and relayed the information to Shannon *Emperor Kanishka* flew on at a ground speed of 519 knots, heading towards the next position, about 50 miles south of Cork in the Irish Republic. Flight 182's routeing then proceeded up the mouth of the Bristol

Air India 747-237B VT-EFO Emperor Kanishka, *one of eleven -237Bs purchased by the airline, delivered on 30 June 1978. This aircraft was lost in the Atlantic Ocean off the Irish coast on 23 June 1985 while en route from Montreal to London, with the loss of all 307 passengers and twenty-two crew. (Boeing)*

Channel, on across the West Country to the VOR radio beacon at Ibsley and from there it would continue on to London. On the flight deck a discussion ensued on the flight purser's requirement for bar seals to lock bars in keeping with customs regulations. Dumasia asked Captain Bhinder to radio ahead to London operations with the request. In the Shannon Air Traffic Control Centre, controllers M. Quinn and T. Lane monitored *Emperor Kanishka's* progress, together with other airliners in the area. Suddenly, at 07.13:01 hours, a clicking sound of a transmit button came over their headsets and as they watched the screen VT-EFO's radar return suddenly disappeared. Unknown to the controllers, *Emperor Kanishka* had disintegrated in mid-air at 31,000 feet. The tail section aft of the wings broke off and as VT-EFO plummeted towards the Atlantic the wings and engines detached and fell in a shower of twisted metal into the sea. There was no warning and no 'Mayday' call: Flight 182 simply disappeared. [37]

Six thousand miles away ground staff at New Tokyo International Airport (now Narita International Airport) unloaded baggage containers from Canadian Pacific Air Lines' Flight 003 which had recently arrived from Vancouver with a total of 390 people on board. With good winds on the ten-hour flight the 747 had made up some time and had landed ten minutes ahead of schedule at 14.15 hours local time. Trucks ferried the containers to the ground floor of the terminal building and luggage handlers removed the bags for passenger collection. At 15.20 hours local time, as bags were being unloaded

from a container, one piece of luggage exploded causing a blast which blew a hole in the concrete floor and the unloading area was extensively damaged. Two Japanese airport staff were killed and another four seriously injured. Had the aircraft been just half an hour late there would there is no doubt that the blast would have caused the destruction of the 747. [38]

Philippine Airlines Flight 434 was the route designator of a flight from Ninoy Aquino International Airport, Pasay City in the Philippines to New Tokyo International Airport, with one stop at Mactan-Cebu International Airport, Cebu. On 11 December 1994 747-283B EI-BWF with a crew of twenty and 273 passengers on board was flying on the second leg of the route, from Cebu to Tokyo, when a bomb planted by terrorist Ramzi Yousef exploded, killing one passenger. By chance this particular 747, formerly operated by SAS Scandinavian Airlines, had a different seating configuration, so that when the bomb exploded it was two rows forward of the centre fuel tank and thus avoided a fiery explosion. A two square foot hole was opened up in the floor above the cargo hold and the passenger who died absorbed most of the blast force and the outer structure of the 747 was spared. The lower half of the body fell into the cargo hold and ten passengers sitting in the seats in front of and behind him were also injured; one needing urgent medical care. Captain Eduardo 'Ed' Reyes, an experienced veteran pilot, was able to land the 747, saving the jet and all the remaining passengers and crew. Additionally, a 38-minute delay in

On 11 December 1994 Philippine Airways 747-283B Combi EI-BWF with a crew of twenty and 273 passengers on board was flying on the second leg of the route, from Cebu to Tokyo, when a bomb planted by a terrorist exploded, killing one passenger. Despite causing extensive damage Captain Eduardo 'Ed' Reyes was able to land the 747, saving the jet and all the remaining passengers and crew. This aircraft was first flown on 17 February 1979 and delivered to SAS on 2 March that year as SE-DFZ Knut Viking.

takeoff from Cebu meant the 747 was not as far out to sea as anticipated, which contributed to the captain's options available for an emergency landing and he and his first officer headed for Naha Airport on Okinawa Island. The flight crew had to disengage the auto-throttles and resort to using the throttles to steer the crippled 747 reminiscent of United Airlines Flight 232, reducing air speed to both control the radius of turns and to allow the jet to descend. Fuel was dumped to lessen the strain on the landing gear. Captain 'Ed' Reyes landed the damaged 747-283B at Naha Airport at 12:45 pm, one hour after the bomb exploded. The other 272 passengers and 20 crew members survived. [39] EI-BWF was later converted to 747-2XBF configuration. It subsequently changed hands several times, always to air cargo companies and was finally placed in storage in 2007. As of 2012 Flight 434 is still used but no longer originates in Manila. It is a Cebu-Tokyo flight using Airbus A330-300 aircraft rather than Boeing 747s. Philippine Airlines still operates a Manila-Tokyo route as flight 434, but using Boeing 777 aircraft.

South African Airways Flight 295 was a Boeing 747-244B Combi [40] ZS-SAS *The Helderberg* that was delivered to the airline in 1980. The aircraft took off at 14:23 on 27 November 1987 from Chiang Kai Shek International Airport, Taipei, Taiwan, Republic of China on a flight to Jan Smuts Airport, Johannesburg, South Africa via Sir Seewoosagur Ramgoolam International Airport, Mauritius. Due to adverse weather and the late arrival of a connecting flight the departure had been delayed by one hour and 23 minutes. Forty-nine year old

Dawid Jacobus Uys served as the captain of Springbok Two-Nine-Five. The co-pilot was 36-year old David Hamilton Atwell. Third pilot was 37-year old Geoffrey Birchall and the flight engineer was 45-year old Guiseppe Michele Bellagarda. Flight 295 had 140 passengers and fourteen cabin crew. The aircraft was configured as a seven-pallet Combi with six pallets of cargo consisting mainly of electrical and electronic components and parts, hardware, paper articles, textiles, medicines and sports equipment in place on the main deck cargo compartment. The master waybills stated that 100,000lb of baggage and cargo were loaded on the aircraft. A Taiwanese customs official performed a surprise inspection of some of the cargo; he did not find any cargo that could be characterized as suspicious.

At some point during the flight, an intense fire developed in the right-hand forward pallet on the main deck and it was probably not extinguished before impact. (The substances involved in the combustion included plastic and cardboard packing materials but the actual source of ignition could not be determined). The fire generated considerable smoke, carbon monoxide and carbon dioxide, which penetrated to the passenger cabin and possibly to the cockpit. At 03:56 the controller cleared the flight for a direct approach to the Flic-en-Flac (FF) non-directional beacon and requested Uys to report on approaching FL 50. At 00:04 Uys said 'Kay'. From 00:08 to 00:39 the Mauritius approach controller called the Combi repeatedly but there was no reply. Later, when the cockpit voice recorder was played back Dawid Uys was heard to say in a surprised tone of voice,

'Wat die donner gaan aan? (What the hell is going on now?') This is followed by a sudden loud sound.

The Helderberg crashed into the Indian Ocean at about 00:07. The local time was 04:07. [41] The time was determined from two damaged wrist watches recovered from hand baggage. The night was dark. The moon had set at 20:16. The 'smoke evacuation' checklist calls for the aircraft to be depressurised and for two of the cabin doors to be opened. No evidence exists that the checklist was followed, or the doors opened. A crew member might have gone into the cargo hold to try to fight the fire. A charged fire extinguisher was later recovered from the wreckage on which investigators found molten metal.

When *The Helderberg* last informed Mauritian air traffic control of its position, its report was incorrectly understood to be relative to the airport rather than its next waypoint, which caused the subsequent search to be concentrated too close to Mauritius. The United States Navy sent P-3 Orion aircraft from Diego Garcia to conduct immediate search and rescue operations in conjunction with the French Navy. By the time the first surface debris was located twelve hours after impact, it had drifted considerably from the impact location. Oil slicks and eight bodies showing signs of extreme trauma appeared in the water. All 140 passengers and nineteen crew on the manifest were killed. The South African Navy sent the SAS *Tafelberg* and the SAS *Jim Fouclie* to assist in the recovery of debris and remains. The ocean tugs *John Ross* and *Wolraad Woltemade* also attended the scene, along with the Department of Environment Affairs vessels RS *Africana* and RS *Sonne*.

Rennie Van Zyl, the head South African investigator, examined three wristwatches from the baggage recovered from the surface; two of the watches were still running according to Taiwan time. Van Zyl deduced the approximate time of impact from the stopped watch. The aircraft crashed at 00:07:00, around three minutes after the last communication with air traffic control. Immediately after the crash, the press and public opinion suspected that terrorism brought down *The Helderberg*. South African Airways was perceived as representing the South African apartheid government as the airline was government-owned and airline offices around the world had been vandalized. Experts searched for indicators of an explosion on the initial pieces of wreckage discovered, such as surface pitting, impact cavities and spatter cavities caused by white hot fragments from explosive devices that strike and melt metal alloys found in aircraft structures. Experts found none of this evidence. The investigators drew blood samples from bodies and found that the bodies had soot in their tracheae.

The South Africans mounted an underwater search, named Operation Resolve, to try to locate the wreckage. The pingers attached to the flight data recorders were not designed for deep ocean use; nevertheless, a two month long sonar search for the pingers was carried out before the effort was abandoned on 8 January 1988 when the pingers were known to have stopped transmitting. Steadfast Oceaneering, a specialist deep ocean recovery company in the USA, was contracted at great expense to find the site and recover the cockpit voice recorder and flight data recorder. The search area is described as being comparable in size to that of the RMS *Titanic*, with the water at 16,000 feet being considerably deeper than any previously successful salvage operation. However against all odds, the wreckage was found within two days of the sonar search of the area commencing. Three debris fields were found, 1.5, 2.3 and 2.5 kilometres apart, which suggested that the fuselage broke up before impact. On 6 January 1989,

South African Airways Flight 295 was a Boeing 747-244B Combi, named The Helderberg *(registration ZS-SAS; c/n 22171) that was delivered to the airline in 1980. The aircraft took off on 27 November 1987 from Taipei Chiang Kai Shek International Airport, on a flight to Johannesburg via Mauritius under the command of Captain Dawie Uys and crashed into the Indian Ocean at about 04.07 local time.*

the cockpit voice recorder was salvaged successfully from a record depth of 16,100 feet by the remotely operated vehicle (ROV) Gemini, but the flight data recorder was never found. Van Zyl took the voice recorder to the National Transportation Safety Board in Washington DC to show his goodwill and to ensure neutral observers. Van Zyl believes that if he kept the CVR in South Africa he could have been accused of covering up the truth. At the NTSB, Van Zyl felt frustration that the degraded CVR, which had been in the deep ocean for fourteen months, did not initially yield any useful information. Around 28 minutes into the recording the CVR indicated that the fire alarm sounded. Fourteen seconds after the fire alarm, the circuit breakers began to pop. Investigators believe that around 80 circuit breakers failed. The CVR cable failed 81 seconds after the alarm. The recording revealed the extent of the fire. Van Zyl discovered that the front-right pallet was the 'seat' of the fire. The manifest said that pallet mostly comprised computers in polystyrene packaging. The investigators said that the localized fire likely came in contact with the packaging and produced gases that accumulated near the ceiling. They also said that gases ignited into a flash fire that affected the entire cargo hold. The cargo fire of Flight 295 did not burn lower than one meter above the cargo floor. The walls and ceiling of the cargo hold received severe fire damage. Van Zyl ended his investigation without discovering why the fire started.

An official commission of inquiry was chaired by Judge Cecil Margo with cooperation from the aircraft manufacturer, Boeing, and the United States National Transportation Safety Board. The official report determined that while *The Helderberg* was over the Indian Ocean, a fire had occurred in the main deck cargo hold, originating in the front right-hand cargo pallet. Aircraft parts recovered from the ocean floor showed fire damage in temperatures over 300°C; tests showed that temperatures of 600°C would have been required to melt a carbon-fibre tennis racket recovered from the crash site, leading Boeing specialist Fred Bereswill to speculate that an oxidant such as ammonium perchlorate was present. The reason for the loss was not specified, but two possibilities were detailed in the official report: Firstly, that the crew became incapacitated due to smoke penetration into the cockpit. Secondly, that the fire weakened the structure and the tail separated leading to impact with the ocean. The commission concluded that it was impossible to allocate blame to anyone for the fire. The manufacturer is quoted in the report as having 'contested' any scenario that involved a break-up of the aircraft and thus the commission did no more than mention the two possible scenarios in its final report as incidental to the primary cause of the accident.

The commission determined that the primary cause of the aircraft's loss was that fire detection and suppression facilities in class B cargo bays (the type used aboard the 747-200 Combi) were inadequate. The accident alerted aviation authorities worldwide to the fact that the regulations regarding class B bays had lagged far behind the growth in capacity of such cargo bays. The exact source of ignition was never determined, but the report concluded that sufficient evidence was found to confirm that the fire had burned for some time and that it might have caused structural damage.

The crash was the first fire incident on the 747 Combi and one of few fires on wide body aircraft. Fred Bereswill, the investigator from Boeing, characterized the Flight 295 fire as significant for this reason. Barry Strauch of the NTSB visited Boeing's headquarters to inquire about the Combi's design. Boeing's fire test in the Combi models did not accurately match the conditions of *The Helderberg's* cargo hold; in accordance with federal US rules, the Boeing test involved setting a bale of tobacco leaves ablaze. The fire stayed within the cargo hold. The air in the passenger cabin was designed to have a marginally higher pressure than cargo area hold, so if a crew member opened the door to the cargo hold, the air from the passenger cabin would flow into the cargo hold, stopping any smoke or gases from exiting through the door.

Investigators devised a new test involving a cargo hold with conditions similar to the conditions of Flight 295; the plastic covers and extra pallets provided fuel for the fire, which would spread quickly before generating enough smoke to activate smoke alarms. The hotter flame achieved in the new test heated the air in the cargo hold. This heated air was more pressured than normal, and overcame the pressure differential between the cargo hold and the passenger cabin. When the door between the passenger and cargo holds was open, smoke and gases therefore flowed into the passenger cabin. The test as well as evidence from the accident site proved to the investigators that the design of the Boeing 747 Combi did not provide enough fire protection to the passengers. The FAA confirmed this finding in 1993 with its own series of tests. After the accident, South African Airways discontinued use of the Combi and the Federal Aviation Administration introduced new regulations in 1993 specifying that manual fire fighting must not be the primary means of fire suppression in the cargo compartment of the main deck. Complying with these new standards required weight increases, which made the 747 Combi economically unviable on some routes but Combi's remained in production until 2002 when the last 747-400 Combi was delivered to KLM.

Northwest Flight 74 was a scheduled flight from Tokyo-Narita Airport (NRT) to Guam (GUM) on 19

August 2005 by 747-251B N627US. The flight up to the approach to Guam was uneventful. About 14:03:28 the local controller at Guam cleared flight 74 for the visual approach to runway 6L and subsequently cleared the flight to land. About 14:05:56, the captain called for 'gear down, flaps 20' and the first officer immediately responded 'gear down.' About 14:06:36, the captain requested, 'flaps 25, the landing check.' The landing gear warning horn then started. The first officer stated, 'oh sorry,' a crewmember stated, 'we didn't get a gear,' and then the captain requested, 'put it back to 20.' About 14:06:47, the second officer stated 'red gear light,' and the landing gear warning horn sound stopped.

About 14:06:54, the captain stated, 'uh, tell 'em we're gonna have to go around. Hold out to the left here. Flaps ten.' About 14:07:02, the first officer called the local controller and advised, 'tower, Northwest 74, we're gonna uh, do a go-around. We'd like to hold out to the west while we work on a problem.' The local controller then cleared the flight to fly the runway heading and climb and maintain 2,600 feet.

During the go-around, the captain asked the second officer, 'what do you have for the gear lights?' The second officer responded, 'four here.' When all gear are down and locked on the Boeing 747-200, the landing gear indication module located on the second officer's instrument panel has five green lights: one nose gear light above four main landing gear lights. The crew then read through the 'Red Gear Light Remains On (After Gear Extension)' emergency/abnormal procedure from the cockpit operations manual to troubleshoot the problem. Although the checklist twice presented in boldface type that five lights must be present for the gear to be considered down and locked, the crew did not verbalize the phrase either time.

The captain did not directly request a count, and the second officer did not verbally confirm, the number of gear down annunciator lights that were illuminated;

instead, the flight crew made only general comments regarding the gear, such as 'all gear,' 'all green,' or 'got 'em all.' Because the crew believed that all of the gear annunciator lights were illuminated, they considered all gear down and locked and decided not to recycle the landing gear or attempt to extend any of the gear via the alternate systems before attempting a second approach. During all communications with air traffic control, the flight crew did not specify the nature of the problem that they were troubleshooting.

The flight then positioned for another approach. About 14:15:27, the first officer radioed the controller, and the flight was subsequently cleared to land on runway 6L.

About 14:18:17 N627US touched down and about 14:18:22 the second officer stated, 'reversers normal.' Three seconds later, the local controller radioed 'Northwest 74 go around. Uh, negative, uh, nose wheel.' Engine rpm increased and the second officer stated, 'seventy percent,' and then the first officer and second officer both stated 'go around' multiple times. About 14:18:37 the local controller queried 'Northwest 74, tower,' but the first officer radioed 'we're unable.' About 14:18:51 and then the captain stated 'standby with the evacuation checklist.' The first officer then radioed the LC, asking if he could see any fire, and the local controller responded, 'negative.' About 14:19:56, the captain informed the passengers via the public address system that the nose gear had collapsed and that they were to remain seated. The captain then 'saw smoke coming from an access hatch and told the flight attendants to evacuate.

The official finding was that 'The flight crews' failure to verify that the number of landing gear annunciations on the second officer's panel was consistent with the number specified in the abnormal/emergency procedures checklist, which led to a landing with the nose gear retracted.'

Northwest Orient's N627US seen on approach in an earlier colour scheme than when it had its accident in 2005.

Former British Airways 747-200B G-BOXJ City of Birmingham *parked at the Dunsfold Aerodrome in Surrey, England. G-BOXJ was delivered to BA on 2 May 1980. It often features in the background during drives by celebrities in a 'reasonably priced car' on BBC TV's* Top Gear *programme.*

As increasing numbers of 'classic' 747-100 and 747-200 series aircraft have been retired, some have found their way into museums or other uses. *The City of Everett,* the first 747 and prototype, is at the Museum of Flight, Seattle, Washington, USA where it is sometimes leased to Boeing for test purposes. Other 747s in museums include those at the National Aviation Theme Park Aviodrome, Lelystad, Netherlands; the QANTAS Founders Outback Museum, Longreach, Queensland, Australia; Rand Airport, Johannesburg, South Africa; Technikmuseum Speyer, Speyer, Germany; Musee de l'Air et de l'Espace, Paris, France; Tehran Aerospace Exhibition, Tehran, Iran; Jeongseok Aviation Center, Jeju, South Korea, Evergreen Aviation & Space Museum, McMinnville, Oregon and the National Air and Space Museum, Washington DC.

Upon its retirement from service, the 747 number two in the production line was disassembled and shipped to Hopyeong, Namyangju, Gyeonggi-do, South Korea where it was re-assembled, repainted in a livery similar to that of Air Force One and converted into a restaurant. Originally flown commercially by Pan Am as N747PA *Clipper Juan T. Trippe* and repaired for service following a tail strike, it remained with the airline until its bankruptcy. The restaurant closed by 2009 and the aircraft was demolished in 2010. A former British Airways 747-200B (G-BOXJ) is parked at the Dunsfold Aerodrome in Surrey, England and has been used as a movie set for productions such as the 2006 James Bond film, *Casino Royale.* The Jumbohostel, using a converted 747-200, opened at Arlanda Airport, Stockholm on 15 January 2009.

Footnotes for Chapter 6

35 *Massacre 007: The Story of the Korean Air Lines Disaster* by Richard Rohmer (Coronet Books- Hodder and Stoughton 1984).

36 *Air Disasters* by Stanley Stewart (Ian Allan Ltd 1986; Arrow 1988).

37 An accident co-ordination centre was set up in Cork and floating wreckage and bodies recovered from the sea were taken there. Eventually, about 5% of the aircraft's total structure was retrieved from the sea's surface and 131 victims of the crash were brought ashore. Kanishka had been destroyed by a bomb. See Air Disasters by Stanley Stewart (Ian Allan Ltd 1986, Arrow 1988).

38 See *Air Disasters* by Stanley Stewart (Ian Allan Ltd 1986, Arrow 1988).

39 Manila police were able to track the batteries used in the bomb and many of its contents from Okinawa back to Manila. Police uncovered Yousef's plan on the night of 6 January and the early morning of 7 January 1995 and he was arrested a month later in Pakistan. He was later convicted of the 1993 World Trade Center bombing.

40 The 747-244B Combi is a variant of the aircraft that permits the mixing of passengers and airfreight on the main deck according to load factors on any given route and Class B cargo compartment regulations.

41 The arrival time at Mauritius was estimated at 00:35.

Chapter 7

Baby Boeings

With the DC-8-62 out of the competition, Boeing decided in 1973 to produce a 747 derivative known as the SP – for Special Performance – a smaller airplane aimed at the long thin routes. The fuselage was reduced by forty-seven feet, while retaining the identical wing and lift devices. The airplane offered extended range, higher cruising altitude, superior takeoff and landing characteristics, lower noise and improved fuel economy.

Boeing: The First Century & Beyond by **Eugene E. Bauer**

During the late 1960s the domestic air traffic in Japan grew at a phenomenal rate of more than 20 per cent per annum, the majority of passengers being carried on a fleet of 727 and DC-8-61 aircraft. By the end of the decade, when the average domestic load factor had reached 85 per cent, the time was rapidly approaching when the Japanese domestic market would swamp the entire system. All Nippon Airlines (ANA) and Japan Air Lines (JAL, later Japan Airlines), began to look for a solution.[42] Boeing, meanwhile, had been busy developing the 747SR, a special short-range version of the 747-100B, ideal for the high-density, short-haul operations on routes between the Japanese home islands. The 747SR needed to be able to operate on the 310-mile Tokyo to Osaka route both ways without having to refuel, but on the longer international routes it would be expected to carry an all-up gross weight of up to 735,000lb and these figures therefore became the measure which Boeing used as the yardstick for SR performance and specification. The initial order for the -100SR, four aircraft for Japan Air Lines - was announced on 30 October 1972. The first 747SR (SR-46, the 221st 747 built) was rolled out at Everett on 3 August 1973 and flew for the first time on 31 August. Power was provided by P&W JT9D-7s, each capable of 43,500lb of thrust (all three engine types were available for the 747SR). Registered as JA8117, it received its certification on 26 September 1973 and was handed over to JAL on the same day. JAL began services on its Tokyo-Okinawa route on 7 October 1973. Altogether, JAL received seven SR-46 versions of the 747-100 and three JT9D-powered versions of the 747-100B. These were designated SR-146B. In 1983 JAL ordered two 747-146B SUDs (stretched upper deck); these can seat twenty-five business-class and 538 economy-class passengers. The first of these aircraft flew on 26 February 1986, being certificated on 24 March and delivered to JAL on the same day. [43]

At first, Japan Air Lines had its aircraft arranged to accommodate 498 passengers, including sixteen in the upper lounge, because fewer galley and toilet facilities are required on short flights, but this was later increased to as many as 528 passengers in a two-class layout. Gross weight was reduced to 570,000lb or (two aircraft only) 610,000lb by the decrease in required fuel. Take-off weights ranged from 520,000lb to 735,000lb. The SR differed from the standard -100B configuration in having a strengthened structure to handle the added stress on the airframe and its systems which would be caused by the greater number of take-offs and landings during a given number of flying hours. (The goal was to give the SR an airframe life capable of 52,000 flights over twenty years of operation, compared to the standard life of a 747 airframe of 24,600 flights over the same period.) The undercarriage and its associated systems, particularly, were strengthened and so too was almost every component. The fin attachment, stabilizer root, wing lower surface, wing/fuselage splice, middle and rear spars, in-spar ribs, flap supports, spoilers and all other flying surfaces were strengthened, while crown splices were applied over the centre body. The wing leading edge and engine nacelle struts were also modified.

In 1971 the Lockheed L-1011 TriStar and the

The SR differed from the standard -100B configuration in having a strengthened structure to handle the added stress on the airframe and its systems caused by the greater number of take-offs and landings during a given number of flying hours. Twenty-eight SR-46, -8I and 146B versions were built for the Japanese home market. 747-246B N1800B/JA8114 Demonstrator which first flew on 23 August 1972 before it was delivered to Japan Air Lines on 3 November 1972. (Boeing)

McDonnell Douglas DC-10 were introduced on continental US routes and the short-to-medium-haul sectors throughout the world. These two first-generation wide-body tri-jets were not really designed for long haul, but were aimed at the middle market situated between Boeing's 169-seat 707 and the 380-seat 747. McDonnell Douglas began developing its intercontinental DC-10-30 and -40 models and the following year these were certificated. Lockheed meanwhile went ahead with plans for an extended-range L-1011. In the L1011 and DC-10, Lockheed and McDonnell Douglas between them saw an opportunity to replace the ageing fleets of 707-320s and DC-8-60s on the short- and medium-haul routes. The arrival of their competitors' first-generation tri-jets was not lost on Boeing or the airline industry as a whole. Boeing knew

SP-44 Z5-SPB Outeniqua *of South African Airways. This aircraft first flew on 10 March 1976 and was delivered to SAA on 22 April that year. It was then leased to Air Malawi for a time in 1985 as 7Q-YKL* Mulanje *and to Luxair in 1987.*

N142UA, which first flew on 10 October 1975 (N347SP) and was delivered to Pan Am as N532PA Clipper Constitution *on 29 March 1976. N532PA was acquired on 11 February 1986 by United Airlines, who finally withdrew this aircraft from service in July 1994. (Boeing)*

it had to compete in this arena and quickly, or their customers would buy tri-jets, but with no off-the-shelf design in sight, what could the company offer?

Initially, Boeing looked to a long-range version of its 200-seat 7X7, but this design was only available on paper and the airlines would hardly wait for the aircraft to be developed when Lockheed and McDonnell Douglas tri-jets were readily available. Also, Boeing would be hard pressed to justify an all-new design with its attendant high development costs. Boeing therefore looked to the 747 with a view to shortening it and possibly deleting two of the wing-mounted engines and

installing the third in the tail, thereby creating its own tri-jet design. Although this concept was received in certain places with incredulity, the idea was not without merit. A short-bodied derivative of the 747 had to be a better and less costly option than a whole new design and commonality with existing models in service would prove to be a bonus for the carriers concerned.

Apart from anything else, operational and maintenance costs, spares and also crew-training expenses would be minimal compared with the introduction of an all-new aircraft. Even so, it all boiled down to the age-old problem of seat-per-mile costs.

747-SPJ6 first flew on 14 February 1980 and was delivered to the Civil Aviation Administration of China fifteen days later. It was delivered to Air China as B-2442 on 15 July 1988.

SP-31 A6-SMR of the Government of Dubai (operated by Dubai Air Wing).

Also, Boeing would have to produce a design that would deliver lower aircraft-per-mile costs than that of the 747-200B: that is, the cost in dollars of operating an aircraft on a per-mile basis as a breakdown of airframe, engine and equipment costs, crew expenses, fuel burned and so on. Put more simply, the Boeing design would have to be faster, more economical, longer ranging and capable of carrying a bigger payload, than either the L-1011 or the DC-10-30/40.

One of the means of saving weight would have been to remove the fourth engine from the 747 wing and mount two on one side, the third on the other. Another, more conventional proposal, was to bury the number two engine in the root of the tail-fin as in the 727

configuration. This was not unlike the 747-300 preliminary design which Boeing had rushed through in 1968 in an abortive attempt to head off sales of DC-10s to Northwest Orient. But whatever way one worked it, removing an engine from the wing meant that the wing itself would have to be completely redesigned to take into account the different stress and loading characteristics and all the advantages of flexibility and lightness would be lost. Keeping it simple therefore, the designers finally opted to retain the four engines and original wing, while creating a short-bodied fuselage.

Early in 1973 the short-bodied 747 project took on added urgency with the news that long-standing and valued Boeing customer Pan Am was looking to place

N142UA, which first flew on 10 October 1975 (N347SP) and was delivered to Pan Am as N532PA *Clipper Constitution on 29 March 1976. N532PA was acquired on 11 February 1986 by United Airlines, who finally withdrew this aircraft from service in July 1994. (Boeing)*

SP-21 N747SP which first flew on 4 July 1975 and was the first of ten SP-21s for Pan Am, (N530PA Clipper Mayflower) when it was delivered on 26 April 1976. N530PA was acquired by United on 11 February 1986. The registration was cancelled in September 1995 and in February 1996 the aircraft was stored at Ardmore, Oklahoma. The aircraft had flown a total of 78,312 hours. (Boeing)

an order for new aircraft on its short-to medium-haul routes. Moreover the rumours were that the DC-10-30/40 or -30SB was the leading contender. Lockheed, predictably, countered with their L-1011 TriStar, but although the California Company failed in its sales pitch, it later sold Pan Am a fleet of long-range, short-bodied TriStar 500s. Joe Sutter and his team were convinced that the four-engined 747 short-body - or 747SB - was the answer to the competition, although initially the Boeing management and Pan Am were not so sure. (Pan Am dubbed the SB 'Sutter's Balloon', which led to the project being changed to 'SP' for 'Special Performance.) Boeing sized the 747SP to carry 281 mixed-class passengers (the 747-100s and -200Bs

Air Malawi 747 SP-44 7Q-YKL Mulanje which was leased from South African Airways for a short time in 1985 when it was pictured at Heathrow. This aircraft first flew on 10 March 1976 and was delivered to SAA as Z5-SPB Outeniqua on 22 April that year. After operation by Air Malawi this aircraft returned to SAA in May 1985 and was operated by the airline until November 1987 when it was leased by Luxair as LX-LGX.

SP-09 B-1862 of Mandarin Airlines (formerly N8290V of China Airlines, its parent company) approaching Kai Tak on 28 April 1998. Mandarin operated two of the four SPs originally delivered to China Airlines, B-1882 being owned by First Security Bank and N4522V by Sanwa Business Credit. (Graham Dinsdale)

carried 385 passengers). In August 1973 it was predicted that 214 747SPs could be sold during 1976-85, producing a net increase in 747 sales of 183 aircraft and total sales revenue of $5.9 billion. Equally importantly, it was estimated that the SP would replace only thirty-one anticipated 'conventional' 747s and that McDonnell Douglas would lose potential sales of 149 DC-10-30/40s valued at $4.8 billion. It was considered that the main US customer for the SP would be Pan Am, with twenty aircraft, while overseas, JAL, El Al and QANTAS would account for a further twenty-eight SPs. Total SP sales during 1976-78 were expected to be around 85-143 aircraft. At the beginning of September 1973 Boeing decided to put the SP into production and late that same month Pan Am, now convinced of the benefits of the SP over its rivals, placed a firm order for ten 747SPs valued at $280 million (including spares and an option for fifteen more SPs) with deliveries to begin in 1976.

In simple terms, Boeing shortened the 747 fuselage by 48 feet 4 inches to 176 feet 9 inches. However, this process was not as straightforward as it may have appeared. The nose section remained unchanged, but two straight sections of fuselage and one tapered section had to be removed. A section of fuselage forward of the

front-wing spar was removed, as was the roof section of the next section back. This latter was deleted in order to make room for the fairing of the raised upper deck, which now became flush with the fuselage over the mid-chord position of the wing rather than by the leading edge. Lastly, the large wing-fuselage fairing was replaced with a smaller, or 'cropped', fillet. (During flight-tests, this was found to create a local shock wave and was therefore redesigned with more contouring over the top of the wing.)

Additional stiffeners and sound-proofing were also added to the upper lobe section, mainly because of its proximity to the wing and the front-wing spar/fuselage frame was also modified. Cabin doors were reduced to four per side. Major weight savings changes were made by using reduced-gauge materials for the spars, ribs, skin and stringers in the wing box and centre section, while the original triple-slotted trailing-edge flaps were replaced with single units. The span of the tail-plane was increased by ten feet and a taller fin was added, 24 inches taller than the basic 747's tail, with double-hinged rudder. Seating was reduced to twenty-eight first-class passengers and 271 tourists on the main deck, plus thirty-two passengers on the upper deck.

The lighter-weight materials and some innovative engineering meant that the SP weighed in at about 42,000lb lighter than the empty weight of the 747-100. Almost 12,500lb of this was saved on the wing as a result of much simpler single-slotted flaps in place of the standard 747 triple-slotted arrangement. A shorter fuselage body accounted for a further 11,000lb of weight loss. However, the improved tail unit added about 1,500lb and the improved nose-wheel gear added a further 230lb; but overall, 44,100lb was lost and the SP delivered an operating empty weight of 315,000lb. In comparison, the 747-100's operating empty weight was 360,000lb. Fuel capacity was increased to 50,359 US gallons (190,609 litres). Gross weight was reduced to 663,000lb. Several versions of two powerplants were available: General Electric CF6-45A2 or -50E2-F of 45,000lb thrust, or Rolls-Royce RB.200-524B2, -52422 or 524D4 with 50,100lb or 43,100lb of thrust.

The first SP (N747SP) rolled out of the Everett factory on 19 May 1975. On 4 July - American Independence Day - Jack Waddell and his crew took SP-21 N747SP aloft from Paine Field and for three hours and four minutes they really 'wrung it out'. The crew carried out a preliminary evaluation of handling and systems, airspeed calibration and fuel consumption, they proved that the new flap system was trouble free and then put the aircraft through the full speed range from stall right up to Mach 0.92. The SP-21 reached 30,000 feet and 630mph. Confidence was such that later that day it was taken up again on a second test flight lasting fifty-two minutes. By August 1975 the first two SPs (N247SP was the other) were flying, but problems encountered during the test programme with the cropped wing-fuselage fillet and stabilizer trim resulted in the certification target date of December 1975 having to be moved back to the following February.

N747SP established a number of record-breaking long-distance endurance records. On 12 November 1975 N247SP flew non-stop from New York to Tokyo with 200 passengers in a flying time of thirteen hours 33 minutes. On board was a fifteen-strong party of representatives from JAL. The Japanese airline operated DC-8-62s on the same route, with a refuelling stop at Anchorage, Alaska. For a month after, other demonstration flights totalling 700,000 miles were made, including a 7,310-mile non-stop flight from Sydney, Australia to Santiago, Chile and a 7,140-mile flight from Mexico City to Belgrade. On 5 March 1976 N533PA *Clipper Freedom* was accepted by Pan Am and N532PA *Clipper Constitution* was delivered on 29 March; the airline placing these two SPs in service during April. A new around-the-world record was set 1-

Executive jet - Arab style! SP-27 A40-SO, operated by the Royal Flight of Oman, in the BA maintenance yard at Heathrow on 31 August 1993 following servicing, shortly before entering the paint shop to have its all-over white livery with green and red cheatline applied. Note the Satcom 'hump' behind the flight deck. This 747SP, the 405th 747 built, was delivered to Braniff Airways in October 1979. As N603BN it was operated for five years by Braniff before being sold to the Omani government, who then spent three years having it converted to its present configuration. Oman acquired a second ex-Braniff SP-27 (N606BN - A40-SP), which was also operated by Pan Am and United. The third ex-Braniff SP-27 (N604BN) was acquired by Qatar Airways (A7-AHM). (Graham Dinsdale)

747 SR46 N1975B first flew on 31 August 1973 and was delivered to Japan Air Lines as JA8117 on 26 September that same year. On 15 April 1988 Boeing Equipment Holding Company bought the aircraft (later registered N911NA) and it was sold to the National Aeronautics & Space Administration (NASA) on 27 October 1988.

3 May by N533PA, specially re-named *Clipper Liberty Bell* for the occasion, when it landed at New York JFK airport after a two-stop (at Delhi and Tokyo), 22,864-mile flight. Elapsed time totalled 39 hours 26 minutes. [44] By the end of May three more SPs were accepted by Pan Am: N747SP (now N530PA) *Clipper Mayflower* on 26 April, N247PA (N531PA) *Clipper Liberty* on 17 May and N534PA *Clipper Great Republic* on 28 May. [45] Further history was made, on 28-30 October 1977, when *Clipper Liberty Bell,* specially re-named *Clipper New Horizon* for the occasion, marked Pan Am's fiftieth anniversary, setting a new speed record for an around-the-world flight, passing over both poles: San Francisco - London - Cape Town - Auckland-San Francisco, in 54 hours 7 minutes and 12 seconds (actual flight time was 48 hours and 3 minutes) for the 26,706 mile flight, from John F. Kennedy Airport, New York and return. It broke the previous record established twelve years earlier by a modified 707 by 8 hours 20 minutes.

But although the SP was technically, a success story, it had little commercial success, only 45 SPs being produced, the last on 9 December 1989.[46]

SP-44 3B-NAG Château du Reduit *under lease to Air Mauritius at Paris-Orly on 31 May 1990. This aircraft first flew on 4 June 1976 and was delivered to South African Airways as ZS-SPC* Maluti *on 16 June 1976. (Graham Dinsdale)*

Tajik Air's 747SP-21 Snow Leopard *on lease from United Airlines as N149US.*

The structural strength of the 747 was indisputably confirmed on 19 February 1985 when N4522V, a China Airlines' SP-09, (call sign 'Dynasty 006') flying from Taiwan Taoyuan International Airport at Taipei to Los Angeles International with 23 crew and 276 passengers, entered into a series of manoeuvres that no other 747 had to endure. N4522V was piloted by Captain Min-Yuan Ho, first officer Ju Yu Chang, flight engineer Kuo-Win Pei, relief captain Chien-Yuan Liao and relief flight engineer Shih Lung Suwere. Flight 006 was a daily non-stop flight departing from Taipei at 16:15 and scheduled to arrive at LAX at 07:00 local time. The SP-09 had covered most of the flight across the Pacific during the night and early part of the dawn. The accident occurred ten hours into the flight, at 10.16am, when the aircraft was 350 miles northwest of San Francisco and about forty minutes from landing at LAX, cruising at 41,000 feet, when it encountered some light turbulence. Met reports had indicated that a stormy weather front extending from the Californian coast was moving out to sea and below the 747 lay the black clouds of this storm front which reached from 11,000 feet at their base to the tops of high cloud at 37,000 feet. The sequence began when the No. 4 starboard (outermost) engine stalled at a low thrust setting and flamed out. [47] After the flameout Min-Yuan Ho instructed Shih Lung Suwere to attempt to restart the engine, while the 747 remained at FL 410 (41,000 feet), with the autopilot still engaged and the Bleed air on. (This was contrary to the flight manual procedure, which required the aircraft to be below 30,000 feet, before attempting to restart a flamed out engine). The restart attempt failed. Ho was under the impression that the wings were level when he disengaged the autopilot, but they were not. (The

747SP-44 ZS-SPE Hantam *of SAA at Bangkok in November 1999. The aircraft first flew on 5 November 1976 and was delivered to SAA on 22 November that same year. (Gerry Manning)*

747SP-94 YK-AHA November 16 t*he first of two Special Performance 747s for Syrian Air, delivered on 21 May 1976 (the other is YK-AHB* Arab Solidarity, *which was delivered on 16 July 1976) on takeoff at Sharjah March 2000. (Gerry Manning)*

autopilot had over-compensated for first the turbulence and then the engine being shut down and it had not been able to prevent the 747 entering a tightening 'aileron roll' to starboard as they dropped through cloud. The airspeed continued to decrease, while the autopilot rolled the control wheel to the maximum left limit of 23 degrees. As the speed decreased even further, the 747 began to roll to the right, even though the AP was maintaining the maximum left roll limit of 23 degrees. By the time the captain disconnected the autopilot, the 747 had rolled over 60 degrees to the right and the nose had begun to drop. Aileron control was the only means available to the autopilot to keep the wings level as the autopilot does not connect to the rudder during normal cruise flight. To counteract the asymmetrical forces created by the loss of thrust from the No. 4 engine, it was essential for the pilot to manually push on the left rudder. However, the captain failed to use any rudder inputs at all, before or after disconnecting the AP.)

As the 747 descended through clouds, the captain's attention was drawn to the artificial horizon which displayed excessive bank and pitch. Because such an attitude is highly irregular, the crew incorrectly assumed the indicators to be faulty. Without any visual references (due to the cloud) and having discarded the information from the ADIs, the crew became spatially disoriented. The 747 entered a steep dive at a high bank angle. Altitude decreased 10,000 feet within only 20 seconds, a vertical descent averaging 30,000 feet per minute. The crew and passengers experienced g-forces reaching as much as 5g. Ho had the control of the aircraft wrenched from his grasp. N4522V performed an extraordinary series of convulsions, rolling until the wings were

vertical, then nose-dived close to the speed of sound - it fell at a rate of 18,000 feet, or over 3 miles a minute - the centripetal forces pinning both passengers and crew to their seats; finally it turned upside down. (The stresses were later calculated to be ten to twelve times the force of gravity.) A scan of all the instruments would have revealed the 747's true flight attitude, but the three remaining engines had all flamed out and Ho's mind concentrated solely on the power dive, to the exclusion of all else.

If the storm front had extended to near the surface of the sea the crew would not have overcome their disorientation and the aircraft would have plummeted into the Pacific. Only after breaking through the bottom of the clouds at 11,000 feet could the captain orient himself and bring N4522V under control, levelling out at 9,600 feet. They had descended 30,000 feet in under two and a half minutes. The flight crew were under the impression that all four engines had flamed out, but the National Transportation Safety Board believed only engine No. 4 had failed. After levelling out, it was found that the three remaining engines were supplying normal thrust. A restart attempt brought No.4 back into use. They began climbing and reported to air traffic control 'condition normal now' and they were continuing on to Los Angeles. They then noticed that the inboard main landing gear was down and one of the hydraulic systems was empty. Because they did not have sufficient fuel to reach Los Angeles with the drag added by the landing gear, Ho diverted to San Francisco. Learning that there were two seriously injured people on board, an emergency was declared and N4522V flew straight in to the airport and landed without further incident.

Parts of the undercarriage and pieces of the control surfaces were ripped off and the APU (Auxiliary Power Unit) in the tail was torn from its mountings. Most affected was the tail, where large outer parts of both horizontal stabilizers had been ripped off. The entire left outboard elevator had been lost along with its actuator, which had been powered by the hydraulic system that ruptured and drained. The wings were permanently bent upwards by two inches, the inboard main landing gear lost two actuator doors and the two inboard main gear struts were left dangling. It is thought that had the pilots, who had been flying for ten hours when the engine was shut down, disconnected the autopilot and taken full manual control in time, they might have prevented the frightening series of events. The incident led to renewed pilot training and an improvement in both the computer-based auto systems.

The 747's strength and sound construction is legendary. Unfortunately, due to improper aircraft repair, structural strength was absent on Japan Air Lines' 747SR-46 JA8119 on Monday 12 August 1985. On this day JA8119 (which first flew on 28 January 1974) had completed four domestic flights when it landed at Tokyo International Airport (commonly referred to as Haneda Airport, HND) at 17:17. The next flight, around the Obon holiday period in Japan, when many Japanese people make yearly trips to their hometowns or resorts, was to be flight JAL123 to Osaka-Itami Airport (ITM). As JA8119 departed Gate 18, 509 of the 528 seats were occupied, mostly by Japanese, but amongst the number were 21 foreigners. Captain Masami Takahama and the 15 crew brought the total number of people on board to 524. Takahama was a training captain of three years' standing. First Officer Yutaka Sasaki was under training for promotion to command and he occupied the left-hand seat in the position of acting captain, while Takahama supervised from the right. Hiroshi Fukuda was the flight engineer. The flight plan route from Haneda for JA8119 was via Mihara, Hakone, Seaperch, airway W27 to Kushimoto, airway V55 to Shinota and then on to Osaka. The planned flight level was 24,000 feet and the estimated flight time was 54 minutes.

JAL123 took off from runway 15L at 18.12 hours local time, 12 minutes behind schedule, and climbed to 24,000 feet and flew southwest over Sagami Bay before turning almost due west over Oshima Island as it proceeded on a direct routeing to Seaperch. At 18.24 hours, while climbing through 23,900 feet at a speed of 300 knots as the aircraft reached cruising altitude over Sagami Bay and as JAL123 approached the eastern coast of Izu Peninsula a loud bang was heard from the rear of the 747. The 'beep-beep' of the cabin pressure warning horn began to sound and then it stopped. An unusual vibration occurred as the rear pressure bulkhead tore open; the resulting explosive decompression tearing away a portion of its vertical fin, measuring five metres together with the section of the tail-cone containing the auxiliary power unit (APU) and severing all four of the

SP-B5 HL7457 on finals at Kai Tak, 27 June 1997. It first flew on 30 January 1980 and was delivered to Korean Air on 18 March 1981. (Graham Dinsdale)

747SP-38 QANTAS SP-38 VH-EAA City of Gold Coast Tweed *first flew on 11 January 1981 and was delivered to the airline on 19 January that same year. (Boeing)*

hydraulic systems. (A photograph taken from the ground some time later confirmed that the vertical stabilizer was missing). [48] Decompression occurred, the hydraulic pressure dropped and ailerons, elevators and yaw damper became inoperative. All hydraulic fluid had drained away through the rupture. With total loss of hydraulic control and non-functional control surfaces, the aircraft began to oscillate up and down. The pilots managed a measure of control by using differential engine thrust. [49] These improvisations proved helpful, but further measures to exert control, such as lowering the landing gear and flaps, interfered with control by throttle and the jet's uncontrollability once again as the 747 experienced Dutch rolls and phugoid oscillations (unusual movement in which altitude and speed change significantly in a 20-100 seconds cycle without change of angle of attack). The loss of cabin pressure at high altitude had also caused a lack of oxygen throughout the cabin and emergency oxygen masks for passengers soon began to fall. Flight attendants, including Yumi Ochiai, a 26-year old off-duty JAL stewardess flying as a passenger, administered oxygen to various passengers using hand-held tanks. Later she recalled that 'There was a sudden bang. It was overhead in the rear. My ears hurt. Immediately the inside of the cabin became white.' The

section of the aft fuselage that had fractured had caused the cabin to depressurise and to mist the atmosphere. 'No sound of an explosion was heard,' she continued. 'The ceiling above the rear toilet came off.'

JA8119 started to descend to 6,600 feet while the crew tried to control the aircraft by using engine thrust. Upon reaching 6,600 feet the airspeed had dropped to 108 knots. The aircraft then climbed with a 39 degree angle of attack to a maximum of approximately 13,400 feet and started to descend again. With all flying controls and hydraulic systems lost the pilots fought to gain control and Takahama called a continuous series of instructions to co-ordinate their efforts. The engines still operated normally and engine power was their only means of guidance but the aircraft was also still 'Dutch rolling' about the sky. The 747 flew across Suruga Bay and as it did so door five right warning light illuminated indicating that it was unlocked. Flight 123 then turned northwards and proceeded inland towards Mount Fuji. The interphone chimed in the cockpit and a flight attendant from the back of the aircraft reported the damage to the flight engineer.

Juggling with the power Takahama and Yutaka Sasaki succeeded in turning onto an easterly heading and as they passed to the north of Mount Fuji they

747SP-94 YK-AHA November 16 *the first of two Special Performance 747s for Syrian Air, delivered on 21 May 1976 (the other is YK-AHB* Arab Solidarity, *which was delivered on 16 July 1976) on takeoff at Sharjah March 2000. Bahrain Royal Flight 747SP A9C-HMH. (Graham Dinsdale)*

gingerly attempted to commence descent. A problem arose in controlling the fast speed and Takahama suggested lowering the landing gear. Since all hydraulic power was gone, the alternative system was used and up-locks were electrically released in order to allow the gear simply to fall into place by gravity. The lowered gear seemed to dampen the motion slightly and the 747 settled in descent. At about 20,000 feet Takahama momentarily lost complete control and the aircraft banked sharply and turned a full circle in three minutes over Otsuki City before rolling out again on an easterly course. Passing 10,000 feet JA8119 then turned north again towards the mountainous terrain. As full power was applied to arrest the rate of descent the aircraft began to gyrate wildly, pitching up and down, with the speed increasing and decreasing rapidly. Desperate attempts were made to get some response from the controls but the effort was in vain. Suddenly the speed began to drop rapidly.

Despite a gallant effort to control pitch, the 747 continued to descend and the flaps were lowered on the alternative electrical system to 5° to help aid recovery. The process took almost four minutes, but had the desired effect and with increased power the aircraft managed to start climbing. At about 18.53 hours the altitude peaked at 11,000 feet and Flight 123 began to descend again. Takahama changed frequency to Tokyo Approach Control and verified that the aircraft was out

of control. He then requested his position. The rate of descent now increased to 1,350 feet/minute with the mountains dangerously close. Using flaps and power the crew tried desperately to control the stricken airliner. It was incredible amazing that Flight 123 had stayed in the air for so long but at 18.56:15 the 747 took a final plunge earthward and the ground proximity warning system (GPWS) blared: Pull up, pull up, pu ... pu u ...

Thirty-two minutes had elapsed from the time of the bulkhead explosion to the time of the final crash, long enough for some passengers to write farewells to their families. JA8119 almost totally disintegrated on impact at a height of 4,780 feet into the side of Mount Osutaka at about 70 miles northwest of Tokyo in the Gumma prefecture. JA8119 brushed against a tree covered ridge, continued and struck the Osutaka Ridge, 16.3 miles SW of Ueno Village, Tano District and north-north-west of Mount Mikuni, bursting into flames as fuel tanks ignited. All 15 crew members and 505 out of 509 passengers died, resulting in a total of 520 deaths.

United States Air Force controllers at Yokota Air Base situated near the flight path of Flight 123 had been monitoring the distressed aircraft's calls for help. They maintained contact throughout the ordeal with Japanese flight control officials and made their landing strip available to the aircraft. After losing track on radar, a US Air Force C-130 from the 345th Tactical Airlift Squadron was asked to search for the missing airliner.

The C-130 crew was the first to spot the crash site 20 minutes after impact, while it was still daylight. The crew radioed Yokota Air Base to alert them and directed a USAF Huey helicopter from Yokota to the crash site. Rescue teams were assembled in preparation to lower Marines down for rescues by helicopter tow line. The offers by American forces of help to guide Japanese forces immediately to the crash site and of rescue assistance were rejected by Japanese officials. Instead, Japanese government representatives ordered the US crew to keep away from the crash site and return to Yokota Air Base, stating the Japan Self-Defense Forces

In in a joint venture of NASA and DLR a former Pan Am 747SP was modified to Stratospheric Observatory for Infrared Astronomy (SOFIA) to carry a large infrared-sensitive telescope. High altitudes are needed for infrared astronomy, so as to rise above infrared-absorbing water vapour in the atmosphere. Boeing assigned serial number 21441 to the airframe that would become SOFIA. The aircraft had previously flown with Pan Am, then United Airlines. On 30 April 1997, the Universities Space Research Association (USRA) purchased the aircraft for use as an airborne observatory. On 27 October 1997 NASA purchased the aircraft from the USRA who then conducted a series of flight tests that year, prior to any heavy modification of the aircraft by E-Systems. To ensure successful modification, Raytheon purchased a section from another 747SP,

registration number N141UA, to use as a full-size mock-up. Commencing work in 1998, Raytheon designed and installed an 18-foot-tall (arc length) by 13.5-foot-wide door in the aft port side of the aircraft's fuselage that can be opened in-flight to give the telescope access to the sky. The telescope is mounted in the aft end of the fuselage behind a pressurized bulkhead. The telescope's focal point is located at a science instruments suite in the pressurized, centre section of the fuselage, requiring part of the telescope to pass through the pressure bulkhead. In the centre of the aircraft is the mission control and science operations section, while the forward section hosts the education and public outreach area.

(JSDF) were going to handle the entire rescue alone.

Although a JSDF helicopter eventually spotted the wreck during the night, poor visibility and the difficult mountainous terrain prevented it from landing at the site. The pilot reported from the air that there were no signs of survivors. Based on this report, JSDF ground personnel did not set out to the site the night of the crash. Instead, they were dispatched to spend the night at a makeshift village erecting tents, constructing helicopter landing ramps and engaging in other preparations, all 63 kilometres from the wreck. Rescue teams did not set out for the crash site until the following morning. It was not until nearly 09.00 hours local time - over 14 hours after the crash - that the firemen reached the area and were joined by paratroopers sliding down ropes from helicopters hovering overhead. The 747 had broken apart on narrow ridge and sections had catapulted into ravines on either side. One fireman searching in a gully detected movement in the debris and to his amazement found Yumi Ochiai, the off-duty JAL stewardess, who was jammed between seats but alive in an intact section of the fuselage wreckage. The only other survivors were 34-year old Hiroko Yoshizaki and her eight-year-old daughter, Mikiko and Keiko Kawakami a 12-year-old girl, who was found wedged between branches in a tree. Kawakami's parents and younger sister died in the crash and she was the last survivor to be released from hospitalization. All four survivors had been seated together in the centre of row 56. Medical staff later found bodies with injuries suggesting that the individual had survived the crash only to die from shock or exposure overnight in the mountains. One doctor said 'If the discovery had come ten hours earlier, we could have found more survivors.' 50

It was the worst single accident in aviation history and second only to Tenerife in 1977. Without admitting liability, JAL paid ¥780 million to the victims' relatives in the form of 'condolence money'. Its president, Yasumoto Takagi, resigned, while a maintenance manager working for the company at Haneda killed himself to apologize for the accident.

Improper repairs to a 747 was evident again, sixteen years' later. China Airlines Flight 611 (call sign Dynasty 611) was a regularly scheduled flight from Chiang Kai-shek International Airport (now Taiwan Taoyuan International Airport) in Taoyuan to Hong Kong International Airport in Hong Kong. On Saturday 25 May 2002 747-209B B-18255 disintegrated in mid-air and crashed into the Taiwan Strait just 20 minutes after taking off; killing 225 people. The cause of the crash was improper repairs to the aircraft 22 years earlier. The accident was particularly disturbing to the public because the Taipei to Hong Kong route was and is to this

day one of the most heavily-travelled routes on Earth; it is so profitable that it is even referred to as the 'Golden Route'. The flight on, 25 May 2002 took off at 14:50 local time and was expected to arrive at Hong Kong at 16:28. The flight crew consisted of Captain Ching-Fong Yi, First Officer Yea Shyong Shieh and Flight Engineer Sen Kuo Cbao. About 25 minutes after takeoff the aircraft disappeared from radar screens, suggesting it had experienced an in-flight breakup at FL350 (approximately 35,000 feet or 7 miles) near the Penghu Islands in the Taiwan Strait. The crash occurred at a time between 15:37 and 15:40; Chang Chia-juch, the Taiwanese Vice Minister of Transportation and Communications said that two Cathay Pacific aircraft in the area received B-18255's emergency location-indicator signals. All nineteen crew members and all 206 passengers died.

The flight data recorder from Flight 611 shows that the jet began gaining altitude at a significantly faster rate in the 27 seconds before 747-209B broke apart, although the extra gain in altitude was well within the airliner's design limits. 747-209B was supposed to be levelling off then as it approached its cruising altitude of 35,000 feet. Shortly before the breakup, one of the aircraft's four engines began providing slightly less thrust. Coincidentally, the engine was the only one recovered from the sea floor. Pieces of the aircraft were found in the ocean and on Taiwan, including in the city of Changhua.

The final investigation report found that the accident was the result of metal fatigue caused by inadequate maintenance after a previous incident. The report indicated that on 7 February 1980, the aircraft used on the flight had a tail-strike accident while landing in Hong Kong. Part of the jet's tail was damaged in the incident. The aircraft was de-pressurized, ferried back to Taiwan on the same day and a temporary repair done the day after. A more permanent repair was conducted by a team from China Airlines from 23 May to 26 May 1980. However, the permanent repair of the tail strike was not carried out in accordance with the Boeing Structural Repair Manual (SRM). The area of damaged skin in Section 46 was not removed (trimmed) and the repair doubler plate that was supposed to cover in excess of 30% of the damaged area did not extend beyond the entire damaged area enough to restore the overall structural strength. Consequently, after repeated cycles of depressurization and pressurization during flight, the weakened hull gradually started to crack and finally broke open in mid-flight on 25 May 2002, exactly 22 years to the day after the faulty repair was made upon the damaged tail. An explosive decompression of the aircraft occurred once the crack opened up, causing the complete disintegration of the aircraft in mid-air. 51

Footnotes for Chapter 7

42   ANA would place orders for six Lockheed L-1011 TriStars at the end of October 1972.

43   In 1987 JAL also took delivery of four short-range (SR) derivatives of the 747-300. The first 747SR (SR-81) version for All Nippon Airways (ANA) was JA8133, the 346th 747 built, which first flew on 9 December 1978; it was delivered to ANA on 21 December 1978. The SR-81 version differs from the SR-46 version of the 747-100 in having 46,500lb-thrust General Electric CF6-45A engines. Altogether, ANA received seventeen SR-81 versions.

44   In 1980 N533PA was renamed *Clipper Young America;* in September 1983 it became *Clipper San Francisco;* in 1984 it was renamed *Clipper New Horizons;* in April 1985 it was renamed *Clipper Young America.*

45   The five remaining SP Clippers were accepted during 1977-79; the last, N540PA *Clipper White Falcon,* being delivered on 11 May 1979. Two other SPs allocated to Pan Am, including N535PA *Clipper Mercury,* were later cancelled. Stratospheric Observatory for Infrared Astronomy (SOFIA) - a former Pan Am Boeing 747SP was modified to carry a large infrared-sensitive telescope, in a joint venture of NASA and DLR. High altitudes are needed for infrared astronomy, so as to rise above infrared-absorbing water vapour in the atmosphere.

46   The 44th 747SP was delivered on 30 August 1982. In 1987 Boeing re-opened the 747SP production line after five years to build one last 747SP for an order by the United Arab Emirates Government. In addition to airline use, one 747SP was modified for NASA Dryden Flight Research Center's SOFIA experiment.

47   That engine had failed twice during previous flights (both while cruising at FL 410 & 430, respectively). In each of those cases, the engine was restarted, after descending to a lower altitude. The maintenance response to the logbook entries that noted the problems included engine inspection, fuel filter drainage and replacement, vane controller inspection and replacement, water drainage from Mach probes, insufficient modules, and other filter replacements. None of those acts fixed the recurrent stalling and flameout problem of the No. 4 engine.

48   On 2 June 1978 the aircraft operated on a flight to Osaka-Itami. It floated after touchdown and on the second touchdown the tail struck the runway. The aircraft sustained substantial damage to the rear underside of the fuselage. The rear pressure bulkhead was also cracked. The aircraft was repaired by Boeing. Engineers replaced the lower part of the rear fuselage and a portion of the lower half of the bulkhead. The subsequent repair of the bulkhead did not conform to Boeing's approved repair methods. Boeing technicians fixing the aircraft used two separate doubler plates, one with two rows of rivets and one with only one row when the procedure called for one continuous doubler plate with three rows of rivets to reinforce the damaged bulkhead. This reduced the part's resistance to metal fatigue by 70%. According to the FAA, the one 'doubler plate' which was specified for the job (the FAA calls it a 'splice plate' - essentially a patch) was cut into two pieces parallel to the stress crack it was intended to reinforce, 'to make it fit'. This negated the effectiveness of two of the rows of rivets. During the investigation Boeing calculated that this incorrect installation would fail after approximately 10,000 pressurizations; the aircraft accomplished 12,318 successful flights from the time that the faulty repair was made to when the crash happened. In fact the improper repair was strong enough to survice 6,500 takes offs and landings before the bulkhead gave way. The resulting explosive decompression ruptured the lines of all four hydraulic systems and blew off the vertical stabilizer. With the aircraft's flight controls disabled, the aircraft became uncontrollable.

49   Subsequent simulator re-enactments of the mechanical failures suffered by Flight 123 failed to produce a better solution or outcome and none of the four flight crews in the simulations was able to keep the 747 aloft for as long as the 32 minutes achieved by the actual crew.

50   China Airlines Flight 611 involved a China Airlines' 747-209B that crashed in Taiwan Strait in 2002 on a flight from Taipei to Hong Kong, also because of faulty maintenance done on damage caused by a tail-strike accident long before the crash date, finally causing the aircraft's structure to fail and disintegrate in flight. United Airlines Flight 232 was another case where all control surfaces failed. Dennis E. Fitch, a DC-10 instructor who had read about the JAL 123 crash and had practiced flying with throttles alone in a simulator, used a steer-by-throttle technique to guide the United airliner to an emergency landing at Sioux City, Iowa. Although a wing struck the ground at touchdown and the plane broke up and caught fire, 185 out of 296 passengers and crew survived. DHL shoot-down incident in Baghdad when an Airbus A300 was struck by missile causing a total loss of hydraulics. The crew managed to land the crippled aircraft safely using the throttles.

51   China Airlines disputed much of the report, stating that investigators did not find the pieces of the aircraft that would prove the contents of the investigation report. One piece of evidence of the metal fatigue is contained in pictures that were taken during a routine inspection of the plane years before the crash. The photos showed visible brown nicotine stains around the doubler plate. This nicotine was deposited by smoke from the cigarettes of people who were smoking about seven years before the disaster (smoking was allowed in a pressurized plane at that time). The doubler plate had a brown nicotine stain all the way around it that could have been detected visually by any of the engineers when they inspected the plane. The stain would have suggested that there might be a crack caused by metal fatigue behind the doubler plate, as the nicotine slowly seeped out due to pressure that built up when the plane reached its cruising altitude. The stains were apparently not noticed and no correction was made to the doubler plate, which caused the crash to happen.

Chapter 8

Pan Am Flight 103

I should have been the 271st victim and I still feel terrible for all the other people who died.

Jaswant Basuta in an interview with the BBC in 2008

Before boarding Pan Am Flight 103 on 21 December 1988, Sony Mitchell's father purchased a watch at the Duty Free shop at London Heathrow. He was in a hurry. *Clipper Maid of the Seas*, which earlier had left Frankfurt am Main Airport in West Germany, was due to take off for New York's John F. Kennedy International Airport.[52] But it took longer than expected to get the links taken out of Mitchell's watch and the delay caused him and his baby son to miss the flight. Motown group 'The Four Tops' had been scheduled to return to the United States for Christmas after completing their European tour, but they were late leaving a recording session and overslept. Punk rocker John Lydon aka Johnny Rotten of the 'Sex Pistols' and Public Image Ltd and his wife Nora were also booked on Pan Am Flight 103, but missed it due to delays. The 1988 world tennis No. 1 Mats Wilander had made a reservation but did not take a seat on the flight. The actress Kim Cattrall was also booked on the flight but changed her reservation shortly beforehand in order to complete some last minute gift shopping in London. Music producer Ed Stasium and recording engineer Paul Hamingson had planned to be on the flight but were delayed while finishing a recording session with the rock band 'The Muscle Shoal' at Comforts Place Studio in Lingfield, Surrey. They departed from Heathrow the following day on a different Pam Am flight. The South African foreign minister Pik Botha and a minor delegation of 22 was supposed to board Pan Am 103, but managed to take the earlier Pan Am 101 flight. They were on their way to New York to sign the tripartite agreement whereby South Africa agreed to hand control of Namibia to the United Nations.

Flight 103's 243 passengers and their luggage on the feeder flight from Frankfurt transferred directly onto the 747 at Heathrow, along with interline luggage not accompanied by anyone. Prominent among them was the 50-year-old UN Commissioner for Namibia, Bernt Carlsson, who was due to attend the signing ceremony at UN headquarters on 22 December of the New York Accords. Volkswagen America CEO James Fuller and Volkswagen America Marketing Director Lou Marengo were returning from a meeting with Volkswagen executives in Germany; English musician Paul Jeffreys and his wife Rachel and poet and former girlfriend of musician Robert Fripp, Joanna Walton, credited with writing most of the lyrics on the 1979 album Exposure. Jonathan White was the son of David White who played Larry Tate on the sitcom Bewitched. Thirty-five of the passengers were students from Syracuse University returning home for Christmas following a semester studying in London at Syracuse's London campus.

At least four US government officials were on the passenger list, with rumours, never confirmed, of a fifth on board. On 5 December the Federal Aviation Administration (FAA) had issued a security bulletin saying that on that day a man with an Arabic accent had telephoned the US Embassy in Helsinki, Finland and had told them that a Pan Am flight from Frankfurt to the United States would be blown up within the next two weeks by someone associated with the Abu Nidal Organization. He said a Finnish woman would carry the bomb on board as an unwitting courier. The anonymous warning was taken seriously by the US government. The State Department cabled the bulletin to dozens of embassies. The FAA sent it to all US carriers, including Pan Am, which had charged each of the passengers a $5 security surcharge, promising a 'programme that will screen passengers, employees, airport facilities, baggage and aircraft with unrelenting thoroughness'. Warnings of possible terrorist action however, had not deterred Matthew Gannon, the CIA's deputy station chief in Beirut, Lebanon, who was sitting in Clipper Class, or Major Chuck 'Tiny' McKee, an army officer on

Pan Am 747-121/SCD N739PA Clipper Maid of the Seas.

secondment to the Defense Intelligence Agency (DIA) in Beirut, who sat behind Gannon in the centre aisle. Two Diplomatic Security Service special agents, Ronald Lariviere, a security officer from the US Embassy in Beirut and Daniel O'Connor, a security officer from the US Embassy in Nicosia, Cyprus, acting as bodyguards to Gannon and McKee, were sitting in economy. The four men had flown together out of Cyprus that morning. On 13 December, the warning was posted on bulletin boards in the US Embassy in Moscow and eventually distributed to the entire American community there, including journalists and businessmen. As a result, a number of people allegedly booked on carriers other than Pan Am, leaving empty seats on PA 103 that were later sold cheaply in 'bucket shops'. Just days before the flight, security forces in a number of European countries, including Britain, were put on alert after a warning from the Palestine Liberation Organization (PLO) that extremists might launch terrorist attacks to undermine the then ongoing dialogue between the United States and the PLO.

Jaswant Basuta, a 47-year-old car mechanic of Indian nationality was checked in for the flight, but he arrived at the boarding gate too late. Having attended a family wedding in Belfast, Basuta was returning to New York to start a new job. Friends and relatives from nearby Southall came to see him off at the airport terminal and bought him drinks in the upstairs bar. When 'gate closing' flashed on the departure screen, Basuta hurried through security and sprinted to the gate, but the room was empty except for Pan Am ground staff who denied him access to the aircraft.

Clipper Maid of the Seas pushed back from the gate at 18:04 and the 55 year old Captain James Bruce McQuarrie, a veteran with 11,000 flight hours, lifted off at 18:25. Beside him sat 52 year old First officer Raymond Ronald Wagner and 46 year old flight engineer Jerry Don Avritt. The flight deck crew was New York/JFK based while the sixteen cabin crew was based at London Heathrow. Flight 103 flew northwest into the Daventry departure over the Midlands and levelled off at 31,000 feet about 25 miles north of Manchester at 18:56. At 19:01 UTC, air traffic controller Alan Topp watched Flight 103 approach the corner of the Solway Firth on his screen and observed as it crossed the coast at 19:02 UTC. On his scope, the aircraft showed transponder code or 'squawk' - 0357 and flight level - 31O. At this point *Clipper Maid of the Seas* was flying at 31,000 feet on a heading of 316 degrees magnetic and at a speed of 313 knots. At that moment, the airliner's 'squawk' flickered off.

Topp tried to make contact with Captain MacQuarrie, with no response. Over in the Oceanic Clearance Office, ATC assistant Tom Fraser tried as well and asked a nearby KLM flight to do the same, but there was no reply. Where there should have been one radar echo on Topp's screen, there were five and as the seconds passed, the echoes began to fan out. Comparison of the cockpit voice recorder with the radar returns showed that eight seconds after the explosion, the wreckage had a one-nautical-mile spread. British Airways pilot Captain Robin Chamberlain, flying the Glasgow-London shuttle near Carlisle, called Scottish authorities to report that he could see a huge fire on the ground. The destruction of PA103 continued on Topp's screen, by now full of returns moving eastward with the wind. The explosion punched a 20-inch-wide hole on the left side of the fuselage, almost directly under the 'P' in the 'Pan Am' logo painted on it. The disintegration of the aircraft was rapid. Later, investigators from the

US Federal Aviation Administration (FAA) were lowered into the cockpit in the wreckage before it was moved from the crash site and while the bodies of the flight crew were still in it. Investigators concluded that no emergency procedures had been started. The pressure control and fuel switches were both set for cruise and the crew had not used their oxygen masks, which would have been required within five seconds of a rapid depressurization of the aircraft. Investigators from the Air Accidents Investigation Branch (AAIB) of the British Department for Transport concluded that the nose of the aircraft separated from the main section within three seconds of the explosion. The cockpit voice recorder in the tail section of the 747 was found in a field by police searchers within 24 hours of the bombing. There was no evidence of a distress signal: a 180-millisecond hissing noise could be heard as the explosion destroyed the aircraft's communications centre. Although the explosion was in the aircraft hold, the effect was increased by the large pressure difference between the aircraft interior and the outside air.

Shock waves from the blast ricocheted back from the fuselage skin in the direction of the bomb, meeting pulses still coming from the initial explosion. This produced Mach stem shock waves, calculated to be 25% faster than and double the power of, the waves from the explosion itself. These Mach stem waves pulsing through the ductwork bounced off overhead luggage racks and other hard surfaces, jolting the passengers. A section of the 747's roof, several feet above the point of detonation, peeled away. The nerve centre of a 747, from which all the navigation and communication systems are controlled, is located below the cockpit, separated from the forward cargo hold by a bulkhead wall. Investigators concluded that the force of the explosion broke through this wall and shook the flight- control cables, causing the front section of the fuselage to begin to roll, pitch and yaw. The shock waves of the explosion rebounded from one side of the aircraft to the other, running down the length of the fuselage through the air conditioning ducts and splitting it open. This in turn snapped the reinforcing belt that secured the front section to the row of windows on the left side and it began to break away. Then the whole front section of the aircraft, containing the flight deck with crew and the first class section, broke away altogether, flying upwards and to starboard, striking the No.3 engine as it snapped off. With the disruption of the control cables, the aircraft went into a steep dive. When the fuselage disintegrated, the cabin depressurised to a quarter of ground-level pressure, leaving the passengers fighting for breath. Because of the sudden change in air pressure, the gases inside the passengers' bodies would have expanded to four times their normal volume, causing their lungs to swell and

then collapse. The explosion knocked out the power, plunging the passenger cabin into darkness. A Scottish Fatal Accident Inquiry, which opened on 1 October 1990, heard testimony that, when the cockpit broke off, the fuselage became an open cylinder. Tornado-force winds tore up the aisles, slamming into passengers' chests, making it even more difficult to breathe and stripping their clothes off. Some were thrown to the rear. Other people and objects not fixed down were blown out of the aircraft into the night at temperatures of -46°C, their 31,000-foot fall through the night-time troposphere lasting about two minutes. Some passengers remained attached to the fuselage by their seat belts, crashing to earth strapped to their seats.

Investigators believe that within three seconds of the explosion, the cockpit, fuselage and No.3 engine were falling separately. The fuselage continued moving forward and down until it reached 19,000 feet, at which point its dive became almost vertical. As it descended, the fuselage broke into smaller pieces, with the section attached to the wings landing first in Sherwood Crescent, Lockerbie at more than 500 mph. The 200,000lb of kerosene contained inside ignited, the resultant fireball, creating a crater 154 feet long vaporizing the house and its occupants, Dora and Maurice Henry. Several other houses and their foundations were completely destroyed and 21 others were damaged so badly they had to be demolished. Four members of one family died when their house exploded and Kathleen and Thomas Flannigan and their ten year

old daughter were killed by the explosion in their house at 16 Sherwood Crescent. Their son Steven, 14, saw the fireball engulf his home from a neighbour's garage where he had gone to repair his sister's bicycle.

The remains of seven of the eleven residents killed in the inferno on the ground at Sherwood Crescent were never identified. Another section of the fuselage landed about half a mile northeast, where it slammed into widow Ella Ramsden's home in Park Place. Her house was demolished, but she escaped. Her back garden was strewn with bodies and wreckage and a victim was found wedged in the roof still strapped in his seat. Distinctive marks on Captain MacQuarrie's thumb suggested he had been hanging onto the yoke of the jet as it descended and may have been alive when the 747 crashed. The captain, first officer, flight engineer, a flight attendant and a number of first-class passengers were found still strapped to their seats inside the nose section when it crashed in a field by a tiny church in the village of Tundergarth. The inquest heard that a flight attendant was found alive by a farmer's wife, but died before her discoverer could summon help. Of the total of 270 fatalities (259 in the aircraft, eleven on the ground), 189 were American citizens, many of them from New Jersey and New York; and 43 British citizens.

According to a CIA report several groups were quick to claim responsibility in telephone calls in the United States and Europe. Jaswant Basuta, who had narrowly missed the flight was initially considered a suspect as his checked baggage had been on the flight without him. After questioning at a Heathrow police station, he was released without charge. Twenty years later, in an interview with the BBC, he talked about his narrow escape from death: 'I should have been the 271st victim and I still feel terrible for all the other people who died'.

The fuselage of the aircraft was reconstructed by air accident investigators, revealing a 20-inch hole consistent with an explosion in the forward cargo hold. Examination of the baggage containers revealed that the container nearest the hole had blackening, pitting and severe damage indicating a 'high-energy event' had taken place inside it. A series of test explosions were carried out to confirm the precise location and quantity of explosive used. Fragments of a Samsonite suitcase believed to have contained the bomb were recovered, together with parts and pieces of circuit board identified as part of a Toshiba Bombeat radio cassette player, similar to that used to conceal a Semtex bomb seized by West German police from the Palestinian militant group Popular Front for the Liberation of Palestine - General Command two months earlier. Items of baby clothing, which were subsequently proven to have been made in Malta, were also thought to have come from the same suitcase. A circuit board fragment, allegedly found embedded in a piece of charred material, was identified as part of an electronic timer similar to that found on a Libyan intelligence agent who had been arrested ten months previously, carrying materials for a Semtex bomb. Investigators discovered that a bag had been routed onto PA103, via the interline baggage system at Frankfurt, from the station and approximate time at which bags were unloaded from flight KM180 from Malta. [53]

In 1977 Pan Am had celebrated its fiftieth anniversary but by the mid-1980s America's premier carrier was in deep financial trouble. Huge losses on its domestic routes by 1985 brought matters to a head and on 22 April 1986 Pan Am agreed to sell its pacific division to United Airlines for $750 million. The deal included the 747SP fleet and six Lockheed TriStars. On 12 August 1991 a bankrupt Pan Am sold its remaining assets to Delta Airlines for $416 million in cash and the assumption of $389 million worth of liabilities. What was left of Pan Am's once mighty fleet was kept alive by Delta as a proving operation in Florida for flights to South America. On 4 December 1991, the day after Pan Am shed its Chapter Eleven protection, Pan Am was no more. Delta pulled the plug.

Footnotes for Chapter 8
52 747-121 N739PA the fifteenth 747 built and delivered in February 1970, one month after the first 747 entered service with Pan Am) was scheduled, after the transatlantic leg of Flight 103, to take off again for its final destination at Detroit Metropolitan Wayne County Airport at Romulus in Michigan.
53 After a three-year joint investigation by Dumfries and Galloway Constabulary and the US Federal Bureau of Investigation, during which 15,000 witness statements were taken, indictments for murder were issued on 13 November 1991 against Abdelbaset al-Megrahi, a Libyan intelligence officer and the head of security for Libyan Arab Airlines (LAA) and Lamin Khalifah Fhimah, the LAA station manager in Luqa Airport, Malta. In 1992 a US federal court found Pan Am guilty of wilful misconduct due to lax security screening. Alert Management Inc and Pan American World Services, two subsidiaries of Pan Am, were also found guilty; Alert handled Pan Am's security at foreign airports.

Chapter 9

Long Haul

138

A nightime scene at London Heathrow with a British Airways 747 about to depart.

Malaysia and Lufthansa 747s at Frankfurt on 23 February 1990. (Graham Dinsdale)

Top: British Airways 747 City of Belfast *on finals. (Rolls-Royce)*

Bottom: All Nippon Airways 747-481D JA8957 in the 'Pokémon' cartoon scheme at Okinawa in October 2004. On 15 May 2001 the airline announced that it had selected Boeing to convert two ANA 747-400s from its International three-class 367-seat configuration to its two-class, 569-seat domestic configuration. The domestic configuration primarily involved removing the winglets and installing wingtips, as well as modifying the cabin interior with new passenger and attendant seats, in-flight entertainment systems, galleys, toilets, floor coverings, closets and stowage units. (Gerry Manning)

Opposite page: Iberia 747-256B EC-DIB on takeoff at Madrid in September 2002. (Gerry Manning)

Above: A Wardair Canada 747 taxies past the cargo area at London Gatwick.

Below: Virgin Atlantic 747-238B G-VJFK Boston Belle *(Author)*

TWA 747 Skyliner *at London Gatwick on 16 February 1991 bound for St. Louis.* (*Author*)

Middle: Virgin 747-400 Tubular Belle *at LHR on 10 February 1996.* (*Graham Dinsdale.*)

Bottom: Avianca HK2980X, a 747-258B Combi, seen at Frankfurt on 23 February 1990. (Graham Dinsdale)

British Caledonian Boeing 747-211B G-GLYN on finals at Gatwick on 11 July 1987. (Graham Dinsdale)

747-451 N661US, seen here taking off on its delivery flight, was accepted by Northwest Airlines in 1989 as N661US. Fully loaded, a -400 weighs over 250 tons, yet after about fifty seconds from beginning to roll, at a speed of 170 knots, it will rise into the air at about a mile down the runway. Once the eighteen wheels are retracted, the -400 will climb at over 3,000 feet per minute and at 1,500 feet the flaps are retracted and speed increased to 250 knots. With declining air pressures the rate of climb reduces to around 1,000 feet per minute and the cruising altitude of about 35,000 feet is reached after around thirty minutes. (Boeing)

Top: Corse Air 747 taking off from Brussels on 4 May 1989. (Graham Dinsdale)

Middle: All Nippon Airways' 747 climbing out at HKG on 29 April 1998. (Graham Dinsdale)

Bottom: 747-287B LV-MLP Aerolineas Argentinas at Miami in October 1981. (Gerry Manning)

Top: 747-346 HS-UTW
Orient Thai Airlines at
Bangkok in November
2010. (Gerry
Manning)

Middle: Air France
747-400 is caught by
the camera just a the
point of lift-off from a
wet runway.

Bottom: An early
British Airways' 747
departs on another
long-haul flight.

QANTAS 747-438 VH-OJR Longreach *on finals*.

Boeing 747-200 C-FCRE of CP Air Empress of Italy *arrives at London Gatwick before starting a return flight to Tononto*.

Chapter 10

Freighters

Nowadays, giant aircraft such as the Boeing 747 and others of similar ilk have the wide-body, 'well-fed' look...

Although the 747-100 was designed to carry freight from the very outset and was offered in all-cargo and passenger-cargo convertible configurations, no Model 747-100s were ever built as such. Orders were received for both versions, but these were subsequently cancelled or converted to all-passenger aircraft before delivery.

Originally, Boeing had confidently expected that up to half of the first 400 747s bought by airlines would be cargo-carrying aircraft. This projection was based mostly in the belief that the introduction of SST aircraft would see passenger yield moving to the new generation supersonic aircraft, leaving the early 747s to be converted to cargo-carrying aircraft. The supersonic revolution never really materialized, however and for the first three years of the 747's life, Boeing received only one firm order for a cargo-carrying aircraft and this was a new-build -200F, for Lufthansa. Also, the early

engines used to power the 747-100s, which grew ever heavier as modifications and increased fuel loads were added to their gross weight, were just not powerful enough to deliver the thrust and take-off speed margins required by freight-carrying 747s fitted with nose and/or side doors.

This situation only began to change in 1973-74 when the oil crisis caused world economic recession which saw a rapid downturn in passenger loads, especially on the transatlantic routes. As a result, fleets generally were forced to cancel or unload some of their existing large aircraft such as the 747-100s onto the second-hand market. After conversion, many were put into service as cargo-carrying aircraft.

The conversion of 747-100s from passenger-carrying to cargo-carrying aircraft was carried out at the Boeing-Wichita Modification Responsibility Center in

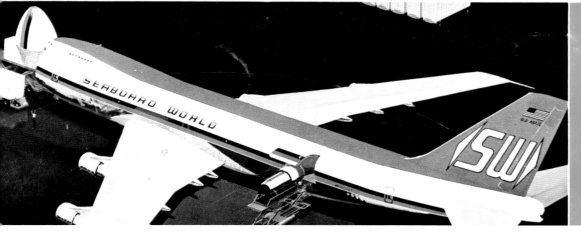

A 29 feet 6 inch long conveyor frame of a Conway Mucker weighing 9,700lb being lifted to the main deck of a Seaboard 747 containership. All four -245F containerships were subsequently acquired by Flying Tigers. (Seaboard World Airlines)

Kansas. Starting in 1974, the cabins on ex-United Airlines' -100s for cargo carrier Flying Tigers were gutted and rebuilt with a strengthened main cargo-deck floor, a cargo-handling system was installed and a 120 x 134 in side cargo door was created in the left side between the trailing edge of the wing and the tail. These modifications increased the maximum take-off weight to 755,000lb. Eventually, twenty-four aircraft were converted to 747-100SF configuration, with the others being prepared for Pan Am and the Imperial Iranian Air Force. In addition, early in 1974 two 747-129s were converted by Boeing-Wichita for SABENA with the addition of a strengthened aft deck to carry up to six freight pallets and a side cargo door 11 feet 2 inches wide and 10 feet 3 inches high on the left side of the fuselage behind the wing. To keep rain from running in from the top of the fuselage when the door was open, a rain deflector strip was installed above the door, projecting several feet to each side.

The added door allows main-deck combination - or 'Combi' - loading: either all passengers, all cargo, or passengers and up to twelve pallets or containers. Containers up to 8 feet high can be carried forward of the cargo door and containers 10 feet high can be carried aft of the door if the normal passenger ceiling is removed. Cargo and passenger areas are separated by a

747-2B5BFs HL7452 and HL7451, the first two of five 747 freighters for Korean Air Cargo, which took delivery of both aircraft on 25 June 1980. (Boeing)

removable bulkhead, the passengers being seated forward of the cargo. By early 1977, more than forty 747s had been delivered with, or modified to have, the side cargo door.

The 747-l00s were not powerful enough to carry an upward-hinged nose door and to operate efficiently as pure freighter aircraft; however, when the higher thrust P&W JT9D engine became available Boeing could at last press ahead with a pure freighter version of the 747 and in 1970 committed $54.2 million into developing the -200A to this end - it was the first 747 to feature straight-in loading of bulk cargo through a hinged-up nose-hatch which Boeing termed a 'visor'. The width of the cabin permits two 8 feet wide by 8 feet high (containers - the longest of which is 40 feet and a 747-200F can carry six - to be loaded side by side through the nose. A further $15 million was spent developing an optional 11 feet x 10 feet side door which allows containers ten feet high to be loaded on board and carried in the rear part of the cabin. At first there seemed little chance of a sizeable return on these huge investments, because for the first two years only one of these big aircraft was put into service. Sales eventually

picked up, however and the company's faith in the pure freighter design was rewarded, with seventy-three -200Fs being built over twenty-one years before production switched to the 747-400F in 1991.

Distribution of the cargo as it is loaded is by means of a powered transfer- system built into the cabin floor. With a central station at the nose door, two people can distribute and stow upwards of 250,000lb of main-deck cargo in half an hour. An automatic weight-and-balance computer makes it unnecessary to calculate manually the weight and movement of each container. If the load is distributed beyond limits, the distribution system shuts down. Cargo loading is normally by means of mobile ground equipment, but to serve airports without such facilities Boeing developed an on-board cargo loader that is carried in the nose of the aeroplane. This can lift units of up to 30,000lb through either the nose or the side door. The 29 feet-long unit, which weighs 14,000lb is carried in the forward end of the cabin. It does not entirely displace cargo in that space because it can contain two 8 x 8 x 9 feet containers.

In addition, the fuselage was revised to delete all passenger doors except one and five on the left side of

View looking forward of the rear cabin of a 747-100C, which has its ceiling removed. Conversion of 747-100s from passenger-carrying to cargo-carrying aircraft was carried out at the Boeing-Wichita Modification Responsibility Center in Kansas. Starting in 1974, the cabins on ex-United Airlines' -100s for cargo carrier Flying Tigers were gutted and rebuilt with a strengthened main cargo-deck floor, a cargo-handling system was installed and a 120 x 134 inch side cargo door was created in the left side between the trailing edge of the wing and the tail. (Boeing)

747-230F D-ABZF Lufthansa Cargo at Sharjah, March 2000 in a special scheme showing times and locations around the world and how cargo flights can connect them. (Gerry Manning)

the aircraft. All passenger windows are also deleted except the windows in doors one and five. Three small windows were added on the left side and two on the right side for viewing the wing- and cargo-loading operations. The aircraft systems, such as the air-conditioning system were revised to suit freighter use.

D-ABYE, the first -200F (its temporary US registration during certification testing was N1794B) was rolled out on 14 October 1971 and first flew on 30 November. Following certification on 7 March 1972, with the designation 747F as a pure freighter, D-ABYE *Cargonaut* was accepted by Lufthansa two days later, entering service on the Frankfurt-New York route on 19 April. *Cargonaut* could carry a maximum payload of 260,000lb - three times that of the 707 - nearly 3,000 miles. This aircraft is still in service, with Korean Air

and was the first 747 to exceed 100,000 flying hours. Late in 1974, JAL, Seaboard World and Air France took delivery of -200Fs (in Air France service they became known as 'Pelicans', a reference to the upward-opening nose door). The first 747-200F to have the side cargo door fitted was -245F N701SW, the 242nd 747 built, which was delivered to Seaboard World Airlines on 31 July 1974. The later availability of the Pratt & Whitney JT9D-70A engine permitted an increase in aircraft take-off weight from the original 785,000lb to 820,000lb, so the -245F was returned to Everett for conversion. The seventy-third and final -200F built was a -281F received by Nippon Cargo Airlines on 19 November 1991.

The 747 used as a freighter brought about a major revolution in the large-scale airlift of cattle. Previously, the animals had been walked singly up a ramp and into

The lower cargo container compartments were powered similarly to the main deck system. Electrically driven pneumatic wheels move the containers and/or pallets inside the aircraft.

747-2B5BF HL7452 of Korean Air Cargo being loaded.

the aeroplane cabin, where they were tethered. Obsolescent aeroplanes, or others near the ends of their service lives, were usually used for this work because of the severe airframe corrosion resulting from animal wastes. The 747, with its large cabin and side-door loading, changed because the animals could be containerized: now, up to six cows can be loaded into one leak-proof, open-top container and lifted aboard; up to 118 cows can be carried in a single 747. The speed and range of the 747, even for trans-Pacific flights from the United States to the Orient via Alaska, make it unnecessary to unload the animals at intermediate stops

and thanks to the containers, the aeroplane is relatively clean at journey's end. The major change to a 747 used regularly for cattle lift is an increase in the capacity of the cabin air-conditioning system.

At the start of the 1970s Boeing looked at several ways of creating a high-capacity passenger and freight aircraft to revitalize the sagging 747 freight market. Though ways could be found to increase the payload of the 747, each method employed incurred a penalty in that the 747's range would be reduced as a result. And once again, Boeing was restricted by the limitations imposed by the engine technology then currently

Flying Tigers' 747 freighters at Hong Kong on 10 September 1987. (Graham Dinsdale)

747-228F F-BPVR (N1783B), which first flew on 28 September 1976, one of seven -228Fs purchased by Air France, delivered on 13 October 1976. In Air France service 747 freighters are known as 'Pelicans', a reference to the upward-opening nose door. The sixty-seventh and final 200F built (F-GCBK) was received by Air France in October 1991. (Boeing)

available. To increase the payload by 75,000lb to 275,000lb, for instance, would involve stretching the 747 fuselage and at the same time place reliance on Pratt & Whitney to develop the JT9D engine further to deliver 53,000lb of thrust. (The P&W JT9D-7F/7FW engine, which produced 48,000lb dry/50,000lb wet thrust, finally became available in 1975, followed by the 54,000lb-thrust JT9D-7R4G2.) However, this would effectively reduce the 747's range to 3,450 statute miles which would prevent the new aircraft flying the lucrative transatlantic freight routes between the USA and Europe. To overcome the range limitations, Boeing proposed wing-root extensions, or using an extended wing and mating it to a double-deck body. However, this would have raised the super freighter's gross weight to more than 1,000,000lb and a payload of 300,000lb and this combined weight increase would have required much more powerful engines than were at first envisaged. Studies into higher-capacity passenger-freight aircraft were finally consigned to the waste-paper basket when it was realized that to power the new super freighter, the engines would each have to produce between 65,000-75,000lb of thrust, something that was clearly impossible at this time.

Early in the 1990s an alarming engine-mounting problem was diagnosed on some 747s, the first being -2R7F LX-ECV, the 482nd 747 to be built and which first flew on 30 September 1980. It was delivered to Cargolux on 10 October, who used it until the aircraft was bought by China Airlines on 26 February 1985,

Flying Tigers' 747 freighters at Hong Kong on 10 September 1987. (Graham Dinsdale)

747-123F/SCD N672UP of United Parcel Service (UPS) on approach to Kai Tak on 28 April 1998. This aircraft is the 119th 747 built: it flew for the first time on 17 March 1971 and was delivered to American Airlines on 16 April 1971. (Graham Dinsdale)

when it was re-registered B-198. After almost seven years' operation by Air China, on 29 December 1991 B-198 crashed into the Taiwanese mountains. Crash investigators discovered that the right wing inboard engine was missing: using state-of-the-art underwater diving equipment, it was eventually found in July 1992 on the seabed in the Formosa Straits; when it was raised to the surface, the strut assembly was found to be missing (it was finally discovered in April 1993).

The loss of a second -200F on 4 October 1992 heightened fears that there were structural problems with the 747's engine mountings. This time -258F 4X-AXG, belonging to El Al, lost both its starboard engines shortly after take-off from Amsterdam, Holland. (The aircraft had first flown on 7 March 1979 and had been delivered to the Israeli airline twelve days later.) It crashed at Bijlmermeer while the pilot was trying to return to the airport and all four crew and more than sixty people travelling on the aircraft died.

A third incident involving 747 engine mountings occurred in March 1993 when an Evergreen International Airlines' 747-100F lost an engine just after take-off from Anchorage International Airport in Alaska. The engine fell into a car park of a shopping mall, though fortunately no one was injured and the aircraft was able to land safely. The subsequent inquiry placed the blame for the accident on severe turbulence causing the entire engine pylon to fail.

By this time the engine mountings on all 900-plus 747s in service were being closely inspected. The engines were connected to the wing in four places: an upper mount was attached to the front spar, a rear

N7449WA on lease to Korean Airlines in January 1977. This aircraft was delivered to World Airways on 10 June 1974 and is currently operated by Evergreen International Airlines as N470EV.

Thought to be Boeing 747-273C (c/n 21841/396) wearing what could be called a triple colour scheme! Operated by Flying Tigers, in partial Seaboard World livery, operating for VIASA.

diagonal brace to an under-wing fitting and two mid-spar mounts beneath the wing. Inspection revealed that the engine-mounting 'fuse' (or break-point) pins were particularly corroded, especially in the structure of the early 747 models, though even the pins on the newer aircraft were clearly showing signs of corrosion. Originally Boeing had designed the engine mountings so that in the event of serious problems in flight, or impact in a crash on the ground, the engines would break off and fall away to prevent any further structural damage to the wing or rupture of the fuel tanks.

A major redesign of the engine mountings was instigated and in June 1993 Boeing publicly stated that the modification involved inserting two 9.5 inch stainless-steel mountings manufactured from corrosion-resistant steel instead of carbon steel, in between the mid-spar fitting. The two new mountings were designed to take over from the four existing connections, so that if these were to fail, the two new mountings would stop the engine falling off in flight. At the same time, new mid-spar fittings of a larger size were installed, while a stronger diagonal brace and upper link was used on new-production -400s. At a cost of about $1 million per aircraft, each 747 had to have all four pylons removed, the wing root and ribs inspected and repaired and the modified pylons reattached. The total cost of the repairs and inspection was shared jointly between Boeing and the airlines, whose aircraft were effectively out of action for between thirty-five and forty-two days. Some of the major 747 carriers opened up their own modification centres and carried out the repairs and inspections themselves and on behalf of other airlines.

Cargolux freighter on turnaround. (Rolls-Royce)

444

747-3H6 B-KAC Dragonair Cargo on takeoff at Manchester in August 2003. (Gerry Manning)

While passengers can conceivably be carried on the upper deck of the 747-200F, this is rarely done and Boeing realized that if it could offer carriers a more versatile 747-200C, one which could be configured for either an all-passenger, an all-freight, or a combination load, there was the distinct possibility that additional 747 sales would result. Such an aircraft could be used for just passengers in the summer when cargo traffic was low and for freight-carrying during winter months when the situation was normally reversed. Boeing therefore committed $14.6 million into developing the 747-200C

to operate in five different cargo- and passenger-loading arrangements. Also fitted with a hinged nose, it has a cargo distribution system built into the main deck floor and the passenger flooring is installed above the cargo rollers. Conversion from all-passenger to all-cargo requires that the aircraft be out of service only twenty-four hours or less. Partial changes can be made more quickly, frequently within the time that is required for normal routine maintenance. Gross weight is 833,000lb with either Pratt & Whitney JT9D-7R4G2 or General Electric CF6-50E2 engines.

China Airlines Cargo at Kai Tak, 27 June 1997. (Graham Dinsdale)

747-4R7F LX-FCV of Cargolux is caught by the camera making a very sharp turn to land on Runway 32 at Zurich in August 1998. (Gerry Manning)

The first aircraft, 747-273C N747WA, the 209th 747 built, was rolled out at Everett on 28 February 1973 and was flown for the first time on 23 March. After certification on 24 April it was delivered to World Airways on 27 April. The aircraft was later leased to several carriers, including Pan Am, where it was named *Clipper Mercury;* it was finally retired by owners Evergreen in November 1988. Unfortunately the convertible never fully realized its sales potential, with only thirteen being sold between 1973 and 1988.

Although sales of the 747-200 freighter and -200C passenger/freighter were disappointing, airlines such as Air Canada, KLM and SABENA have taken to Boeing's -200M Combi version, largely because it offers six main-deck cargo positions, which permit the same passenger capacity as a wide-body DC-10 or TriStar and the cargo capacity of a DC-8 or 707 freighter. No Model 747-200M has been built as such from new: the designation in fact applies to 747-200Bs, usually without the nose-loading feature, that have been modified to incorporate a side-loading cargo door in the fuselage, aft of the wing.

The first production 747-200B Combi-233M C-GAGA for Air Canada, the 250th 747 built - was rolled out at Seattle on 30 October 1974 and it flew for the first time on 18 November. The aircraft could carry 365

747-243BC Combi I-DEMC Taormina *first flew on 14 November 1980 and was delivered to Alitalia on 26 November 1980. (Boeing)*

Lufthansa Cargo D-ABZF at Sharjah 1997. (Graham Dinsdale).

passengers in its all-passenger configuration, or it could take a maximum main-deck cargo load of 176 passengers and twelve cargo pallets; it was delivered on 7 March 1975 and put into service on the London-Toronto route where it replaced a stretched DC-8. By the end of 1987, sixty-five 747-200Bs had been converted to 747-200Ms. Altogether seventy-eight series 200 Combis were delivered between 1975 and 1988. Three aircraft were lost between 1983 and 1987: 747-2283M HK-2910X, on lease to Avianca (Aerovias Nacionales de Columbia), crashed on approach near Madrid in November 1983. An Air France -228B Combi, F-GCBC, ran off the runway at Galeao International at Rio de Janeiro, Brazil, on 2 December 1985 and was damaged beyond economical repair. And on 28 November 1987 ZS-SAS *Helderberg*, a South African Airways -244B Combi en route to Mauritius, crashed into the Indian Ocean 137 miles north-east of

the island after a cargo fire.

The loss of the Avianca 283M Combi with 182 people on board on 27 November 1983 occurred late at night at the end of the flight from Paris to Madrid's Barajas Airport. The captain had over 23,000 hours' flying experience and he and his first officer were very familiar with the airport. As the Combi reached the last part of the flight the crew were advised by air traffic that they were cleared to descend for an approach to Runway 33. At 9,000 feet the first officer checked his ILS approach chart which gave the exact height of Barajas Airport as 1,906 feet. At this point the captain told his first officer to switch to the marker. His first officer did so and gave the final approach heading and ILS localizer frequency, which the captain repeated. The first officer then said that the crossing altitude of the marker was 2,382 feet. This, however, was incorrect, the correct crossing altitude of the maker being 3,282 feet: the

747-48E HL-7415 Asiana Cargo at Anchorage in September 2008. (Gerry Manning)

Ex-Air Afrique (TU-TAP) 747-2S4F Hl7474 of Korean Air Cargo climbing out of Kai Tak on 29 April 1998. (Graham Dinsdale)

officer had transposed the first two digits, effectively putting the Combi 900 feet below the safe height.

The captain accepted the incorrect height and continued on the descent. Controlled by the autopilot, the Combi descended until it was at about 80 feet below the incorrect safe height given by the first officer. The captain, oblivious to the error, continued - and he was not even concerned when the ground proximity warning system instructed him to 'Pull up: terrain!' He discounted it and continued as if nothing was wrong, disconnecting the autopilot and slightly reducing his rate of descent. The Combi crashed into the ground at 139 knots at an altitude of 2,249 feet. There was only one survivor.

ZS-SAS, the South African Airways -244B Combi which caught fire and crashed into the Indian Ocean with the loss of the crew and more than 150 passengers on 28 November 1987, highlighted several inadequate practices. The last word received was that the crew reported smoke on the flight deck and this was borne out by wreckage recovered from the subsequent deep-sea salvage operation several months later; the board of enquiry later concluded that a freight pallet in the main deck area had caught alight and that the fire had quickly spread to other parts of the aircraft. The smoke detectors were inadequate and the fire-fighting equipment fitted could not hope to contain the fire. Furthermore, the

UPS freighter landing at Hong Kong's Kai Tak aiport on 29 April 1998. (Graham Dinsdale)

enquiry concluded that the pressure lock between the cargo compartment and the main passenger cabin was incapable of preventing smoke seeping through. The enquiry's report led to a tightening-up of fire precautions, more powerful fire-fighting equipment and the installation of higher-standard fire-resistant materials in the ceiling and side walls. Subsequently all cargo had to be transported in flame-penetration-resistant containers with built-in smoke detectors and fire-extinguishing systems.

On 22 December 1999 Korean Air Cargo 747-2B5F HL7451 took off from Gimpo International Airport, Seoul bound for Milano-Malpensa Airport. The flight crew consisted of 57-year-old Captain Park Duk-kyu, 33-year-old First Officer Yoon Ki-sik, 38-year-old Flight Engineer Park Hoon-kyu and 45-year-old maintenance mechanic Kim Il-suk. The jet made its first stopover at Tashkent International Airport in Uzbekistan before taking off again for London-Stansted. Following the departure from Tashkent one of the inertial navigation units (INUs) partially failed, providing erroneous roll data to the captain's attitude director indicator (ADI or artificial horizon). The first officer's ADI and a backup ADI were correct, a comparator alarm called attention to the discrepancy and in daylight the erroneous indication was easily identified. The ADI's input selector was switched to the other INU and the correct indications returned. At Stansted, the engineers who

attempted to repair the ADI did not have the correct Fault Isolation Manual available and did not think of replacing the INU. One of them identified and repaired a damaged connecting plug on the ADI. When the ADI responded correctly to its 'Test' button, they believed the fault had been corrected, although this button only tested the ADI and not the INU. The ADI's input selector was left in the normal position. It was dark when the jet took off from Stansted, with the captain flying. When the captain tried to bank the 747 to turn left, his ADI showed it not banking and the comparator alarm sounded repeatedly. The first officer, whose instrument would have shown the true angle of bank, said nothing, although the flight engineer called out 'bank'. Captain Park Duk-kyu made no response and continued banking further and further left. At 18:38, 55 seconds after take-off, Flight 8509 plunged into Hatfield Forest near the village of Great Hallingbury at a speed between 250 and 300 knots, in a 40° pitch down and 90° left bank attitude killing all four crew.

Following a cargo flight from Luxembourg-Findel Airport on 27 November 2001 9G-MKI, a 747-246F of MK Airlines, descended towards Port Harcourt Airport in Nigeria and the 747 freighter crashed about 700 metres short of the runway. The front section broke away from the fuselage, a fire erupted in the main fuselage and one of the thirteen-crew was killed. Company policy stipulated that approaches to Port

Polar Air Cargo 747 freighter at Hong Kong on 30 April 1998. (Graham Dinsdale)

G-GSSD, a Boeing 747-87UF in the colours of British Airways World Cargo. Three of the freighters will be flown by Global Supply Systems, a subsidiary of Atlas Air Holdings, to cargo hubs in Asia, Africa, India and the United States. (Author)

Harcourt were to be flown by the captain. In this case first officer was pilot flying during the approach. He was following a non-standard autopilot approach, tracking a localizer radial inbound and descending using vertical speed mode. MK Airlines company policy was to not use the autopilot below 2,000 feet above ground level (agl). There were other indications of non-adherence to procedures, including the failure to make appropriate calls between the pilot flying and pilot not flying. A lack of situational awareness due to poor cockpit coordination was apparent and there was a problem interpreting the visual references on the approach.

On 14 October 2004 MK Airlines flight number 1602, operated by 9G-MKJ (previously *Waterberg* of South African Airways) a 747-200F cargo flight from Halifax Stanfield International Airport, Nova Scotia, Canada to Zaragoza Airport, Spain, crashed on take-off killing the crew of seven. The jet lifted off from Halifax but struck the ground shortly beyond the runway. Following lift-off the tail of the jet bounced twice off the tarmac near the end of the runway and separated from the jet when it hit a mound of earth 300 metres beyond the end of the runway. The 747 then headed forwards in a straight line, breaking into pieces. Over eighty fire-fighters and twenty pieces of apparatus from Halifax Regional Fire and Emergency responded to the call. An investigation into the crash revealed that the flight crew had used the incorrect speeds and thrust setting during the take-off attempt, with incorrect take-off data being calculated when preparing the flight (incorrect V speed calculation, as the result of the crew re-using a lighter take-off weight of 240,000 kg from the aircraft's previous take-off at Bradley, instead of the correct weight of 353,000 kg). The official report blamed the company for serious non-conformances to flight and duty time, with no regulations or company rules governing maximum duty periods for loadmasters and ground engineers, resulting in increased potential for fatigue-induced errors.

Footnotes for Chapter 10
54 The aircraft was involved in the incident at Filton Airfield, England on 10 October 2004, four days prior to the accident.

Chapter 11

Military and Multifunctional

With NASA pinpointing the space shuttle as its number one priority, loss of the prime contract [to North American Rockwell on 26 July 1972] simply increased Boeing's determination. The Company initiated three key programs to support those operations...the second was the adaptation of a 747 airplane to carry the shuttle piggyback in conducting earthbound landing tests, as well as to return shuttles to the Cape after landing in California.

Eugene E. Bauer, *Boeing: The First Century & Beyond*.

On 18 July 1974 the National Aeronautics and Space Administration (NASA) obtained 747-123 N9668, the eighty-sixth 747 built, from American Airlines. After using it for wake vortex investigation, NASA sent it to Boeing in 1976 for modification as a carrier for the forthcoming space shuttle; it was subsequently designated a 'Shuttle-Carrier Aircraft', or SCA. The aircraft, now serialled N90SNA, was stripped of all airline equipment, although the original American Airlines red, white and blue striping was retained. The fuselage was reinforced to support the weight of the 150,000lb shuttle and removable large end-plate fins were added to the tail-plane to improve directional stability when carrying the orbiter. These and the modified support structures protruding from the fuselage roof reduced the 747's performance. An all-up weight limit of 710,000lb was laid down. With or without the shuttle on top, the 747's crew were restricted to Mach 0.6 and 26,000 feet, or about 250 knots IAS. The JT9D-3A engines were modified to JT9D-7 AH standard to increase take-off thrust to 46,900lb. [55]

Two missions were planned for the SCA: carrying the shuttle aloft for initial aerodynamic testing, followed by launch into free-gliding flight; and ferrying it from the US west coast, where it is built and where it usually lands, to the launch site at Cape Canaveral in Florida. The first use was made of the SCA in February 1977 when N905NA began a three-phase flight-test programme with space shuttle *Enterprise* at NASA's Dryden Flight Research Facility at Edwards AFB, California. The shuttle was mounted on top of the SCA by being hoisted under an overhanging gantry, after which the SCA is wheeled into place beneath it. The shuttle was then lowered into the cradles on top of the SCA. The gross weight of the combination was 584,000lb. The three rocket motor nozzles of the shuttle were covered by a Boeing-built fairing After the initial taxiing tests of the 747-orbiter combination had taken place, the first flight was made on 18 February; this was with the shuttle unmanned and not to be released. A second captive phase with two crew aboard the shuttle was tested and finally a third phase, which started on 13 August 1977, tested the shuttle's ability to be released off the 747's back. Launch procedure for the shuttle called for the 747 to climb to 25,000 feet and when it reached 200 knots, to enter a shallow dive at full power. The separation point was reached at 240 knots, at which time the 747 pilot pulled the engines back to idle and deployed the speed brakes. When the necessary airspeed was attained, the crew of the shuttle released the latches and lifted free of the SCA. Chuck Yeager, the first man to fly faster than the speed of sound, must take the credit for proposing that the shuttle be mounted on the back of the 747 with a positive angle of attack: this helped to provide some lift and on launching, the airflow built up quickly and enabled the shuttle to fly easily away and clear of the back of the 747.

If things went wrong and the 747 crew needed to evacuate their aircraft, they could use a chute-type slide that was installed behind the flight deck and which exited below the nose section. The exit hatch was fitted with an explosive device to blow out the door and the crew, who would be

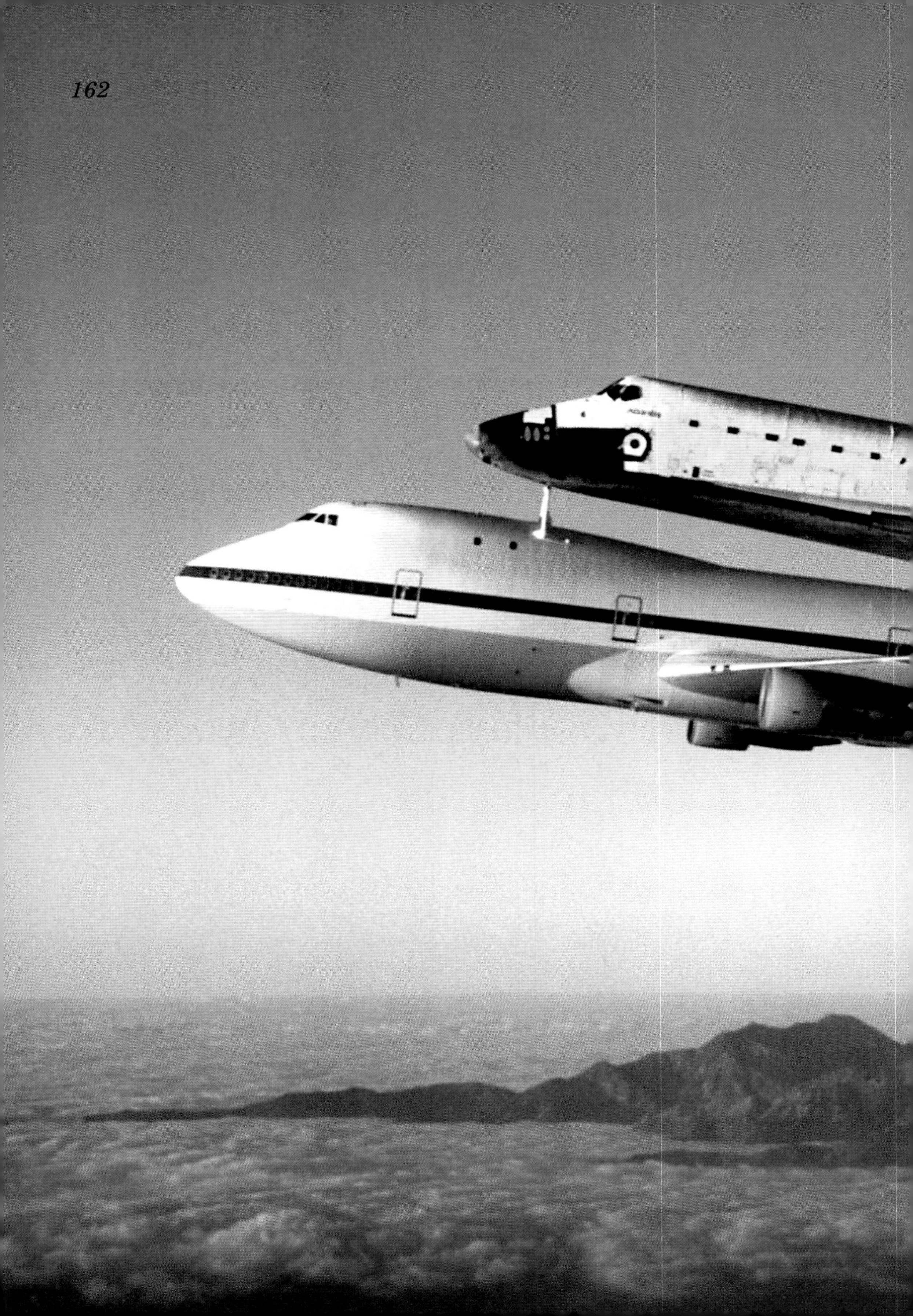

Shuttle Atlantis *atop the 747 Shuttle Carrier aircraft. Two 747s were modified to carry the Space Shuttle. One is a 747-100 (N905NA) and the other is a 747-100SR (N911NA). On 18 February 1977 N905NA made its first flight carrying the space shuttle* Enterprise *unmanned at NASA's Dryden Flight Research Facility at Edwards AFB, California and has since carried all Space Shuttles.*

Formerly known as the National Emergency Airborne Command Post (referred to colloquially as 'Kneecap') the E-4B is now referred to as the National Airborne Operations Center (NAOC). E-4B 75-0125 operated by the 1st ACCCS, 55th Wing. The E-4B first flew on 29 April 1975, with delivery to the USAF on 4 August with less than full equipment. This was installed over several years by organizations contracted to the USAF Oklahoma City Air Logistics Center. The fully equipped E-4B was redelivered to the Air Force (SAC) on 21 December 1979 and its first operational mission was flown in March 1980. (Boeing)

wearing parachutes, would then have bailed out. (As another safety measure, the hydraulic system on board the 747 was fitted with close-valves to prevent all pressure being lost throughout the system if the shuttle collided with the tail as the two separated.) In the event, all the combination tests proved successful and the crew had no call to use the precarious slide.

In 1975 the pre-revolutionary Imperial Iranian Air Force (the IIAF - later, the Iranian Islamic Air Force) acquired eleven used 747 airliners and arranged for the then Boeing Military Aircraft Company in Wichita to militarize them. Five were 747-131s purchased from TWA, two were

ex-Continental Airlines 747-124s and four were 747-125s that Eastern Air Lines had bought from Boeing but had immediately sold to TWA. While at Wichita, all were fitted with side cargo doors and three with Boeing in-flight refuelling booms. These received three-digit IIAF serial numbers preceded by the figure 5. In 1976, these were all replaced by four-digit numbers prefixed by 5. In 1977 and 1978, the IIAF ordered five additional 747-2J9Fs new from Boeing, although the last of these five was never delivered, going instead to Northwest. Some of these aircraft were also adapted to carry Beech refuelling pods under the wings for the in-flight refuelling of receiver aircraft.[56] The IIAF

The first E-4B built as such, with the added Super High Frequency radio housing on the fuselage. First flown on 23 April 1975 and delivered to the USAF less than fully equipped on 4 August 1976, the aircraft was re-delivered on 21 December 1979. (Boeing)

The Imperial Iranian Air Force KC-747 5-8105 seen before delivery. Note the refuelling boom. (Boeing)

747s were used regularly on flights between Iran and USAF bases to pick up military stores and equipment, but all this ended in 1979 when the Shah of Iran was deposed. All the Iranian 747s were eventually disposed of, the -200s being transferred to Iran Air.

On 23 February 1973 the USAF's Electronic Systems Division awarded Boeing a $59 million fixed-price contract for two E-4A (747-200B) Advanced Airborne Command Post aircraft. These are logical successors to the various KC-135/EC-135 aircraft used to support the National Emergency Airborne Command Post (NEACP) - known as 'Kneecap' - as flying command posts. The greater capacity of the 747 allows the carriage of more equipment and a larger battle staff, plus built-in 'hardness' features designed to protect the aircraft and its equipment from the effects of nuclear blasts. A third E-4A was ordered in the early summer of 1973 at a cost of $27.7 million. The fourth and final aircraft, an E-4B, with more advanced engines and equipment, was contracted in December at a cost of

$39 million. All three E-4As had their command, control and communications equipment fitted by E-Systems (later part of Raytheon). As an interim measure this was equipment removed from the EC-135 aircraft. 73-1676, the first of three EAAs, was powered by JT9D engines and first flew on 13 June 1973; it was delivered to Andrews AFB, Maryland, on 16 July, after which much of the classified equipment was installed. 73-1677, the second EAA, first flew on 11 September and was delivered on 3 October; and 74-00787, the third, which was also the first production 747 to be powered by GE CF6 engines, first flew on 6 June 1974 and was delivered on 15 October. Later, the first two E-4As were re-engined with the CF6 and later still, with the more powerful 52,500lb-thrust CF6-50E2.

A fourth aircraft (75-0125) was made on the original E-4A order, but it incorporated many refinements, such as nuclear thermal shielding (hardening), including electromagnetic pulse, additional generators for increased electrical capacity for the equipment and a larger battle

The 747 Aircraft carrier proposal. (Boeing)

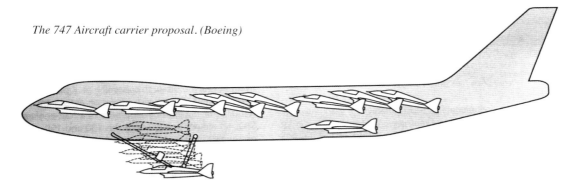

The E-4B has increased internal fuel for missions in excess of twelve hours' duration, but it can also be refuelled in flight to extend endurance to seventy-two hours. All three E-4As were subsequently upgraded to E-4B standard. (Boeing)

staff. It first flew on 29 April 1975 and was delivered to the USAF on 4 August as an E-4B with less than full equipment. (This was installed over several years by organizations contracted to the USAF Oklahoma City Air Logistics Center.) The fully equipped E-4B was redelivered to the Air Force (SAC) on 21 December 1979 and it flew its first operational mission in March 1980. All three E-4As were subsequently upgraded to E-4B standard, with the first redelivered to the Air Force on 15 July 1983.

The E-4B has increased internal fuel for missions in excess of twelve hours' duration, but it can also be refuelled in flight to extend endurance to seventy-two hours. The increased fuel load and other modifications, give the aircraft an all-up gross weight of 800,000lb. The E-4B has a 1,200-kilovolt-amp electrical system, compared with the 240-kilovolt-amp systems on the standard 747s, driven by two 150-kilovolt-amp generators mounted on each of the engines. Altogether, ninety-four crew members can be carried on three decks. The upper deck contains the flight deck and a 330 square feet flight-crew rest area, while the 185 feet long main deck is divided into compartments for an NCA area, briefing and conference rooms, a battle-staff work-area for up to thirty crew, communications and technical control centres and a crew rest area.

As first delivered, the E-4B was outwardly indistinguishable from the E-3As, but when the super-high-frequency (SHF) satellite link was installed, a large and distinctive blister was added to the top of the fuselage at the rear of the upper deck to house the dish antennae. At the opposite end of the radio frequency range is the dual very-low-frequency (VLF) and low-frequency (LF) communications equipment which uses two trailing-wire aerials, the longer of which is 5 miles long when fully deployed. (The forward and rear lobes on board the aircraft

SP-Z5 N60697 of the United Arab Emirates at London-Heathrow on 27 July 1989. This aircraft is now operated as A6-ZSN. (Graham Dinsdale)

NASA 905, an Ex-American Airlines' 747-123 used as a test bed seen in 1974 undergoing vortex tests accompanied by a Learjet and a Cessna T-37. (NASA/DFRC)

house electronic equipment, a maintenance workshop and a small station in the tail for the VLF antenna winch operator.) Altogether, the aircraft has thirteen external communications systems operating through no fewer than forty-six different antennae.

Most of the functions that can be performed in the air relative to communication with ground facilities throughout the world can be performed while the E-4B is on the ground when appropriate connections are made to the aircraft. The improved satellite communications system and communications processing equipment have anti-jam features and support operations in a nuclear environment over extended ranges. The E-4B is capable of tying into commercial telephone networks and has the potential to be used for radio broadcasts to the general population. Improvements have included a data-processing capability and more survivable command, control and communications' equipment, including initial Milstar modification. All four E-4Bs are operated by the 55th Wing, Air Combat Command and the main operating base is currently Offutt AFB, Nebraska.

From 1985 to December 1989, eighteen Pan Am 747s (fourteen -100s and four -200Bs, each converted at a cost of up to $20 million by Boeing Wichita) were made

In 1974 the National Aeronautics and Space Administration (NASA) obtained 747-123 N9668 from American Airlines and after using it for wake vortex investigation, in 1976 it was modified as an SCA carrier for the Space Shuttle programme. (Boeing)

Above: The Evergreen 747 Supertanker, N740EV, is a 747-200 modified as an aerial application platform for fire fighting using 20,000 US gallons (76,000 litres) of fire-fighting chemicals. To date two aircraft have been converted. The tanker made its first American operation on 31 August 2009, and has also been deployed to Israel to fight an uncontrolled fire on Mount Carmel. Right: A close-up of the four retardent exit points - the Evergreen Supertanker's tank system can be configured for segmented drops, allowing the contents of the tank to be released at multiple intervals while in flight.

available to the Civil Reserve Air Fleet (CRAF) as a ready reserve of heavy-lift transports (designated C-19A by the US Air Force) in times of national emergency. The Air Force contracted with Pan American World Airways to modify these 747s with side cargo doors, reinforced main-deck flooring and a cargo distribution system, all of which added 13,000lb to the empty weight of the aircraft. Because of a corresponding reduction in payload, the USAF paid compensation to Pan Am during commercial passenger operations. The first C-19A conversion (Air Force serial numbers were not assigned) was completed on 31 May 1985. If called into service by the US Air Force, these passenger aircraft could be converted to freighters in less

than 48 hours. When the aircraft were no longer used, Boeing-Wichita subsequently converted five of them to full freighter configuration.

Two 747-2G4Bs powered by four CF6-80C2B1s (F103-GE-102s), each developing 56,750lb of thrust, were purchased by the DoD under the designation VC-25A, to replace the two former primary and back-up VC-137Cs (707-320C) that had served as presidential aircraft, the first since 12 October 1962 and the other since 1972. The first VC-25A was rolled out in September 1989 and both aircraft were delivered to the 89th Airlift Wing at Andrews AFB, Maryland, in August and December 1990. The aircraft can carry up to 70 passengers and 23 crew members. The VC-

Ex-TWA 747-131/SCD 5-8101 of the Imperial Iranian Air Force being refuelled in flight by IIAF 747 tanker. In 1975 the pre-revolutionary Imperial Iranian Air Force (IIAF; later this stood for the Iranian Islamic Air Force) acquired twelve used 747 airliners and arranged for the then Boeing Military Aircraft Company in Wichita to militarize them (5-8105/5-284). Five were -131s, purchased from TWA, three were ex-Continental Airlines -124s and four were -125s that Eastern Air Lines had bought from Boeing but had immediately sold to TWA. While at Wichita, all were fitted with side cargo doors and three with Boeing in-flight refuelling booms. After the Shah of Iran was deposed in 1979 all the Iranian 747s were eventually disposed of. (Boeing)

25As had a Bendix Aerospace EFIS-10 electronic flight instrument system and state-of-the-art on-board worldwide communications equipment, two galleys and an emergency medical facility. A pair of self-contained air-stairs are located on the left side and a built-in baggage loader on the right side. Together with a second Garrett GTCP331-200 auxiliary power unit (APU) in the tail, they allow the aircraft to be practically self-sufficient and reduces the need for ground-support equipment. Despite their long range (7,140 miles), the VC-25As can also be refuelled in the air. Each carries a crew of twenty-three and can carry up to seventy passengers. Maximum take-off weight on a long-range mission is 803,700lb.

In addition, six 747SP series have been, or are being used in a military or military-operated role by the countries of Abu Dhabi, Oman, Saudi Arabia, United Arab Emirates (UAE) and Dubai.

Apart from the E-4, Boeing saw additional potential for the 747 as a military tanker, transport aircraft and even as a missile launcher. During the height of the Cold War, data was prepared and service trials were conducted, but not one aircraft was ever purchased by the USAF, although the Imperial Iranian Air Force did show some interest in the 747 in the joint freighter-tanker role and at least two were so converted. Boeing saw the 747 as a tanker that could refuel B-52 bombers with 230,000lb of fuel after both aircraft had flown 4,600 statute miles. This would have added about 2,990 miles more range than if the Stratofortresses had been refuelled by a KC-135. A 747 was modified with a flying-boom and trials involving dry hook-ups took place with a B-52, SR-71 Blackbird and an F-111 as the receiver aircraft. The trials were funded by the US military and were successful, but nothing came of the 747 tanker project.

Nothing came of the proposed MC747 concept which appeared in 1972, either: this promoted the idea that the -200F could be modified as a launch platform for four Minuteman intercontinental ballistic missiles (ICBMs).

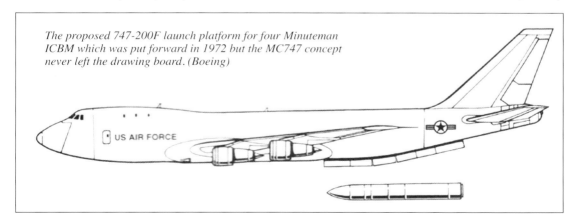

The proposed 747-200F launch platform for four Minuteman ICBM which was put forward in 1972 but the MC747 concept never left the drawing board. (Boeing)

VC-25A 28000, the first of two used by the 89th Airlift Wing at Andrews AFB, Washington DC flying over Mount Rushmore, near Keystone South Dakota. VC-25 is the US Air Force Very Important Person (VIP) version of the 747-200B. The US Air Force operates two in VIP configuration as the VC-25A. Tail numbers 28000 and 29000 are popularly known as Air Force One, which is technically the air-traffic call sign for any United States Air Force aircraft carrying the US President. Although based on the 747-200B design, they include several innovations introduced on the 747-400. Partially completed aircraft from Everett, Washington, were flown to Wichita, Kansas, for final outfitting. Two 747-2G4Bs (c/ns 23824/5) were purchased under the designation VC-25A, to replace the two former primary and back-up VC-137Cs that had served as presidential aircraft, one since 12 October 1962 and the other since 1972, The first VC-25A (82-8000, formerly 86-8800) was rolled out in September 1989. This and the second VC-25A (92-9000, formerly 86-8900) were delivered to the 89th Airlift Wing at Andrews AFB, Maryland, on 23 August and 20 December 1990 respectively. (USAF)

The missiles would have been released backwards or forwards from a bay in the aft section 46, modified with bomb-bay doors. When dropped facing backwards either the MC747 would have to be flying away from the target, or the missiles would rotate up and over the aircraft to head for their target. If they were launched facing forwards, then they would drop underneath the 747 and ignite before streaking towards their target 5,000 feet ahead of the aircraft.

Not surprisingly perhaps, the MC747 concept never left the drawing board. Neither did Boeing's other equally ambitious bomb-carrying versions, where it was calculated that up to seven 57,000lb missiles could be carried in bomb-bays forward and aft, or that two 200,000lb missiles could be dropped from a bomb-bay more than 65 feet long. An air-launched, cruise missile

(ALCM), carrier version was proposed whereby the 747 would carry forty-three ALCMs and launch them from the rear of the aircraft after they had been loaded onto carriage racks through the nose door. However, this scenario never reached fruition; not did another proposal, whereby the ALCMs would be launched from rotary launchers or stack racks, like those used on the B-52.

In the early 1970s the service entry of heavy transports like the Lockheed C-5A Galaxy led to studies involving aerial aircraft carriers. In 1973 Boeing engineers began investigating the possibility of using a 747 AAC (Aerial Aircraft Carrier) to carry ten Boeing model 908-625 tailless, supersonic 'advanced micro fighters' armed with a rotating 25mm cannon and air-to-air or air-to-ground missiles. [57] With a double-decker hangar and two launching bays, it was believed that the scheme might actually prove

The YAL-1A which first flew on 18 July 2002, taking off from Edwards AFB on a test flight. The YAL-1A is a 747-400F modified by Boeing for the US Air Force as a platform for a powerful airborne chemical oxygen iodine laser (COIL) that can potentially be used to destroy enemy missiles flying at several times the speed of sound. (DoD).

Inset: The nose-mounted high-energy laser turret. (DoD)

cheaper than establishing a short-term land base. It was envisaged that not only would the tiny aircraft be launched from the mother plane, but that they would also return to it, be refuelled and rearmed and launched once again. These tasks were expected to last no more than about ten minutes per fighter. The studies, which went on until 1975, involved a variety of different, configurations. However nothing came of the AAC project or its complementary 747 AWACS version, which would have carried two of the 'microfighters' for reconnaissance.

In view of the long-standing problems with the C-5A, Boeing proposals in the late 1970s and early 1980s to use the 747-200F as an airlifter for the USAF seemed to have merit, especially when fatigue cracks were found in the Galaxy's wings. Boeing even developed a special nose-jack to reduce the sill height of the nose door by 6 to 10 feet off the ground to enable tanks and vehicles to be loaded and offloaded. The device was successfully tested in 1980 using a Flying Tigers - 200F, but the US government, probably acutely embarrassed by the vast fortune it had already spent on the much-maligned Galaxy, did not show any tangible interest in the 747 transport. After contracting Lockheed to develop new wings for the C-5A, in 1982 the military ordered fifty C-5B versions instead.

During the 1970s the proposed 747 KC-33A was also adapted as an aerial refuelling tanker and was bid against the DC-10-30 Advanced Cargo Transport Aircraft (ACTA) programme that produced the KC-10A Extender. Before the Khomeini-led revolution, Iran acquired four 747-100 aircraft with air-refuelling boom conversions to support a fleet of F-4 Phantoms. Since then, other proposals emerged for adaptation of later 747-400 aircraft for this role. [58]

In the early 1990s Boeing saw another opportunity to promote the 747 transport when cost-overruns on the McDonnell Douglas C-17 Globemaster III programme persuaded the Department of Defense to invite proposals for an off-the-shelf non-developmental airlift alternative (NDAA). No fewer than eleven aerospace companies came up with proposals for airlifter versions of existing aircraft. Boeing proposed a Pratt & Whitney 4056-powered 747-200F airlifter, designated the C-33A, which had an increased weight of 920,000lb and an 8,970-mile range. Their bid was helped in 1991-92 during Operation Desert Shield and Operation Desert Storm, which saw a massive increase in 747 cargo operations. During and after the Gulf War, 747s flew 3,700 missions, transporting no fewer than 644,000 troops and 220,000 tons of equipment and supplies. In 1995 Boeing and Pratt & Whitney's joint PW4056-powered C-33A proposal emerged successful from all of the competitors - but none of the new aircraft was ordered. Instead, the DoD favoured additional C-17 Globemaster III aircraft - which, ironically, was subsequently produced by Boeing after its take-over of McDonnell Douglas.

The 747 CMCA variant was considered by the US Air Force as a Cruise Missile Carrier Aircraft during the development of the B-1 Lancer strategic bomber. It would have been equipped with 50 to 100 AGM-86 ALCM cruise missiles on rotary launchers. But this plan was abandoned in favour of more conventional strategic bombers. Because of the US military's experience gained in the Gulf War, when Patriot missiles were launched to intercept theatre ballistic missile such as the Soviet-built Scud, the DoD sought alternative methods whereby incoming missiles could be destroyed by an airborne high-energy megawatt-class laser weapons system (ABL). In 1994 Boeing, with Northrop Grumman (TRW), manufacturers of the Chemical Oxygen Iodine Laser (COIL) and Lockheed-Martin, who build the optics and detectors, became one of two consortiums selected to study ways of implementing such a system for the Ground-based Mid-course Defense (GMD) programme and mounting it in a turret in the nose of an aircraft.[59] Under ABL, the COIL; the first such weapon to be carried on an aircraft, could be fired against an incoming ballistic missile while it and the aircraft are in flight.

The platform the consortium chose was a prototype derivative of the 747-400F called the YAL-1A. The life potential of an aircraft of this size had immediate benefits for the project in that it can carry sufficient oxygen and iodine for up to thirty bursts of five seconds each. The range of the COIL (180-360 miles) and the accuracy of the optics and detectors (which can lock onto a missile as it enters the boost phase during the first 30-140 seconds of flight) are such that the YAL-1A can fly at altitudes in excess of 40,000 feet, several hundred miles from its target and still destroy in-flight missiles within seconds of them being launched. Laser tests carried out showed that a five-second burst of energy fired at the missile by the COIL so soon after take-off would cause the propellant tanks to explode and thus scatter the debris in the vicinity of the launch site, an ideal deterrent.

On 12 November 1996 the US Air Force initiated its Airborne Laser (ABL) programme by awarding a series of development contracts totalling $1.1 billion over 6½ years to Boeing, Lockheed Martin and TRW (known as 'Team ABL') covering the building of a YAL-1A and the mounting and test-firing of the ABL. Team ABL was tasked to design, produce, integrate and flight test the first prototype ABL demonstration system and to perform a successful boost-phase shoot-down of a theatre ballistic missile. The DoD expected that the first test to destroy a theatre ballistic missile would take place by late 2002. If the first part of the programme proved successful, Boeing anticipated winning a $4.5 billion follow-on contract to build a further six AL-1A production aircraft, the first scheduled to be fully operational by 2006, with the rest in service by 2008. This number of aircraft was arrived at because of the need, in times of international crisis, for at least one AL-1A to be airborne at any one time.

In January 2000 the YAL-1A was flown to Boeing-Wichita to be fitted with a controllable nose turret for directing the laser beam and in July 2002 flight testing began. The COIL was ground tested in Southern California and delivered it to Edwards AFB in February 2003. The testing of the Airborne Laser's Beam Control/Fire Control (BC/FC) system was completed in April 2004.[60] Lockheed Martin then began final integration of the flight turret assembly, including the 1.5-metre telescope/beam director. On 12 November 2004 'Team ABL' fired a laser beam for the first time using the flight laser modules in the ABL System Integration Laboratory at Edwards Air Force Base. When fully configured, the YAL-1A would serve as the prototype for a family of weapons to defend against the threat of rogue missile attacks in the 21st century.

Footnotes for Chapter 11

55   On 27 October 1988 NASA acquired from Boeing, N747BL, the former JAL SR-46 (JA117), the 221st 747 built, for use as a second shuttle-carrier after suitable modification.

56   Originally the -2J9Fs were assigned continuing four-digit numbers, but in 1984 all but three of the IIAF 747s were given civil registrations.

57   Lockheed was simultaneously working on a comparable adaptation of its C-5 Galaxy. The micro fighters were to be 8.84 metres long with a wing span of 5.33 metres and weighing 3,760kg.

58   The Evergreen 747 Supertanker was a 747-200 modified as an aerial application platform for fire fighting using 20,000 US gallons (76,000 litres) of fire-fighting chemicals.

59   For the GMD programme, Boeing would develop the ground-based interceptor, X-band radar, upgraded early warning radar and interfaces to space-based infrared system satellites - as well as battle management, command, control and communications.

60   The BC/FC system accurately points and fires the laser with sufficient energy to destroy a missile while it is still in the highly vulnerable boost phase of its flight profile, before separation of its warheads. The conformal window, the large piece of glass on the forward side of the turret ball, is one of the largest transmissive optics ever coated.

Chapter 12

'Megatop' - the 747-400 Series

In addition to the long-range, all passenger model, seating from 350 to 400 passengers, there are three complimentary models in the 747-400 family. All four share the benefits of superior range and payload capability, low fuel consumption and outstanding crew efficiency. Airplane fuel efficiency is not generally measured in the same terms as automobile fuel efficiency. But when it is, the result surprises a great many people. A Boeing airplane with 70 per cent of the seats occupied is more fuel efficient that a new automobile carrying two people.

Boeing Marketing Brochure

By the early 1980s Boeing's seemingly unconquerable 747 was under threat from market forces and it must have seemed too many in the industry that the 747 had reached the end of its development. By 1984 production stood at just one 747 a month, down from seven a month in 1979-80. In the United States and Europe, McDonnell Douglas and Airbus Industries respectively, were emerging as strong contenders vying for the crown that Boeing had worn for almost twenty years. The MD-11, a much bigger and much modernized version of the DC-10-30/40 series, made its appearance at the 1985 Paris Air Show. Airbus was also fast developing its range of state-of-the-art, long-range, high-capacity A330/340 aircraft. Boeing countered these very competitive high-tech designs with new, twin-engined aircraft of their own, but while the 757 and 767 kept pace with the latest avionics, lighter carbon-composite materials, higher-aspect ratio wings and systems, its elder statesman, the 747, still relied heavily on electro-mechanical instruments and systems little changed from the late 1960s. It was obvious from the lessons learned with the launch of the 747-300 that what the airlines wanted was not simply an 'advanced series 300', which evolved in 1984, but rather, a radically new approach with modern avionics, longer range and higher capacity.

In May 1985 Boeing announced the development of the new Model 747-400, an advanced and greatly improved long-range version of the Model 747-300. Apart from a quantum leap in technology, if the 747 was

to remain competitive against the all-comers, Boeing recognized the need greatly to improve the aircraft interior, range, fuel-burn and operating costs. These were daunting targets to apply to an aircraft design that was almost twenty years old. Replacing the interior with the latest fire-resistant materials, upping the fuel capacity and adopting the latest engines would go a long way to achieving many of these goals, but initially, Boeing baulked at changing the flight deck completely, choosing instead to retain the original electro-mechanical instrumentation and to keep the same autopilot. At first, Boeing's whole approach to the -400 was to avoid wholesale change, particularly on the flight deck, principally to help minimize aircrew retraining. At first therefore, only a reduction in the number of conventional electro-mechanical instruments took place. Boeing were greatly influenced in this approach by Cathay Pacific, one of the launch customers from a consultative group formed by Boeing which also included British Airways, KLM, Lufthansa, Northwest, QANTAS and Singapore Airlines.

Boeing's decision to utilize technology used on the 757 and 767 twins changed in 1985 after pressure from most of the other airlines in the consultative group who by now were enjoying significant technological advances in their operation of the advanced Airbus A320 aircraft, which used the latest digital avionics. They persuaded Boeing to update the 747-400 with the latest 'glass' or digital avionics, including improved EFIS

The first 747-400ER takes off on its maiden flight on 31 July 2002.
It began a three-month flight test programme that culminated with
certification and delivery to launch customer QANTAS Airways.
(Boeing)

(electronic flight instrument systems) displays with their fault warnings and corrective actions, collision avoidance, datalink, wind-shear warning, 4D navigation (a calculation of whether or not the -400 can reach a certain altitude by a certain navigational waypoint) and digital electronic engine control (known as 'power by wire'). Out went the flight engineer's panel and an all-new flight deck operated by a two-man crew was adopted. (In the early days of 747 operation Pan Am had a system whereby pilots, after retiring as such at the mandatory age of sixty, could continue flying as flight engineers.) The 400 pilots and engineers and 200 ground staff who visited the 747-400 flight simulator were almost unanimous in their praise for the revised and much simpler instrument layout and finally, even Cathay Pacific was won over.

A significant weight-saving of 4,200lb had been achieved through the use of new, lighter, high-strength aluminium-lithium alloys with improved fatigue life incorporated in the upper and lower skins of the wing torsion box, stringers and lower-spar chords. A further 1,800lb was saved by the replacement, on the -400's huge five- truck, eighteen main landing-gear wheels, of steel brakes with BF Goodrich carbon brakes and new wider wheels (the sixteenth version of the 747 wheel, with the diameter increased by two inches to 22 inches to house the new brakes) with low profile tyres so that the same overall diameter of 49 inches could be maintained. All areas of the structure which have previously been prone to fatigue cracks have been strengthened, the large front end having thicker frame, skins and doublers to obviate expensive repair procedures. Metal flooring previously used in the passenger cabin has been replaced by light, tough graphite floor panels. Corrosion protection is further improved by white epoxy paint in the under-floor areas, especially in the areas below and around the toilets and galleys.

The rudder had an increase of five degrees movement to 30 per cent over earlier 747s and new rudder actuators decrease the runway minimum control speed by 10 knots. The large epoxy composite fairing which covers the join between the fuselage and the wing has been re contoured to reduce drag. Unladen wingspan has been increased to 211 feet 5 inches by the use of upward-pointing six feet high winglets, which immediately distinguish the -400 from earlier models, with a sweep back of 60 degrees, canted out at an angle of 22 degrees. (When the -400 is fully fuelled, due to the flexible wing structure and the winglets, the span actually grows by almost two feet to 213 feet!) The new winglets, which are graphite (carbon-fibre and epoxy honeycomb sandwich skin), increase the aspect ratio of the wing, thereby reducing induced drag and increasing the range of the aircraft by a calculated 3 per cent, or a 7 per cent fuel consumption reduction per

passenger mile. This also aids the -400's take-off characteristics and permits higher cruising altitudes to be flown. To further improve take-off and landing performance, an additional leading-edge flap is fitted to the wing extension.

The improvements to the 747-400 include more powerful engines with up to 58,000lb-thrust, with a choice of three powerplants in four versions: the Pratt & Whitney PW4056, which utilizes single crystal turbine blades; the 58,000lb-thrust General Electric CF6-80C2B1F; or the 58,000lb-thrust Rolls-Royce RB211-524G/60,000lb-thrust -524H. Since 1983 all three engines have reduced fuel-burn by 5-10 per cent and each one is capable of full authority digital engine control (FADEC). To further increase range, by 403 statute miles, an additional 3,300 US gallons (12,490 litres) of fuel can be carried in new tanks between the front and rear spars in the horizontal stabilizer (tail-plane). The -400 can carry more than 57,000 gallons (215,745 litres) of fuel and over 400 passengers in excess of 8,050 statute miles, 1,150 statute miles further than the -300. Depending on engines and other variables, the gross weight of the 747-400 ranges from 800,000 to 850,000lb with an option offered to 870,000lb. Thanks to the added fuel, the more fuel-efficient engines and the new wing-tips, the 747-400 has a range of up to 8,400 miles. With Pratt & Whitney PW4056 engines, 412 passengers and baggage and required fuel reserves, the range is 7,945 statute miles. With Rolls-Royce RB.211-524Hs, up to 426 passengers and 37,400lb of cargo, the range is 7,178 miles. The 747-400's range makes possible non-stop service with typical full (420) passenger, three-class payload on such routes as London-Tokyo, Singapore-London and Los Angeles-Sydney.

Interiors of the 747-400 have been redesigned to improve passenger convenience and appeal. Ceiling and side-wall panels have been re-contoured with new, lighter-weight materials that provide an open, airy look. Passenger stowage capacity has grown to 15.9 cubic feet in each 60 inch outboard stowage bin, or 2.95 cubic feet per passenger. New laminate materials, phenolic glass or carbon composite, able to withstand a heat release of 65W/m square, have replaced epoxy/ glass for partitions, doors, closets, galleys, toilet walls and major surfaces. A new thermoplastic blend in place of polycarbonates reduces smoke and toxicity levels in the event of fire and upper-deck ceiling panels are made of improved polyester and phenolic sheet-moulding materials instead of standard polyester. Interior flexibility permits airline operators to relocate class dividers and galley and toilet modules more quickly to serve market requirements. [61] Thanks to a number of utility hook-ups, airlines can also locate their galleys in

747-400 series aircraft in production at Seattle in 2002. (Boeing)

up to twelve different areas, offering a total of 157 possible locations. These 'quick change features' allow major rearrangements within forty-eight hours, while seats and compartments can be changed overnight. A revised -400 air distribution system increases the main-deck cabin air-distribution zones from three to five and ventilation rates can be regulated based on passenger density in each zone.

Crew rest is a new flight-deck feature, the dedicated flight-crew rest area with two bunks and the decor of the flight deck having been enhanced, while the aft-adjustment or seats and stowage has been increased. For the first timer on any airliner, an optional overhead cabin crew rest area uses space in the rear of the fuselage above the aft toilets. This area, which can be configured for eight bunks and two seats, provides privacy as well as comfort for off-duty flight attendants. By using this compartment, ten more profit seats are available on the main deck of the aircraft. (The crew-rest module introduced at the rear of the -300 cabin will take up twenty passenger seats.)

A new Pratt & Whitney Canada (P&WC) 1,450hp auxiliary power unit (APU) was chosen to replace the earlier Garrett (Allied Signal) APU. The PW901A APU, which drives two generators to produce a total of 180 kilovolt amps, provides an estimated 35 to 40 per cent

reduction in fuel consumption (saving an airline an estimated $125,000 per annum), better air pressurization performance on hot days, higher electrical output and reduced noise levels over the prior APU. These units, mounted in the rear fuselage of 747s, supply pressurized air for air conditioning and engine starting while me aircraft is on the ground, plus electrical power to operate lights and other requirements, during stops. The new APU can also be retrofitted to earlier 747s.

Significantly, flight deck changes transformed a three-crew-member, analogue cockpit with electro-mechanical instruments - all familiar 747 characteristics - to a full digital, two-crew flight deck with cathode ray tube (CRT) displays, the flight engineer's systems being located in the roof between the two pilots. (The workload is designed to be half to one-third that of the standard 747). Simplified and automated systems have reduced the number of flight-deck lights, gauges and switches from 971 to 365 on the -400, twenty-two fewer than the 757/767 and 100 less than the 737. Streamlined processes and automation further reduce crew workload. There are 68 per cent fewer checklist items for normal procedures (for example, the -400 checklist has thirty-four line items compared to 107 for the earlier aircraft) and 75 per cent fewer steps are required to deal with non-normal procedures - a rapid cabin depressurization and emergency descent requires just three

On 22 October 1985, lead customer Northwest Airlines ordered the first 747-400 (-451 c/n 23719/line number 696), a -451 (N661US), seen here on the Boeing production line at Everett. It was rolled out at Everett on 26 January 1988. N661US flew for the first time on 29 April 1988 and on 26 May completed the longest engineering flight in Boeing commercial aircraft history, lasting more than fourteen hours, as cruise performance was evaluated. (Boeing)

actions, as compared to twenty on older versions. In the event of an engine fire, the -400 crew need to check off four line items, down from fifteen on the -200 or -300. Whereas a cargo fire needed sixteen actions on the older types, only two are needed on the -400. Because of the great differences in the two-crew cockpit and the revised instrumentation, pilots qualified on earlier variants of the 747 must be trained and qualified specifically for the -400.

The major flight information is displayed across six side-by-side (unlike in the 757 and 767, where they are one above the other), interchangeable Collins 8 x 8 inch integrated display system (IDS) screens, or CRTs, which allow more information to be displayed. The Collins central maintenance computer (CMC) is located on the console between the pilots. It interfaces with the -400s digital data bus and constantly monitors seventy individual systems centrally, giving faults in plain English on the CRT. Using this system, both flight and

The first 747-400 under construction at Seattle. (Boeing)

maintenance crews can obtain an update of the aircraft's mechanical condition (previously the information was only available to maintenance workers on the ground), to locate and correct faults. The primary flight display (PFD) or the EADI (electronic attitude director indicator) displays information regarding the aircraft's attitude, altitude, horizon, airspeed, vertical speed and heading, pitch and bank, speed deviation, instrument landing system course and glidescope. Airspeed is displayed in a vertical tape on the left, with barometric pressure, attitude and vertical speed on the right. Aircraft heading is shown on a box on a compass arc at the foot of the screen.

Other data, such as autopilot and auto throttle modes, ground-speed and radio altitude, are also displayed. The navigation display (ND) or EHSI (electronic horizontal situation indicator), which replaces the earlier 'moving map' and which shows track, heading, wind and distance, are duplicated. (On the captain's side the left-hand display unit is the PFD; his right-hand screen is the navigation display. The display screens are reversed for the first officer.) The presentation format capitalizes on the best features of the traditional electromechanical instrumentation and

On 17 June 2002 thousands of Boeing employees gathered in the world's largest building to celebrate the rollout of the first 747-400ER. (Boeing)

747-45EM B16405 of Eva Air at Bangkok in November 2010. (Gerry Manning)

incorporates new features that are only possible on a programmable CRT display.

The EHSI has four modes with approach, VOR, map (with a maximum range of 736 miles) and flight plan, with either the full compass rose or an enlarged quadrant. (The aircraft symbol can be located in the centre to permit the pilot to view all around in busy terminal areas where ATC instructions may involve tight manoeuvres.) Essentially, the ND integrates compass, track, weather and map references into a single display, with all the elements presented in a common scale. In a multi-colour format, it depicts the horizontal position of the aircraft in relation to the flight plan and displays a map that shows navigation features of the surrounding region. This improves crew orientation and allows the pilot to make rapid and accurate flight-path corrections. Wind speed and direction and vertical deviation from the flight path are also displayed. Each pilot may adjust the composition of his navigation display by choosing from a variety of features. Colour weather radar returns

may be selected and presented at the same scale and orientation as the map. Altitude and time of arrival for each flight-plan waypoint can also be displayed. In addition to map mode, a pilot can select plan mode, VOR mode, ILS mode, or (optional) full compass rose mode.

Two engine indication and crew alerting system (EICAS) display units, located centrally, monitor the performance of various systems and alerts the crew of any abnormal conditions. Primary data for aircraft operation is shown on the CRTs and CDUs and includes data from the following three systems: the electronic flight instrument system (EFIS), EICAS and the flight management system (FMS). EFIS contains primary flight data such as altitude, air data and navigation. EICAS presents all engine indication, thrust management and caution and warning displays and can call up the status or schematics of various systems at any time on one of the CRTs. The primary role of the EICAS computers is to monitor the hundreds of signals sent

747-4D7 HS-TGO of Thai Airways at Heathrow, February 2000 in a special scheme which shows the Royal Barge, to promote tourism. (Gerry Manning)

Line up of British Airways' 747s at Heathrow in 1997. The specially commissioned works of art on the tails of BA aircraft instead of one design applied to the whole fleet was revealed on 10 June 1997. The cost of commissioning the controversial artwork and applying the overall design was approximately £2 million and the total cost of the new image about £60 million. The scheme was universally disliked by passengers and crews and Margaret Thatcher the British Prime Minister. Nearest aircraft is Colum then 747-400 Emmly Masanabo (British Airways)

from the engine and subsystem sensors during a flight. Information the crew requires in flight, either full time or on command, is displayed at the flight deck in a multicolour format that can be read quickly and easily. Primary engine data such as fan speed, thrust and jet temperatures and pressures are displayed in the upper screen in either round-dial or tape format. Also displayed is major 'aircraft-status' information about landing gear and flap positions, doors, tyres and fuel states. The lower screen displays more engine data such as compressor speeds, oil pressures and temperatures,

as well as 'synoptics' of the hydraulic, electrical and fuel systems. Circuit-breakers and other functions previously located on the flight engineer's panel are located overhead. On the ground after the flight, the EICAS computer performs an equally vital role in providing maintenance crews with an automatic record of any system malfunction during the flight. In addition, crew can command EICAS to record data for trend analysis, including details pertaining to flight profile, temperature and other conditions that affect the system's performance.

David Hollingsworth, head of customer support at Rolls-Royce, writing in 1994, said: The monitoring of engines in flight has made great strides in the last decade. Early attempts were abortive because of the poor reliability of the sensors and measuring equipment used. There were also problems in analysing the vast amount of data collected. For many years, the warning devices in aircraft were often less reliable than the equipment they were monitoring. For example, pilots were accustomed to false fire warnings. Today that situation has changed. Although sensors are subject to vibration and wide variations in temperature and pressure, modern transducers are much more reliable and accurate than those of the past. Digital systems have led to an increase in the number of parameters being measured, providing the opportunity for condition monitoring in greater depth.

'Modern fuel systems with full-authority digital engine control (FADEC) make it easier to monitor engines via the digital databus used on the latest airliners. Electronic equipment is designed with built-in test equipment (BITE) and a carefully chosen level of redundancy. The BITE enables it to identify internal electronic failures or obviously false sensor signals (for example, a shaft apparently running at 150 per cent of its maximum speed) and to give an indication to maintenance personnel. The redundancy allows the equipment to continue to function to a satisfactory level, even with some failures in the system. The failures can then be fixed at a time convenient to the operator.

'With condition-monitoring today, data is gathered on a sampling basis when the equipment is in use and recorded for subsequent analysis and interpretation. The processing of data converts measurements into useful information. Measurements are made only to provide 'snapshots' of performance and engine behaviour at selected stages of a flight - after lift-off and during climb and cruise. These techniques avoid the costly collection of masses of unnecessary information and thousands of man hours needed for its subsequent analysis.

'Sampled data can be recorded in flight on cartridges or disks which are transferred into ground systems when the aircraft lands. A further enhancement to this system enables information to be transmitted in flight to ground stations and analysed, so that any maintenance action necessary can be taken immediately after the aircraft lands. This is particularly valuable in long-haul operations, when an aircraft may be away from base for several days.

'Ground-based computer systems can now analyse

Cathay Pacific 747 at Hong Kong (Rolls-Royce plc)

For the first time on any airliner, an optional, overhead cabin-crew rest area in the 747-400 uses space in the rear of the fuselage above the aft toilets. This area, which can be configured for eight bunks and two seats, provides privacy as well as comfort for off-duty flight attendants. By using this compartment, ten more profit seats are available on the main deck of the aircraft. (Boeing)

the data gathered in flight and report 'by exception' - signalling only when unusual events are occurring, or trends in engine behaviour are moving close to limits, indicating that maintenance action is necessary.'

The Honeywell (Sperry) flight management computer system (FMCS) stores flight plans to reduce crew workload and navigation errors. It takes a maximum of just three seconds to complete a calculation which took up to twenty seconds on the earlier 747. The system calculates the optimum altitude, speed and routing for a flight, given the relevant inputs from the pilots. Importantly, the FMCS has the capability to carry out '4D' navigation.

In addition, information shown on the three multifunction control display units (MCDU) can be selected by the pilots as required. The MCDUs can display data regarding standby navigation; automatic navigation radio tuning and dual-integrated thrust

management and can access the central maintenance system and a host of other functions. A multipurpose printer is included to provide in-flight printouts of data link information and suchlike. Should a primary flight display fail, the information can be immediately switched to the navigation display panel, with the other pair still operating. Automatic or manual display switching is used as back-up in the event of an individual CRT failure. Conventional electro-mechanical airspeed, altitude, vertical speed and compass instruments are fitted, so if a total failure of all the flight and navigation displays occurs - an unlikely event - the pilots can still operate safely.

Other new flight-deck features include a full-time auto-throttle, streamlined throttle quadrant and dual-thrust management system in the FMC. There is also automatic start and shutdown of the APU and integrated radio communication panels. The Collins autopilot

C-FCRA Canadian Airlines at Bangkok November 1999. The livery shows a goose on the fin and was short lived as they were taken over by Air Canada. (Gerry Manning)

KLM Royal Dutch Airlines' 747-406 PH-BFU Beijing.

flight-director system (AFDS) hardware is basically identical to that fitted to the 757/767, but the FCS-700A has updated software. An important new facility on this full digital triplex system is 'altitude intervention', which can handle an unexpected change of height caused by ATC instruction without the crew having to recalculate the flight plan. The AFDS also controls the auto-land capability of the -400 and is cleared to bring the aircraft in for automatic landings with a decision height of naught feet and a forward view along the runway of under 655 feet.

Travellers always want as much personal space as possible, but the real question is whether the value they place on extra space will generate additional revenue. Comfort is rated four times more important on long-

range than on short-range flights and only first-class and business-class passengers are consistently willing to pay a premium for additional space and amenities. The 747-400 offers more options for passenger comfort. Seating alternatives for high-yield travellers on the upper deck can include twenty-six sleeper seats, thirty-eight first-class seats, or forty-two to fifty-two business-class passenger seats. In addition, up to ninety-one passengers can be seated on the upper deck in an all-economy, 34 inch seat-pitch arrangement.

Most -400 operators have a seating capacity for 380-450 passengers, depending on the ratio of first-class business- or club-class and economy-class seats. KLM 747-400s seat a total of 387 passengers in an 18/105/264 layout, while Air New Zealand seats 396 passengers in

Delta Airlines 747-451 N676NW, with the Delta fleet number 6316 clearly displayed on the nosewheel door.

Above: QANTAS 747-438ER VH-OEH Spijkers.

Left: QANTAS 747-438 VH-OJB City of Sydney *in striking 'Aussie' scheme. This aircraft first flew on 18 August 1989 and was delivered to the airline on 15 September that year.*

a 16/56/324 layout and United Airlines' -400s accommodate 436 passengers in an 18/68/350 configuration. In British Airways' service, the 747-400 carries up to 426 passengers, but the standard configuration is for 401 passengers in a three-class layout (fourteen First, fifty-five Club World, 332 World Traveller). Late in 1995, British Airways' innovative new First service offered passengers, for the first time, their own individual cabins which they can use as a private office or mini-meeting room, also an entertainments centre, a dining room for two, or a bedroom, complete with a flat, 6 feet 6 inches full-length 'flying bed' at the touch of a button. This provides unrivalled levels of privacy and comfort.

The modern upper deck features a large galley with room for twenty food and beverage carts and two or three toilets; it also has nineteen more windows. Two new full-wing doors replace existing 747-200 upper deck exits. An aft straight stair replaces the original 747 forward circular stair. Upper deck passengers also have side-wall stowage that can serve as a table or additional work surface.

The 747-400 interior has ceiling and side-wall panels re-contoured with new, lighter materials that are easier to maintain and the volume of overhead stowage in both side and centre bins has increased dramatically. New materials on partitions, doors, closets, galleys, toilet walls and other interior surfaces meet Boeing goals for fireworthiness. The new, flexible interior allows operators to install sidewall galleys and toilets without changing the ceiling and its support structures. The modular outboard overhead stowage bins can be removed to make way for a new galley or toilet. As passenger seats are relocated, passenger and entertainment services can be reprogrammed using the Advanced Cabin Entertainment and Service System (ACESS).

The lower hold in every 747 has a mechanized loading system for cargo and baggage and 6,025 cubic feet of containerized cargo volume. On-board powerdrive systems and optional pallet-handling hardware in the lower hold can work with a mix of standard containers and commercial and military pallets. One attendant at the compartment doorway transfers cargo modules to their positions over a surface of ball transfer units and rollers. An additional 835 cubic feet of bulk cargo can be loaded into the 20 feet-long bulk cargo compartment of the 747-400, where it is attached to floor fittings or held in position by floor-to-ceiling nets.

On 22 October 1985 lead customer Northwest

The 747 marked its twentieth anniversary on 30 September 1988 when N7470, the first built, followed by the newest model, the -400 (N6038E/PH-BFC Calgary for KLM-Asia Airlines, the 735th 747 built), flew in close formation over each of Boeing's major plants in the Puget Sound area, as well as downtown Seattle, Washington, seen here. On board the lead aircraft as passengers were Jack Waddell, Brien Wygle and Jess Wallick, the original N7470 flight crew. At the time, orders for the 747 stood at 877 (including 161 for the new -400 version, of which 703 had been delivered). (Boeing)

Airlines ordered the first 747-400 and c/n 23719/Line number 696, a -451 (N661US) was rolled out at Everett on 26 January 1988, the same day as the new 737-400 was rolled out of the Boeing-Renton plant - the first double roll-out in the company's long and distinguished history. N661US took off from Paine Field near Everett on 29 April to begin the intensive flight-test programme, which would certify three different engines: the P&W PW4000, the General Electric CF6-80C2 and the Rolls-Royce RB211-524G. In all, four -400s were used for the basic -400 certification. Aircraft numbers one and four

were used for certification with the P&W engines, number two for the GE engines and number three for the Rolls-Royce powerplants. Number 4 was used for aircraft interiors installation requirements and also demonstrated reduced workloads in two-crew operations. It was envisaged that the total programme would require approximately 2,400 hours of testing, of which about half would be in the air. On 26 May the 747-400 completed the longest engineering flight in Boeing commercial aircraft history. This marathon flight lasted more than fourteen hours as cruise performance was evaluated. Forty-nine cruise data points were taken at eight different altitudes and at a series of Mach numbers, making this one of the most productive tests ever. In addition to cruise performance, other tests included a lapse-rate take-off (engine thrust characteristics measured during acceleration), take-off trim evaluation and an auxiliary power unit (APU) performance evaluation.

On 27 June at Moses Lake, Washington, 747-451 - temporarily registered N401PW to publicize the PW4000 engine - set a new official weight record by reaching an altitude of 7,000 feet at a gross weight of 892,450lb. [62]

In late August 1988 the first 747-400 flew to Roswell, New Mexico, to test the lighter, tougher carbon brakes in a series of refused take-offs (RTOs), which contribute to a picture of 747-400 braking characteristics for the FAA. A test is completed by advancing the -400's throttles to full power, releasing the brakes and accelerating to a predetermined ground speed just before a simulated engine failure. The pilots then reduce the 'good' engine power to idle, apply maximum wheel-braking and extend the wing spoilers. Thrust-reversers are not used during the tests. An 870,000lb gross weight RTO was successfully performed in the first week in September 1988 at Edwards AFB in the high desert of Southern California.

In 1986 five more airlines - British Airways, KLM, Lufthansa, Cathay Pacific and Singapore Airlines - placed firm orders for forty-nine -400s. (In Singapore Airlines' service the -400s are known as 'Megatops' and this logo is painted on the forward fuselage - just as the 'Bigtops' logo is on the airline's -300s.) In 1987 a further fifty-eight aircraft were ordered by United Airlines and Air France. By June 1988, Boeing had received orders for 146 -400s from nineteen airlines. The first -400 to be actually delivered to an airline was Cathay Pacific's VR-HOO [63] which arrived at Hong Kong on 28 August 1988. The -400 was finally certificated on 10 January 1989, but because the FAA insisted on further software and other electronic alterations, N661US could not be delivered to Northwest until 26 January. The airline put N661US into service on 9 February on its Minneapolis-Phoenix route.

The Combi version of the 747-400 introduced in 1985 features a large (134 x 120 inch cargo door on the main deck aft of the wing on the left side, plus equipment that allows passenger seats to be removed and cargo tracks to be installed, giving carriers the option of carrying containerized or palletized cargo in the main deck behind the passengers. The large, side cargo door means that cargo can be loaded in the aft section at the same time as passengers are boarded in the forward section; this allows for rapid turnaround and through-stop operations. A locked partition separates the passenger compartment from the cargo area, which is

On 10 September 1993 Boeing celebrated the roll-out of the 1,000th 747, a 747-412 (9V-SMU) for Singapore International Airlines. 9V-SMU flew on 29 September and was delivered to SIA in October. (Boeing)

747-4D7 HS-TGY of Thai Airlines (old livery) at Bangkok in November 2010. (Gerry Manning)

accessible only by the crew. Roller trays on the aft floor facilitate loading of 8-feet-wide containers, or pallets up to 20 feet long. The Combi can handle large-volume shipments such as cars, small boats, heavy machinery, drilling equipment and even small aircraft or helicopters. Environmental control in the cargo area allows transportation of live animals, perishable foods and cut flowers/vegetables, while maintaining separate environmental control of the passenger cabin.

All-passenger or six- or seven-pallet configurations allow carriers to meet seasonal fluctuations in traffic. Typical mixed-passenger and six- or seven-pallet arrangements accommodate 266 passengers and more than 9,000 cubic feet of cargo. The 747-400 Combi provided 1,100 miles greater range, with 12,000lb more payload than previous Combis. It carries more

passengers than a wide-body tri-jet and handles about as much cargo as a 707. Cargo operations do not interfere with passenger service because main-deck cargo loading occurs in an area of the aircraft where there is normally no activity. KLM was the initial customer, ordering four with CF6-80C2 engines in April 1986, for delivery starting in February 1989. Three other airlines have also ordered 747-400Ms. Altogether twenty-one airlines had ordered a total of 161 Model 747-400s by the end of September 1988.

In October 1989 Boeing announced that it planned to build the 747-400 high-capacity Domestic, the latest in the long line of short-range (SR) 747s operated by Japan Air Lines and All Nippon Air Lines. Once again, major structural strengthening was used in the construction to take account of the increased take-off

747-412F 9V-SFG MEGA ARK Singapore Airlines Cargo at Sharjah, March 2000. (Gerry Manning)

JAL 747-446 JA8907 *taking off from Haneda in*
August 2009.

and landing cycles. Externally, the -400D can differ
from the standard -400 in not having the six feet-
winglets fitted, because these tip extensions, being
designed to reduce drag on long haul flights, are
unnecessary on short, intra-flights in Japan (although
carriers have the option of having them fitted). In fact
the fuel saving is so negligible that it is more cost-
effective to dispense with the winglets and their
associated increase in weight. There is no tail-tank fitted
and this has helped reduce the aircraft's gross weigh to
around 600,000lb. The -400D can carry 568 passengers
in all-economy seating, the largest number of passengers
on any commercial aircraft in existence. The first 747-
446D[64] flew on 15 March 1991 and went into
commercial service with JAL (JA8083) on 10 October
1991. By the end of 1998 JAL had received eight -
446Ds and ANA had taken delivery of ten -48ID
versions, of which three were later converted to standard
-446 configuration.

An all-cargo version was added to the 747-400
family in 1989. The 747-400 freighter, which is
equipped with a hinged nose for straight-in freight
loading, can transport more cargo (249,000lb) further
than any other commercial jet freighter. Compared to
the 747-200 freighter, it has 26 tons more payload
capacity, a 1,380-mile longer range, with a 12 per cent
better fuel-burn per lb of pay-load. This increased range
and improved fuel-burn greatly impressed freight
carriers such as Luxembourg-based Cargolux, one of
Europe's largest all-freight airlines, which received the
first -428 freighter on 17 November 1993. Cargolux

Right: Garuda Indonesian Airways 747-400 with MD-11
PH-KCF Annie Romein *on the apron at Schiphol.*
(Author)

A pair of British Airways' 747-436s in formation. The nearest aircraft is G-BNLC City of Cardiff *which first flew in June 1982 and was delivered to the airline on 21 July that year.*

reported that -400F operation would enable them to dispense with about 300 refuelling stops a year.

The 747-400 freighter accommodates all standard airborne pallets, including 8 x 8 feet intermodel containers up to 40 feet long or special cargo up to 180 feet long. It routinely carries cars, long pipe and drilling equipment, live animals, small aircraft, high-bypass-ratio aircraft engines and heavy, outsized machinery and vehicles. The side cargo door accepts loads of up to 10 feet high. Steerable automatic power-drive units rotate 20 feet-long containers or pallets forward of the door, then transfer them laterally so that loads can be positioned along either side of the main deck. No manual handling is required.

Two -400s were written off in crashes in 1993. F-GITA of Air France landed at Papeete on 12 September and then for some reason veered off the runway and came to a halt on the beach where its nose became immersed in shallow water. Fortunately, none of the 272 passengers and crew suffered any lasting injuries. The first major loss of a -400 occurred on 4 November 1993 when B-165, a China Airlines' 747-409 (which had just been recently delivered, on 8 June) ran off the runway at Kai Tak after landing in heavy rain and strong winds caused by a nearby typhoon. China Airlines Flight 605 (call-sign 'Dynasty 605') was a daily non-stop flight departing from Taipei at 6:30 am and arriving at Kai Tak Airport at 7:00 am local time. Flight 605 touched down

Bottom: Air France 747-428 F-GEXA (advertising the World Cup Finals with a different footballer on each side of the cabin) taxiing at Kai Tak in April 1998. (Graham Dinsdale)

747-4D7 HS-TGN of Thai Airways at Phuket in January 2012. (Gerry Manning)

more than 2,100 feet past the runway's displaced threshold, at a speed of 150 knots, following an IGS runway 13 (non-precision) approach. Tropical Storm Ira was generating 20-knot crosswinds on that runway, gusting to 38 knots, from a heading of 070 degrees. The pilots received several computer-generated windshear and glide slope deviation warnings and observed severe airspeed fluctuations, during the last mile before touchdown. The auto brakes were set at only the number two level and then were turned off moments after touchdown, when the Captain elected to use manual braking and thrust reversal. The speed-brakes were extended momentarily, but then retracted. This caused the 747 to 'float', making the brakes ineffective until the speed brakes were extended again. The Captain deliberately turned the 747 to the left when he realized the airliner would go off the end of the runway and into the approach lighting system (ALS) for runway 31. This action caused a 'ground loop', making the 747 slide off the left side of the runway into Victoria Harbour, thereby preventing a collision with the ALS for Runway 31. It finally came to rest in shallow water, with a heading of almost 180 degrees out from the direction of Runway 13. Fortunately it refused to sink, thanks to the inbuilt buoyancy and strength of its construction and all 296 passengers and crew escaped without any serious injuries. A British Airways pilot had refused to make the approach to Kai Tak Runway 13 minutes before the CAL 605 Captain decided to attempt it.

The investigation indicated that the accident was caused by the Captain's failure to initiate the mandatory missed approach procedure when he observed the severe airspeed fluctuations, combined with the wind shear and glide slope deviation alerts. Immediately after the aircraft became submerged in water, crewmembers ensured that all passengers put on life-jackets and evacuated onto eight of the ten main deck emergency exits. These exits (as on all 747s) are specifically equipped with inflatable evacuation slide/rafts for ditching emergencies. The passenger cabin remained completely above water during the evacuation, although eventually sank tail first. Additional damage to the nose and first-class cabin was noted. There were 22 minor injuries among passengers or crew and the 747 was written off as a total hull loss. The vertical stabilizer on B-165 interfered with the accuracy of the ILS signals for Runway 31, so it was removed with dynamite shortly after the crash. That permitted airliners to make safe ILS approaches whenever the wind patterns mandated the use of Runway 31 (the reciprocal

Lufthansa 747-400 D-ABVC.

Northwest 747-451 N670US. This aircraft first flew on 26 July 1990 and was delivered to the airline on 31 August that same year.

direction of Runway 13). B-165 was later recovered, but because of the corrosion caused by the salt water, it could not be put back into service again and the aircraft was stored by the HAECO building to be used for fire-fighting practice.

QANTAS Flight 1 was a passenger flight which was involved in a runway overrun accident at Don Mueang International Airport, Bangkok in Thailand as it was arriving for a stopover in Bangkok on 23 September 1999. QANTAS flights travel between London Heathrow and Australia on a route known as the 'Kangaroo Route'. The Kangaroo Route traditionally refers to air routes flown between the countries of Australia and the United Kingdom, via the Eastern Hemisphere. This flight began at Kingsford-Smith Airport in Sydney earlier that day at 1645 local time and after more than eight hours flying was approaching Don Mueang International Airport at 2245 local time.

During the approach to Bangkok the weather conditions deteriorated significantly, from 8 kilometres visibility half an hour before landing to 750 metres at

the time of landing. The flight crew observed a storm cloud over the airport and ground reports were that it was raining heavily. However these conditions are common at Bangkok. Seven minutes prior to landing a Thai Airways Airbus A330 landed normally, but three minutes before landing another QANTAS aircraft (747-438 *City of Darwin* operating QF15, a Sydney-Rome via Bangkok service) conducted a 'go around' due to poor visibility during final approach. The crew of QANTAS Flight 1, however, were unaware of this. The first officer was flying the jet during final approach. The aircraft's altitude and airspeed were high, but were within company limits. The rain was now heavy enough that the runway lights were visible only intermittently after each windscreen wiper stroke. Just before touchdown the captain, concerned about the long touchdown point (over a kilometre past the runway threshold) and unable to see the end of the runway, ordered the first officer to perform a 'go-around' and the first officer advanced the throttles to TO/GA (Take-off/Go Around) power. Seeing that visibility had increased markedly and the landing

Kuwait Airways 747-469M 9K-ADE.

On 27 June 1988, at Moses Lake, Washington, 747-451, temporarily registered N401PW to publicize the PW4000 engine, set a new official weight record by reaching an altitude of 7,000 feet at a gross weight of 892,450lb. (Boeing)

gear contacted the runway, the captain then decided to cancel the go-around by retarding the thrust levers even though he was not flying the 747. This caused confusion as he did not announce his actions to the first officer who was still flying the jet. When overriding the first officer's actions, the captain inadvertently left one engine at TO/GA power and as a result cancelled the preselected auto-brake settings.

The landing continued, but manual braking did not commence until the aircraft was over 1600 metres down the runway. Company standard operating procedure mandated that idle reverse thrust should be used for landings and that flaps should be set at 25 degrees and not the maximum of 30 degrees. The combination of flaps 25, no auto-braking, idle reverse thrust, a high and fast approach, a late touch-down, poor Cockpit Resource Management and the standing water on the runway surface led to a runway overshoot. The aircraft in fact

accelerated for a few seconds after touchdown. Then it proceeded to hydroplane and skid its way down the runway, departing substantially from runway centre line. It gradually decelerated, but far too slowly to save the aircraft, which proceeded past the runway end, over a stretch of boggy grassland, colliding with a ground radio antenna as it did so and came to rest with its nose resting on the perimeter road. The ground on the other side of the road forms part of a golf course. This incident was QANTAS' most significant incident in fifty years of jet aircraft operation. The aircraft was returned to service and is now nicknamed the 'Golf Buggy'.

The collision with the antenna caused the nose and right wing landing gear to collapse, the nose landing gear being forced back into the fuselage. The aircraft slid along in a nose-down, right wing low attitude, causing some further damage to the nose and damage to the two right engines and their mountings. The intrusion

747-4H6M Combi 9M-MHL of Malaysia Airlines which first entered service in November 1989, taxiing at Frankfurt on 23 February 1990. (Graham Dinsdale)

of the nose landing gear also caused the failure of the cabin intercom and public address system. There were no significant passenger injuries during an orderly evacuation of the aircraft ordered 20 minutes after the rough landing. Thirty-eight passengers reported minor injuries. The aircraft was repaired and was returned to service. QANTAS still operates flight number 1 between Sydney and London; it now travels via Singapore Changi Airport.

On 11 September 2001 after the terrorist attacks on the World Trade Center in New York and other buildings in Washington DC, a call went out for all airliners to return to their airports of origin (or if they did not have enough fuel, to land in Canadian territory). While discussing the day's events with the Korean Air office, the pilot of Korean Air Flight 85 en route to Ted Stevens International Airport in Anchorage, Alaska included the letters 'HJK' (the code for 'hijacked') in an airline text message. When the pilot sent his message, the text messaging service company, Aeronautical Radio, Incorporated (ARINC) noticed the 'HJK' code. ARINC officials, worried that the Korean pilots might be sending a coded message for help, notified North American Aerospace Defense Command (NORAD). Taking no chances, NORAD scrambled two F-15 jets from Elmendorf Air Force Base to intercept the 747, with Alaska air traffic control (ATC) asking the pilots coded questions. Civil airline pilots are trained to answer these questions in a coded way if hijacked. The Korean pilots, instead of reassuring ATC, declared themselves hijacked by changing their transponder signal to the four-digit universal code for hijack, 7500. Worried that a possible hijacked jet might strike a target in Alaska, Governor

Tony Knowles ordered the evacuation of large hotels and government buildings in Anchorage. At nearby Valdez, (also in Alaska), the US Coast Guard ordered all tankers filling up with oil to head out to sea. Lieutenant General Norton Schwartz, who was in charge of the NORAD planes that scrambled to shadow Flight 85, told reporters in 2001 that he was prepared to order the Korean jet to be shot down before it could attack a target in Alaska.

With NORAD telling Anchorage ATC that it would shoot down the airliner if it came near any potential targets, these controllers informed Flight 85 to avoid all population centres and head out of the country to Whitehorse, Canada. NORAD promptly called Canadian authorities seeking the go-ahead to shoot the 747 down over Canadian soil: Prime Minister Jean Chretien said, 'Yes, if you think they are terrorists, you call me again but be ready to shoot them down.' So I authorized it in principle, It's kind of scary that... [there is] this plane with hundreds of people and you have to call a decision like that.. .. But you prepare yourself for that. I thought about it -- you know that you will have to make decisions at times that will [be] upsetting you for the rest of your life'.

Ninety minutes after the Korean pilots changed their transponder signal to the 7500 hijacked code, the 747 landed safely at Whitehorse, Yukon, Canada. Canadian officials evacuated all schools and large buildings before the jet landed. On the tarmac, Flight 85 was greeted by armed Royal Canadian Mounted Police officers who, after interrogating the pilots, learned the whole ordeal was caused by a translation error. The Korean pilot stated that he had been ordered by Air Traffic Control to change the transponder signal while Air Traffic

---

Flight 85 timeline 11 September 2001

Flight 85 takes off from Incheon International Airport in Seoul, South Korea.
8:46:40 am (Eastern Time Zone (ET) - American Airlines Flight 11 is flown into the World Trade Center's North Tower
9:03: 11 am (ET) - United Airlines Flight 175 hits the World Trade Center's South Tower 9:37 am (ET) - American Airlines Flight 77 crashes into the Pentagon
9:59:04 am (ET) - The South Tower collapses.
10:03:11 am (ET) - United Airlines Flight 93, whose ultimate target was thought to be either the United States Capitol or the White House, crashes near Shanksville, Pennsylvania.
10:10 am (ET) - The portion of the Pentagon wall hit by American Airlines Flight 77 collapses.
10:28 am (ET) - The North Tower collapses.
11:08 am (ET) The pilot of Flight 85 includes the letters 'HJK,' a code for hijacked, in an airline text message.
12:00 pm (ET) - ARINC officials notify NORAD about the use of the hijack code.
1:00 pm (ET) - Jets are scrambled from Elmendorf Air Force Base to shadow the plane.
1:24 pm (ET) - The Korean pilots change their transponder signal to '7500', the four-digit universal code for hijacked.
1-2:45 pm (ET) - Alerted that a possible hijacked plane might strike a target in Alaska Governor Tony Knowles orders the evacuation of potential targets.

Control denied having done so. Korean Air still uses Flight 85 on its Seoul-Incheon to New York-JFK route. However, the flight no longer stops in Anchorage.

On 31 October 2000 Singapore Airlines Flight 006 (SQ006) was a scheduled passenger flight from Singapore Changi Airport to Los Angeles International Airport via Chiang Kai-shek Airport in Taiwan [65]. At 23:00 Taipei local time 747-412 9V-SPK with twenty crew and 179 passengers including three children and three infants - mostly Taiwanese and American - left Bay B5 during heavy rain caused by the typhoon. A few minutes' later the CKS Airport cleared the jet to taxi to runway 05L via 'taxiway Sierra Sierra West Cross' and 'November Papa'. At 23:15:22, the airport cleared the 747 to takeoff at 05L. (Many carriers in Southeast and East Asia take off during bad weather). After a six-second hold Captain Foong Chee Kong heard that he needed to take off at 05L, but he turned 705 feet too soon and lined up with 05R (which runs parallel to 05L), which had been closed for repairs. [66]

At 23:17 Kong attempted to take off from the wrong runway during Typhoon Xangsane with fatal results.[67] Due to poor visibility in the heavy rain, the flight crew did not see that construction equipment, including two excavators, two vibrating rollers, one small bulldozer and one air compressor had been parked on runway 05R. In addition, the runway contained concrete jersey barriers and pits. About 41 seconds later, the 747 collided with the machinery and broke into pieces. The fuselage was torn in two and the engines and landing gear separated. A crane tore the left wing from the aircraft, forcing the jet back on to the ground. The nose struck a scoop loader. A large fire followed, destroying the forward section of the fuselage and the wings. Seventy-nine passengers and

crew died on impact and immediately after the crash and two passengers died in hospital. [68]

Many of the dead were seated in the middle section of the aircraft; the fuel stored in the wings exploded and sent balls of flame through that section. Forty-one fire fighting vehicles, 58 ambulances, nine lighting units and 4,336 personnel were dispatched to assist survivors and extinguish the fire. Chemical extinguishing agents rained on the aircraft at about three minutes after the impact. Ten minutes after the impact, the fire was brought under control. At 00:00 Taipei time on 1 November the fire was mostly extinguished and the front part of the aircraft was destroyed. Authorities established a temporary command centre.

British Airways Flight 268 was a regularly scheduled flight from Los Angeles' LAX airport to London Heathrow. On the flight that took off from LAX at about 9:24 pm on 20 February 2005 G-BNLG, a 747-436, was about 300 feet into the air when flames burst from its number 2 engine. The pilots shut the engine down. Air traffic control expected the aircraft to return to the airport and discharge all 351 passengers and 18 crew and deleted the flight plan. However, after consulting with the airline dispatcher, the pilots decided to set off on their flight plan 'and get as far as we can' rather than dump 70 tonnes of fuel and land. (While 747s are certified to fly on three engines, doing so leaves much less room for error). Upon reaching the UK, believing there to be insufficient usable fuel to reach their destination, the captain declared an emergency and landed at Manchester Airport. A safety controversy ensued; the US Federal Aviation Agency (FAA) accused the carrier of flying an 'unairworthy' airliner across the Atlantic. The FAA proposed fining

Air India 747-437 VT-ESN. The distinctive paintwork highlighting the cabin windows, which was first used on the company's -200 series, led to the aircraft being called 'Palaces in the sky'. Late in 1989 Air India brought in a new livery which omitted the 'Palace windows' and caused such a furore that following pressure from religious leaders that they were reinstated on the -437 series. Near the tail are the words 'Your Palace in the Sky'. (Barry Reeve)

British Airways $25,000. British Airways lodged an appeal on the grounds that they were flying according to United Kingdom Civil Aviation Authority (CAA) rules (which are derived from International Civil Aviation Organisation standards). In the end the FAA told British Airways that it was dropping the case based on assurances that airline changes will 'preclude the type of extended operation that was the subject of this enforcement action.' British Airways said that they had not changed their procedures and according to Flight International the FAA said that they 'will recognise the CAA's determination that the aircraft was not unairworthy.'

QANTAS Flight 30 - 747-438[69] VH-OJK *City of Newcastle* - left Hong Kong International shortly after 9:00 am on 25 July 2008 during a scheduled flight from London Heathrow to Melbourne. One hour and seventeen minutes into the flight passengers and crew heard a loud bang when an oxygen tank exploded, causing a fuselage rupture just forward of the starboard wing root. The cabin de-pressurised and a hole in the floor of the passenger deck appeared, as well as a hole in the outside wall of the cargo deck. There were no injuries and passengers reported that, despite the noise and the deployment of the oxygen masks, there was very little panic.[70] The pilots conducted an emergency descent from 29,000 feet to about 10,000 feet to ensure adequate oxygen supply for the passengers and eventually made an emergency landing at Ninoy Aquino International Airport, Metro Manila in the Philippines. The hole in the fuselage - roughly in an inverted T-shape - was up to 2.01 metres wide and approximately 1.52 metres high located on the right side of the fuselage, below cabin floor level and immediately forward of the wing. The wing-fuselage fairing was missing, revealing some palletised cargo in the hold; however the freight forwarder reported that all items on the manifest were accounted for. Other than some items which were located near the cylinder and resulting hole, no other cargo or baggage on the flight was damaged.[71]

Footnotes for Chapter 12

61 Toilet installation is simplified by a vacuum waste system and 2 inch diameter waste pipes running through the length of the main cabin floor, with an extension to the upper deck, enables airlines to choose from up to 21 possible toilet positions around the cabin. Waste is collected in four tanks - two holding 386 litres each and two holding 296 litres each - at the rear of the belly.

62 Northwest put the 400s into service on 9 February 1989.

63 c/n 23814.

64   c/n 25213, line number 844.

65 Now Taiwan Taoyuan International Airport.

66 The airport was not equipped with ASDA, a ground radar which allows the airport controllers to monitor aircraft movements on the ground.

67 SQ006 was the first fatal crash of a Singapore Airlines aircraft; prior to the SQ006 crash, the sole fatal incident involving SIA was the crash of SilkAir Flight 185, operated by subsidiary SilkAir.

68 39 suffered from serious injuries, 32 had minor injuries, while 25 were uninjured.

69 (c/n 25067).

70 The Australian Transport Safety Bureau interviewed passengers who reported problems with the oxygen masks as part of their investigation. Numerous passengers said that some oxygen masks did not deploy, whilst others had deteriorated elastic. Consequently, it was reported that one passenger smashed a panel of the ceiling to attempt to gain access to the masks. These passengers were deprived of oxygen until the 747 was lowered to a breathable altitude.

71 The ATSB sent four investigators to Manila to conduct a detailed inspection of the aircraft, with QANTAS, the US National Transportation Safety Board, FAA, Boeing, the Australian Civil Aviation Safety Authority and the Civil Aviation Authority of the Philippines also involved. Air safety investigators found that an oxygen cylinder in the area of the explosion had not been accounted for, but that it was too early to say that an oxygen cylinder could be the cause of the mid-air explosion on QF30. CASA ordered QANTAS to inspect all of its oxygen cylinders and brackets holding the cylinders on its 747 fleet. The valve and mounting brackets were found, but not the bottle, number four of 13 fitted in that bank. A senior investigator, Neville Blyth, reported that the cylinder valve was found inside the cabin, having punched a hole 'at least 20cms in diameter' through the cabin floor. Because the 747 had remained airborne and operational throughout the incident, the cockpit voice recorder does not contain records of the initial event itself; its 2-hour memory had been overwritten with recordings taking place after this event, during the diversion and landing. The 24-four hour flight data recorder does contain data covering the entire incident. On 29 August the ATSB stated that the initial investigations had found that the aircraft took about 5½ minutes to descend from the decompression event at 29,000 feet to 10,000 feet and that it appeared that part of an oxygen cylinder and its valve had entered the passenger cabin, then impacted with the No.2 right door handle, turning it part way. The ATSB noted that there was no risk of the door being opened by this movement, with the door systems performing as designed. All three of the aircraft's instrument landing systems as well as the anti-skid braking system were unavailable for the landing; the pilots subsequently landed the aircraft without using those systems.

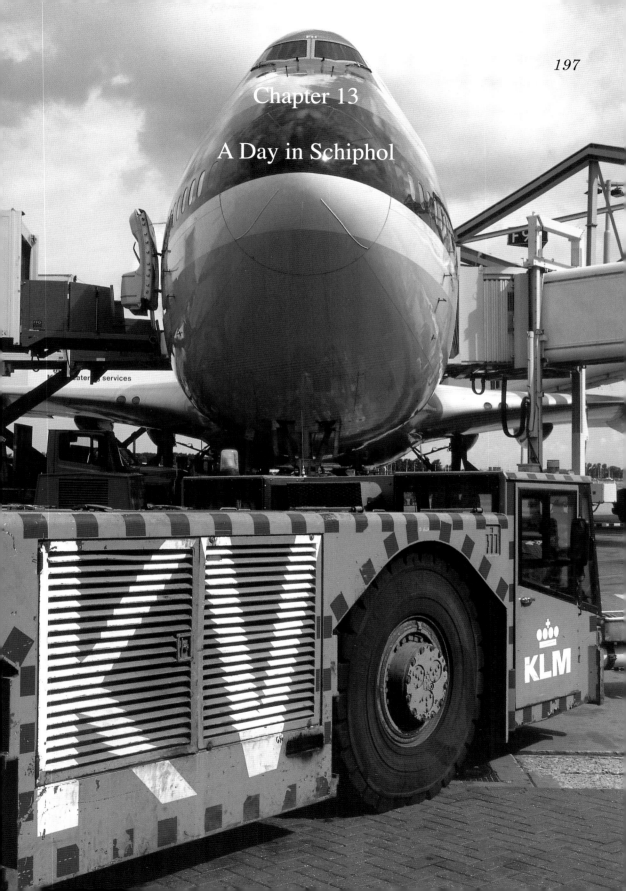

Chapter 13

A Day in Schiphol

Opposite page: Amsterdam-Schiphol Airport.

Right: 747-40M PH-BFY City of Johannesburg *at a misty Schiphol Airport after an early morning arrival from Houston, Texas on 17 October 2003. (Author)*

Below: Rotate! KLM Asia 747-406 PH-BFH City of Hong Kong *leaving Amsterdam-Schiphol. This aircraft first flew on 30 March 1990. (Author)*

Left: KLM 747-306 Combi PH-BUU Sir Frank Whittle. *This aircraft first flew on 15 September 1983 and was delivered to the airline at the end of that month. (Author)*

Right: KLM 747-400 Charles A. Lindbergh *at Amsterdam-Schiphol. (Author)*

Below: KLM Asia 747-406 PH-BFH City of Hong Kong *is replenished at Amsterdam-Schiphol. (Author)*

KLM Asia 747-406 PH-BFH City of Hong Kong *with tow-bars for the respective airliners in the foreground. (Author)*

Below: KLM Asia 747-406 PH-BFM City of Mexico *and other 747s of the Dutch airline at Schiphol. (Author)*

Chapter 14

'Cathay 403, Will You Accept a Visual?'

Captain Mike Rigg

Kai Tak Airport had very definite terrain problems, which ruled out a standard ILS (instrument landing system) approach and presented pilots with an interesting landing pattern, to say the least. A straight-in approach towards the south-east was not possible because of mountains, primarily Lion Rock, lying to the north. Instead, when landing on Runway 13, an approach was made initially on a system similar to an ILS but offset at 47 degrees to the runway and referred to as an 'instrument guidance system' (IGS).

The IGS signals were rejected by pilots at about 700 feet and the aircraft was flown towards a large red-and-white checkerboard at the foot of Lion Mountain, before commencing a sharp 40° turn onto the runway at about 500 feet. The IGS had a paired DME (distance-measuring equipment) with a built-in delay, which gave distance to the landing threshold and on the ground, strobe lights marked out the turn with offset PAPIs (precision approach position indicators) indicating glide path. (In Hong Kong, only aviation danger and

guidance lights are allowed to flash. All commercial advertising lights must be steady).

With the completion of the new Chek Lap Kok International Airport, the approach into Kai Tak is no longer. On 6 July 1998 Cathay's 747-467 8-HUJ was the first airliner to land at Check Lap Kok, after a record-breaking world distance record for the longest commercial flight, from New York, over the North Pole, a distance of over 6,582 miles lasting 15 hours and 24 minutes.

Finals to Kai Tak
'Cathay 403 leaving flight level 350, descending 140.'

'Roger Cathay 403 turn left 260 for separation and call passing flight level 290.'

'403, heading 260, will call passing level 290, where's the traffic?'

'403, your traffic is company L-1011, passing level 280 for 290, in your 10 o'clock 20 miles.'

'Roger, looking.'

China Airlines 747-409 B-18202 on finals for Kai Tak on 1 May 1998. (Graham Dinsdale)

The standard steep turn onto finals for Kai Tak is shown by this Canadian 747...

'What a beautiful day Jim; Christ, you can see forever!'

'Yeah, what a shame to be up here, a man of your talent could be shining the ass of your suit with the tossers on the tenth floor, you don't have to suffer like this Mike!'

'Thanks Jim.'

The big aeroplane, light today by 400 standards at only 238 tonnes (238,000 kilos) with 13 tonnes of that being the remaining fuel, was descending rapidly at 300 knots and around 3,000 feet per minute. Inside the flight deck it was 22 degrees Celsius, very dry, only about 18 per cent humidity and at this speed, the wind noise was moderate. Outside, of course it was very different. A monstrous din in the maelstrom of a 300-knot hurricane with the temperature in the minus 30s Celsius, a wild and turbulent world where no human could survive unprotected. Skin frozen, gut and lungs distended, joints torn asunder and brain starved of oxygen, death would, mercifully, be instantaneous. The long fall to earth would be of no consequence!

'Through all this on she went with hardly a burble, smooth as silk in the stable air mass of a North East monsoon, passengers, even at this late stage, finishing their last drinks, sitting in comfort, many in shirt sleeves, blissfully unaware of the chaos that prevailed a few millimetres from them on the other side of that amazingly thin skin of aluminium.

'Cathay 403, we have the traffic in sight and we're passing level 290.'

'Roger Cathay 403, you are clear of traffic. You are now cleared direct to the Charlie Hotel, maintain flight level 140 and call approach on 119.1.'

'403, direct to Charlie Hotel, 140 and call approach. It's a great day up here!' Jim's 'States' Canadian cheerfully breaking RT discipline; but what the hell, it was a great day up there and it was about to get better.

'Cathay 403 now left the Hong Kong radar frequency efficiently worked by the young 'local' with his clipped, precise and disciplined procedures and only a hint of Chinese accent brushing across his perfect English. They were now being handled by an 'import', an old hand who had arrived from the UK via the Middle East. Procedures maybe not quite so by the book but a man of vast experience. Instant team building, working together, a bond. I don't know why; I think it is in the voice. Exuding confidence, you know he is working for you.

'It is important for the crew of an airliner to build up a mental three dimensional picture of their position, not only relative to the ground but also relative to other aircraft in the pattern. No matter how good the system or the people operating it, mistakes are made. The arbiters over disaster and safety are the crew, the last link in the safety chain. If all else fails their diligence, professionalism, call it what you will, could save the day. A vital aid enabling them to build this canvas is the controller.

On a less dramatic point, by working together they help each other to make a smooth and expedient approach, thereby saving fuel, keeping the accountants happy, satisfying the passengers by avoiding unnecessary delays and the satisfaction of having done a good job permeates the mood. Good material for bullshitting in the bar later too!

'So, as the 747 continued its descent the crew kept their eyes peeled and even more importantly in the modern environment, they listened intently to the transmissions between ATC and other aircraft. They knew where everybody was. They knew where the dangers lay.

'Good afternoon Cathay 403, you are number 4 in sequence, number 1 is just about to touch down, would you like a visual step-down?'

'Is a pig's arse pork? Thoughts, not spoken! Number 1 will be clearing the runway, number 2 must be short finals, number 3 has just left Cheung Chau, we'll cut inside him - 'Tell him yes, Jim and ask him if we are clear up the Lamma Channel.' 'Affirm, you are clear up the Channel and you are 2 in sequence with number 1 on short finals, you are now ahead of the JAL who has just left the CH. Maintain 8,000 feet, QNH 1010 until passing Tathong.'

That mental picture!

The visual step-down approach onto Runway 13 at Kai Tak airport, the old Hong Kong international, was one of the last real aviation experiences of the civil aviation world. No autopilots, no flight directors, throwaway the INS and other navigation aids, even the ATC was minimal. It required good handling skills and Mark 1 eyeball judgement, something a lot of modern aviators never get to practice. Too many, this approach was something to be very wary of, but not to the Cathay pilots, they relished it! It was party time.

The flight path for this approach, if you were lucky, took you over Tathong Point round to the south of Hong Kong Island, passing between Lamma Island and the spectacular and beautiful Repulse Bay, where the Imperial Japanese Army earned themselves such infamy during World War Two and then on to Green Island situated in the Western Harbour. From there you headed for Stonecutters Island (no longer an island I'm afraid, but now joined to the Kowloon Peninsula in that relentless march of progress). From Stonecutters you looked for the Kowloon Magistracy and thence for the famous 'checkerboard', often peering desperately through the industrial pollution that had reduced the visibility to a bare minimum. From the checkerboard you made an almost right-angle turn to line up with the runway.

'Round you went, a couple of hundred feet clear of

... that leads to the short finals onto the runway over and through the crowded housing that was so close to the airport as demonstrated by this Cathay Pacific 747.

Singapore Airlines' 'Megatop' (747-412 9V-SMJ) coming into land at Kai Tak in 1996. (Graham Dinsdale)

Cathay Pacific 747 on approach to Kai Tak.

apartment blocks and Mrs Wong's 'smalls' hanging out to dry, with Lion Rock looming ominously over your left wing and then a nasty little South Wester chucking you about and trying like a Chinese dragon to blow you through the centre line. Yes, 747s are affected by the wind, not even they can defy the laws of nature.

'On a seemingly benign and lovely day, windshear at this juncture could catch the unwary and lead to the very least, an embarrassment and much mirth from one's fellow aviators and in the worst case - it does not bear thinking about.

''Hell, it must be six months or more since I was offered a visual and what a day!' The Captain was ecstatic, like a teenager on a motor bike and he only had half a year to retirement!

'Godammit, I haven't done one of these for over a year, you jammy-assed bastard.'

Jim's North American vocabulary would never let you down.

'Fun it might be, but an observant onlooker would have noticed that things were starting to happen, everything was now on fast forward. The atmosphere on the flight deck had thickened, a sense of pleasure, yes, relaxed yes, but something tangible was there; you could touch the urgency.

Mike at the controls, with the autopilot still engaged for the moment, had wound up the speed, the aircraft was accelerating rapidly towards 380 knots indicated air speed. With the first indication that a visual approach might be on, through all the jocularity, his brain had dropped down a 'cog' and had begun to rev at high speed, the professional was at work...

Why, you may ask, this change, this metamorphosis, what is it all about?

The reason is quite simple. The crew had planned for an Instrument Guidance Approach, an IGS, which basically required the aircraft to cross over a beacon, the CH, situated on Cheung Chau Island at around 8,000 feet and at a speed of 250 knots, or thereabouts. With the visual approach, especially one through the Lamma Channel, the track miles to touchdown had been drastically reduced. This meant the aircraft, or rather its crew, had much less time to get rid - of the height, much less time to calculate, less time to think.

A new plan had to be devised and quickly. So the first action was to dive off some of that height, hence the increase in airspeed. Having done away with the excess altitude, the next problem would be to decelerate the aircraft. This would not be too difficult today as the aircraft was light. Surprisingly, to the layman, the

Cathay Pacific 747 at Kai Tak, Hong Kong in 1997. (Graham Dinsdale)

heavier an aeroplane is, the further it will glide and, not surprisingly, the harder it is to slow down. Even 8,000 feet at Tathong was a bit high, especially if you were carrying more than 300 knots.

'Passing 150 for 8,000!' Jim's voice was strident in order to ensure the Captain heard his check call over the now roaring wind noise.

'Check 150 for 8,000, setting QNH 1010, now passing level 142.' Mike's acknowledgement was loud and clear as he reset his altimeter to the regional pressure setting.

'That checks, QNH 1010 set and cross checked' retorted the first officer. It sounds simple enough, but many a hull has been lost because the crew had set the wrong pressure setting on their altimeters. Sound procedures and adherence to them are a great enhancement to flight safety. That is what this little ritual was all about. They were now only 20 nautical miles from Tathong Point, they still had 6,000 feet to dispose of and all that speed, it was going to be tight!

With 15 miles to go Mike eased back on the stick, reducing the rate of descent, although there was still another 4,000 feet to lose, but he had to get rid of some of that speed! With his right hand he reached out and grasped the spoiler lever, pulling ever so gently (don't want to spill those drinks) back, the panels on the upper surface of the great mainplanes began to rise, disrupting the airflow and reducing the lift. Now, by raising the nose of the aircraft he compensated for the loss of lift but increased the drag. Like a powerful hand, the turbulent airflow grabbed at the airspeed and the knots began to fall away rapidly. They cross Tathong at 10,000 feet but the speed was decreasing through 280 knots, soon they would be below flap limiting speed when other drag devices would come into play.

'Cathay 403, do you have Cheung Chau in sight?' The approach controller was checking their ability to continue with the visual.

'Affirm, Cathay 403, CH in sight' was the clipped reply.

'OK, 403 you are clear up the Lamma Channel for the visual approach.'

The first officer gave a brief acknowledgement; he now had other work to do.

'Autopilot disconnected, flight directors away, Jim.' Jim switched off the instruments leaving the Captain with little in the way of electronic aids.

He didn't need them, he didn't want them, they would only be a distraction, although the DME (distance measuring equipment) would be handy for distance to touchdown and that would be prominently displayed on the navigation display TV screen.

Mike was now hand-flying the aeroplane in a gentle right-hand turn with the thrust levers back at idle. Stretched out before them was a wonderful panorama, the whole of the British territory was laid out like one of those topographical models used to show the attributes of fancy housing projects. The visibility was unusually good with only a trace of the yellow pollution layer that so often blighted the view. From Macau to

China Airlines 747 landing at Kai Tak, Hong Kong on 30 April 1998. (Graham Dinsdale)

Shenzen it was as clear as a bell. Not that either crew member had time to sit and ponder, they were both looking at Green Island, just off the Western end of Hong Kong Island, thinking how close it was. They needed to cross abeam this point at around 3,000 feet, not much higher or they would be looking at an embarrassing 'go-around'!

Mike eased in the spoilers, gently so as not to alarm the passengers with the accompanying trim change and called for the first flap selection. The aircraft burbled as pneumatic pressure forced out sections of the leading edge flaps, increasing the lift, disturbing the airflow and allowing it to fly safely at a lower airspeed.

'Flap 5; Flap 10; Flap 20.' The Captain called the flap in sequence as he reduced the speed further. The first officer obliged, acknowledging each selection. Adrenalin flowed, heart rates were up in the 160 region. Must get that height off! 'Gear down.' Mike needed more drag. Now the aircraft really did rumble and roar in protest as the huge doors in its belly opened and disgorged the 16 big main wheels on four 'bogies', with the nose wheels, making a total of 18, a lot of rubber, courtesy of Messrs Goodyear Ltd.

Now at 220 knots with gear and flap 20 extended,

the big machine fell like a stone, they were going to make that gate at Green Island.

The tension eased, Jim sat the cabin crew down and Mike called for the landing check-list. Another of those quaint rituals common to aviation that have served to make the safest form of transport on Earth.

With Green Island approaching fast, Mike slowed the rate of descent, bringing the speed back steadily towards the flap 20 target. Anticipating, he eased the thrust levers forwards bringing the power up, carefully to make sure the thrust was balanced across all four of those huge Rolls Royce RB211s. The speed stabilized at 160 knots, there was little trim change.

Every time he flew it, the Captain marvelled at how beautifully the big aircraft handled. The pitch was light, the ailerons powerful and precise and the whole package so responsive to the sensitive touch. Just like a much smaller aircraft, this was no machine to be brutal with, it required caressing. It had no vices and loved to be flown, such harmonization Mr. Boeing had not achieved before.

'Cathay 403, call passing Green Island on Tower, good day.'

With a brief acknowledgement, Jim switched the

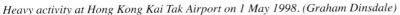

Heavy activity at Hong Kong Kai Tak Airport on 1 May 1998. (Graham Dinsdale)

VR-HOS of Cathay Pacific at LHR on 4 October 2009 for the run to Hong Kong's Chek Lap Kok International Airport. VR-HOS first flew on 25 April 1990 and was delivered to Cathay the following month. On 6 July 1998 Cathay's 747-467 B-HUJ was the first airliner to land at the new airport after a record breaking world distance record for the longest commercial flight, from New York, a distance of over 6,582 miles, lasting 15 hours and 24 minutes. (Author)

radio onto 118.7 megahertz, the tower frequency.

'Good morning Cathay 403, you are clear to land, Runway 13. Surface wind 190 at 12 knots, QNH 1010. Jim acknowledged and then joined the Captain in his visual search for the Kowloon Magistracy and the 'checkerboard'. They were somewhere out there, buried amongst all that expensive high rise.

Over Stonecutters now and bang on target. 'Give me flap 30 and complete the landing check-list, Jim.' They completed the ritual.

1,200 feet, check-list complete and 155 knots, everything was 'hunky dorry'. Remember that windshear!

The checkerboard stood before them like dogs' whatsits now.

Allow for the wind, start the turn just that little bit early. Don't get blown through the centre line, it looks bloody awful. Every approach was a matter of professional pride, flown as though the whole world was watching, stacked with self-criticism.

'500 feet, plus 10.' The first officer made his safety call and with his North American exuberance added 'Looking real good!'

The 747 was in the right turn with the wing tip appearing to scrape the apartment blocks. And right there, sure enough was the washing, on the line, hung out to dry and being doused in aviation paraffin. Poor old Mrs. Wong, she won't be sorry when they move to Chek Lap Kok!

The aircraft was bouncing about as she met those swirling dragons off Hong Kong Island, the speed was up and down 10 knots and this was a quiet day - what about in typhoon conditions? But that is another story! Hands relaxed, small, rapid control movements, try to leave the power alone and look for the far end of the runway.

A large black kite, scavenger of the East swept past only a few yards away, a bit close for comfort, he tumbled in the vortices. An every present hazard, ingest one of those and your Royce may stop rolling.

The animated voice from the radar altimeter, agonizingly American, '60 feet, 10 feet.'

Mike had eased back on the stick putting the aircraft into the landing attitude. Hold it and ease the power off. She touched down like a cat peeing on velvet and the spoilers deployed automatically, killing all that lift and sticking her firmly to the tarmac. A touch of reverse thrust, save the engines but make sure it is there, just in case. Automatic braking did the rest.

They turned off the runway, 'cleaned up' the aircraft and taxied to the terminal. Time for a beer but don't forget, like the man leaving the toilet, the job is not finished till the paperwork is complete!' Oh that bloody paperwork.'

A beautiful view of a 747-400 banking on finals to Kai Tak, June 1997. (Graham Dinsdale)

Chapter 15

Wings Across the Prairie From the Flight Deck

It is essential, in order to remain competitive in this important sector, that we have the best equipment for our customers. The Boeing 747-400 will do that. It is state-of-the-art and it will ensure that British Airways remains pre-eminent in the long-haul market.

British Airways

Rain and strong winds hardly make a trip to the office any more enjoyable on a Monday morning, especially when heavy traffic and delays cause added frustration. However, knowing that your office will soon be at 30,000 feet and heading 4,941.55 statute miles westwards from Gatwick Airport, London to Denver, Colorado, via snow-covered Iceland and Greenland, does offer compensations! On 1 March 1999 G-BNLR, one of a fleet of fifty-seven British Airways' 747-400s, had the honour of flying the first BA 747-400 flight into Denver International Airport.

British Airways is one of the world's biggest carriers of international airline passengers and has a scheduled route network covering around 170 destinations in almost eighty countries. On average, a BA flight departs from an airport somewhere in the world every ninety seconds, contributing to a total of over a quarter of a million flights in a full year, carrying over 30 million passengers and half a million tonnes of cargo. BA is one of the leading operators of 747 series aircraft, introducing the first of its 747-100 series aircraft in 1971 and the 200 series in 1977. On 15 August 1986 the airline placed its initial order for sixteen 747-436s and by the summer of 1988 this was increased to nineteen firm orders, with options on a further twelve aircraft, an investment of $4.3 million each, the highest value aircraft order ever placed up to that time. In July 1990, BA signed their biggest ever contract with Boeing, for up to thirty-three additional Series 436 aircraft (twenty-one firm orders, plus options on a further twelve) valued at about $6.4 billion. (Not surprisingly therefore, on average, each 747-436 is in use 14.42 hours every day - an average of 4,900 hours' utilization per year - while the Series 100 aircraft is used 11.34 hours per day and the Series 200 10.84 hours per day. The airline's last remaining 100s were gone by the end of 1999 and the 200s were due to be withdrawn by 2002.) In early July

1989 British Airways' crews began training on their first 747-436 (G-BNLA) and the company introduced the aircraft on its routes at the end of May 1989.

The captain of Speedbird 2019 (otherwise known as G-BNLR *Rendezvous*) for the inaugural Denver flight, 1 March 1999 was 49-year old John R. Downey MRIN, flight manager 747-400 fleet, who has over thirty years' commercial airline experience, including 4½ years piloting Concorde. Here he explains the routine:

'For operational reasons, the Triple 7s [Boeing 777s] have been substituted by 747-400s for six weeks on the Denver route. We operate the 747-400 as a two-crew aircraft - captain and co-pilot - under normal circumstances. All the drills and so on are planned around that crew complement, but on longer flights, to provide in-flight rest, we carry either one extra member or sometimes a complete double crew, depending on the length of the flight. [The primary crew is referred to as the 'operating crew' and the secondary crew is known as the 'heavy crew'.] Denver is such that it triggers one extra crew member. We have three members so that we can play 'musical chairs' and get some rest during a long flight. [It is standard procedure for the operating crew to fly the 747 for the first few hours of the flight, while the third pilot rests and each can do this by either taking a nap on one of the two bunks in the cabin immediately behind the flight deck, or one of the very comfortable, fully reclining seats in Club Class.]

The CAA lays down rules and regulations for how long you can fly with a two-crew, a three-crew or a complete double crew and there is also an industrial agreement between the company and BALPA,[72] the pilots' union, which also controls the crew complement. [The over-riding legal restriction for flight crew is 100 actual flying hours in any twenty-eight-day period.] A short trip from say, London to New York, would be a two-crew operation, but as the flight extends out to Denver, where flight time is over

Captain Downey and Senior First Officer Alan Emery go through their pre-flight check-list. These duties are divided between the 'handling pilot' and the 'non-handling pilot'. For the flight to Denver the handling pilot was Alan Emery, and Captain Downey was the non-handling pilot, so the latter performed the scan check and prepared the performance calculations, while the senior first officer programmed the flight management computer with the route and appropriate performance data. Then the two pilots come back together as a team to read the check-lists and to go through various procedures. The check-lists confirm that the data that has been loaded is correct, and that the pilots are prepared for engine start. (Author)

nine hours, we require three and if we are going to Buenos Aires or Singapore/Australia, then it would require a double crew. The crew will bid for their work and they do this about a month ahead of the normal schedule. When they've got their trips, that's their planned roster for the month. Because the Denver operation is a substitution for a Triple 7, the trips went into the system relatively late and in fact one of the two co-pilot slots was not covered until the day before the flight and someone available was given it.

This slot was filled by 34-year old Dominic Boyle, who until 2½ years before was a 70 Squadron RAF Hercules pilot. Captain Downey's senior first officer for the Denver trip was Alan Emery (46), a pilot with over twenty years' flying experience. Although Captain Downey is in overall command of the flight, the operation of the 747-400 is a team effort. Apart from the flight crew, the sixteen cabin crew are on board to help ensure the safety of and to look after the 401 passengers seated in First (fourteen passengers), Club World (fifty-five) and World Traveller (332) (British Airways does not use the word 'class'). The captain and first officers are required to complete a set number of take-offs and landings over given periods to maintain their currency. This is quite difficult to achieve on the long-haul direct flights, such as Gatwick to Denver,

where flying hours often reach 9.5 hours outbound and about 9.02 hours inbound. To qualify for a flight, it might be necessary for a pilot to operate the flight simulator if he or she has not carried out a landing within the last twenty-eight days. For the same reason, automatic landings are only carried out when it is necessary, since only manual landings keep the crew member qualified.

Captain Downey continues: The crew meet at a report centre at Gatwick and receive their briefing. Some of this is pre-prepared and the briefing officer would just hand most of the paperwork over for self-briefing. [A comprehensive briefing summary is given to the captain for flight BA2019 on a ten-page computer printout, together with another ten-page printout giving up-to-date local weather at all the airfields and alternates along the route.] One of problems we had was that the computer system we used to check in to actually acknowledge the fact that we'd turned up for the trip, was unserviceable, which caused lots of other problems. Eventually, we got all our paperwork. At that stage we look at the AIS [Aeronautical Information Service] information and the weather information for our flight. This is collated into one document by British Airways systems and is called the 'New Brief'. That has all the NOTAMS and the

Delays put Speedbird 2019's take-all back from 10.35 to 12.05 and in that time burned an extra tonne of fuel. After push-back G-BNLR taxied out to Runway 26L. Virgin Atlantic's G-VMIA 747-123 Spirit of Sir Freddie *developed a technical fault just before take-off and had to return to its stand. This aircraft, the eighty-seventh 747 built, was delivered to American Airways in 1970 as N9669 and subsequently operated with Air Pacific (N14939), Cargolux (LX-NCV), Highland Express (G-HIHO), Qantas (VH-EEI) and Aer Lingus (El-CAI), before being obtained by Richard Branson's airline in 1990. At first VMIA was named* Miami Maiden, *and then in July 1992 it was renamed* Spirit of Sir Freddie *in honour of Sir Freddie Laker, a man who did more than most to promote cheaper air travel across the Atlantic. (Author)*

After take-off it was climb out and away up to the Moray Firth and Scottish Isles via the Midlands for its eventual departure across the Atlantic. First Officer Alan Emery maintains the throttle levers as the altimeter shows 13.400 feet and the airspeed indicator registers 350 knots. (Author)

meteorological information that we require for the flight. It's fine-tuned, filtered if you like, so that we do not end up having to look at every single piece of information that might be picked up on NOTAMs for Gatwick. It will just be the things we are interested in and it's the same for all the other airports on the route. That document is still quite long for a flight to Denver. The flight plan itself has already been computed using a system call SWORD, a computer system which resides in our reservations mainframe computer using the same language. The system takes meteorological data from Bracknell, Berkshire and Washington, for all the upper winds. [Both Met Offices have a Cray computer which runs a mathematical model of the upper wind data for the whole of the world. Each can carry out several billion floating-point calculations a second. They 'talk' to each other and provide back-up for each other as well.]

This, then, gives all the meteorological information we need. Load control will have worked out how many passengers they have got and the dispatch process will know what weight and what payload, the aircraft is looking to carry. That will be fed into the flight planning system along with the wind conditions on the route that will give us the fuel required. We look at that and also at the structure of the reserves that are given to us (that's because we need sufficient fuel to fly from Gatwick to Denver, but we also need sufficient fuel for any en-route contingencies that may occur. For example, there could be delays at the airport and the winds may not be quite what we expect. We also have to have sufficient fuel to fly from our destination to a suitable alternative, which for the Denver flight is Salt Lake City, Utah. So, all that added together comes up with the final fuel figure required - just under 120 tonnes. [73] We then confirm that that is the amount of fuel we require and that is then signalled out to the aircraft support team at the gate who make sure that the refueller knows that figure. This all happens at departure minus one hour.

'It was a day that did not start terribly well because of a bus delay, we actually arrived at the aircraft [at Remote Stand 65, far enough away from the North Terminal that both passengers and crew have to be bussed out to the 747], about thirty-five minutes before departure. Normally it is fifty-five minutes before departure. [This and a technical problem with an engine fire detection loop resulted in about an hour's delay getting the 747 away. Take-off was originally scheduled for 10.35am and during the delay and long taxi out, Speedbird 2019 burned about a thousand kilograms of fuel. This in itself was not a problem because a corresponding amount of fuel is always allowed for in the fuel plan at briefing.]

'When we arrive at the aircraft we have various checks to perform. One of the team [usually the pilot who is flying the aircraft on the route, i.e. the take-off and landing] will walk around the outside of the 747 and ensure that everything is serviceable, making sure that no trucks have been moved into the side of the aircraft, that no pitot head covers have been left on, that the tyres are in good condition, that there are no hydraulic leaks and so on. It is the same as a walk round on any other aeroplane, really.

'Meanwhile, if, on arrival in the cockpit, the ground engineers have not activated the 747's electrical and air supply, this will have been done by the crew. A safety check will have been made to ensure that the hydraulic pump selectors are off, the landing gear lever is selected 'down' and that the flap-lever position selector agree with the flaps. On the flight deck, the three inertial reference systems (IRS) are selected to navigation mode (NAV). Then the crew perform the cockpit pre-flight systems and equipment check, otherwise called a 'scan check'. Captain Downey explains: 'Basically, this is done using the instrument panel itself as a check-list and scanning around the panels in a pre-determined order, making sure that all the switches are in the right place, prior to departure. For the overall systems checks, the on-board computers combined with the EFIS (electronic flight instrument system) displays can be used for determining serviceability. Each check is called up on the EFIS and has to be satisfactory before the crew move on to the next item. Because two flight-crew operate the aircraft, the flight engineer duties have been built into the computers. The primary flight instruments are duplicated for both the captain and the first officer so that either can fly the 747 and the communications and systems are located centrally for easy access by both crew. Generally, the communications and navigation controls are located on

It's 14.45 and at 33,000 feet Iceland looms on the horizon. It is literally the icing on the cake for the flight crew, who have never seen Iceland this clear in the past thirty years. Ten minutes later the first pilot change is made when Dominic Boyle takes over from John Downey for his 'shift'. (Author)

a central console between the pilots, while the aircraft systems, such as fuel flow, air conditioning and electrics and so on, are mounted above the pilots in the cockpit ceiling. Additional controls on the central panel are for the Rolls Royce RB211-52224H engines, including thrust levers, starting and fuel cocks, plus trims for the ailerons and elevators. Captain Downey continues: 'The duties are divided between the 'handling pilot' and the 'non-handling pilot.' For the flight to Denver the handling pilot was Alan Emery and I was the non-handling pilot, so I performed the scan check and prepared the performance calculations, while Alan programmed the flight management computer with our route and appropriate performance data. Then we come back together as a team to read the check-lists and to go through various procedures. The check-lists confirm that the data that has been loaded is correct and that we are prepared for engine start. It means going through all sorts of things, basically a cross-checking process. That one person has loaded the route and someone else checks it, ensures that the distances between each position are correct and so on. It is quite a detailed cross-checking process, not necessarily for the whole route at this stage, but for sufficient so that we have time to go back into it in detail once we are in the cruise. You have at least made sure you are covered, up until entry into oceanic airspace. Quite often the routes are changed once you are in oceanic air-space anyway.

We then go into negotiating with ATC (air traffic control), which can be quite protracted. This is because aircraft going in particular directions have slot times, which is a way of controlling the number of aircraft in particular bits of airspace. In Europe, a particular bit of airspace or area can only accept a certain number of aircraft at a time. One of the ways of controlling congestion is by only allowing aircraft to take off for, say, Brussels, at a particular time, so there is always a gap in the airspace for the aircraft to enter. This means that aircraft that do not have particular constraints - and we were one of those - end up being pushed to the back of the queue. Gatwick is, to be honest, creaking at the seams: there is just one runway, but as many movements as at several large international airports with multiple runways. But ATC do a fantastic job.

'To add to the frustration, when we finally managed to get everything sorted out and on our way we had a minor technical problem: one of the fire detection loops on one of the engines was found to be unserviceable. The system is a dual logic system, so that if you have two loops working, you have to get warning on both of the loops to confirm a fire. If you have just one loop giving a warning it is considered a fault. When you have only one loop active, if that fire loop detects a warning you get a fire warning. Basically it means you could get a possible false

Greenland looks picturesque but distinctly uninviting as Speedbird 2019 passes majestically above the barren, rocky landscape at 34,000 feet. Outside air temperature at this height is -60°F (-51°C) - even the fuel temperature is -64°F (-53°C). (Temperature falls with altitude by about 3°F every 1,000 feet, reaching about -65°F (-54°C) by 36,500 feet before rising slightly after this.) With the 747's cruising speed of Mach 0.84, the temperature differences between outside air and surfaces (which are warmed by friction caused by the high-speed airflow) are 158°F (70°C). (Author)

warning. However, it is a perfectly acceptable thing to despatch the aircraft with.

'Once we get clearance to start up and push the aircraft back from the gate, we then go into another check-list, to make sure that we have appropriate hydraulics systems pressurized (to provide braking and steering for the body gear). Then we push the aircraft back and start the engines. These are started by the non-handling pilot; the handling pilot basically just keeps an overall watch on what's going on and communicates with the ground crew initially and the pilot starting the engines talks to the ground crew while the engines are actually starting. [The engines are started in the sequence: four, three, two, one, as number four engine normally powers the hydraulics which supply the main brakes.] We have a system on the 747-400 called Autostart, which enables us to start two engines at a time. The system automatically selects fuel and monitors the start sequence and will take action if any start malfunctions occur. On previous Jumbos we had to select fuel and monitor the engines ourselves. Usually, the engines on the Classic were started by the non-handling pilot and the flight engineer working together. The APU's [auxiliary power unit] pneumatics provides the air for starting the engines. [The APUs on the -400 each consists of a small turbine engine located in the rear portion of the tail-cone, which exhaust to the rear, driving two generators. With this unit running, electrical power is provided for the aircraft systems and pneumatics for the air-conditioning and cabin lights to either cool or heat the cabin.] If something like the EGT (exhaust gas temperature) gets too high [the maximum is 600°C] during the start, it will automatically cut the fuel off and cool the engine down before trying to restart it. If, for some reason, it is unsuccessful, it will come up and say 'I've tried my best and can't cope'. We would then look to do something manually. It is a very good system and it means that a very large aeroplane like a 747-400 can have all four engines running very quickly as we push back.

'As soon as the tug puts us in the position where he wants to disconnect, we have usually reached the stage where both pairs of engines are running. We then get clearance to taxi out, which is usually given as a sequence of coded letters for the appropriate taxiways, either numbers or letters (at Gatwick it is numbers). You have to make sure you taxi out on the centre lines you are supposed to and on a congested apron it is also important to keep a very good look Out [three pairs of eyes are used here] to make sure you don't have something parked where it is not supposed to be parked. Once you get out into more open taxi ways, it is usually not a problem. There are lots of other aircraft around at Gatwick - it's a very crowded place; even when you get out to the holding point (they have four different holding points at Gatwick to allow planes to overtake each other to meet various take-off departure

constraints) it is quite a complicated area.

'One of the other things you have to be very careful of with a large aircraft is the amount of thrust that you need to move. Exhaust velocity is significant and you have to be very careful about where you point it. If you are turning away from the terminal, with the exhausts of the engines pointing towards it, it is very important that you have only idle power on, as the exhausts play over the building. Otherwise you could get into terrible trouble - you could blow a car over if you put too much thrust on. Certainly things like empty containers can blow around on very low power settings.

'We get ourselves out to the holding point and then we are just in sequence for departure, awaiting our turn. When ATC give us clearance to line up, we taxi onto the runway. At the same time we perform the last part of the before-take-off check-list - the last-minute items, configuring the air-conditioning system and switching on the appropriate lights and warning the cabin crew that we are just about to take off. We do this by virtue of a chime that they can hear.

'The air-conditioning is quite interesting. On all commercial aeroplanes with large fan engines the air is bled off the engines to provide air-conditioning. On the 747-400 we have three packs which provide air-conditioning, but of course when they are operating you are actually taking air away from the engines, which under normal circumstances is compressed and mixed with fuel to provide extra thrust. So for take-off, you don't really want to have the air-conditioning on at all, because you want maximum thrust. However, for passenger comfort it is quite nice to be able to have one air-conditioning pack on, because then you don't get the sudden step-change that you notice on some of the short-haul aircraft where the air-conditioning suddenly kicks in. What we do is to use air from the APU to run one of the packs, so we have one pack running and the other two packs switched off for take-off. Then once we are airborne and have made the power reduction to climb-power, we can reinstate the other packs and shut down the APU.

'Once we are cleared for take-off, the technique is a matter of keeping the aircraft straight on the runway. You use what is called rudder fine steering; the rudder pedals also move the nose-wheel, so you use the rudder pedals in the same sense as you would to keep the aircraft straight with rudder, but that's also using the nose-wheel as well. Because there was a blustery wind and a slight crosswind, we also required a little bit of aileron into the wind to keep the wings level and you pre-set this to a guesstimated amount, so that you can then modulate it. Effectively, we fly the wings level down the runway; as the gusts come and you see a wing try a lift, you push it back down again.

You set the power by advancing the throttles manually until the engines have spooled up to a suitable stabilised power setting to enable you to accelerate the engines in unison.

'The handling pilot (Alan) does the take-off and landing and I will fly the approach into Denver and hand over control for the landing. One person flies the approach for the other pilot. When you 'stand the throttles up' you advance the throttles just enough until the engines have accelerated to about 1.1 to 1.2 EPR (exhaust pressure ratio). When we apply take-off power, we get smooth acceleration of all the engines [each of the four RR RB.211-524Hs is capable of producing 60,600lb thrust]. If we just put the throttles straight up to take-off power, one engine might well accelerate quicker than another from idle. You would end up with asymmetric power set and end up doing a very quick pirouette on the runway! This has happened. People have left the paved surface, more so in the early days with the classic engines. The older Pratt & Whitney engines were erratic in the way that they accelerated; but stabilizing the engines is something that we still do because it is important that you get smooth acceleration. You advance the power and the handling pilot just presses the take-off/go around (TO/GA) switches and that then programmes the auto-throttle to go up to the appropriate power settings. We derate power. We work out what the aircraft would actually take off at on that runway in representative conditions. If the aircraft is lighter than that performance limit, we can reduce the amount of thrust and this improves engine life. Basically, the hotter the engines get, the more effect on their life. If you can keep the thrust down and hence the turbine

inlet temperatures down, the engines last longer. You don't have to do a 'wheel spinning get-away from the traffic lights' every time!

Once we are accelerating down the runway, the next things to be looking at are the performance considerations - whether we can stop, or whether we have to continue. This is done during flight planning by calculating the speed to which the aircraft can accelerate (at its weight for the flight) and still be able to brake within the length of runway available. This speed is called 'V1'. It is also the speed at which, if one engine fails, you can still accelerate sufficiently to climb away safely from the runway on three engines. If the take-off has to be rejected prior to V1, the handling pilot closes the throttles, which engages autobrake RTO (rejected take-off): this routes full hydraulic pressure (3,000 psi) to the brake units. The brakes on a 747 are carbon-fibre, much the same as a Formula One racing car except that there are sixteen individual brakes, one on each of the main wheels and the brakes are actually multiple disk and pad packs, so you have rotors and stators, all made of carbon and they are all clamped together by hydraulic pressure. So effectively, you have got a lot more disks than a Formula One car, even though basically it is the same sort of technology. The brakes have to absorb the energy for a rejected take-off of the aircraft at the maximum take-off weight of just under 400 tons and travelling at about 180 knots. You can imagine the amount of energy this involves: it is an awful lot of juggernauts.

Speedbird 2019 lands at 14.28 local time and is directed to its stand (which incorrectly displayed '777' - this was the first flight of a BA 747 into DIA). Alan Emery taxied in perfectly, the engines were shut down and Captain Downey flicked the switches on the overhead panel. BNLA would be prepared for another crew and flown back to the UK on the next scheduled flight. After a lay-over in Denver, Captain Downey and his crew would board another 747 for an early evening departure for London-Gatwick. (Author)

'At V1 you are committed to take off. The handling pilot then removes his hands from the throttle levers and puts them on the control column. When we get to 'rotate' [VR] (we again use a calculated speed depending on the weight of the aircraft), the handling pilot initially pulls the column back smoothly to pitch the aircraft up to 12½ degrees; we do this over a period of about six seconds. If we rotate too quickly and pull the stick back sharply, there is a risk of striking the back of the aircraft on the ground; also, the aircraft will not accelerate to the correct speed, which is V2 (engine out safety speed), plus 10 knots. [VR and V2, calculated by the computer, are displayed on the flight management system (FMS)]. Conversely, if you rotate the aircraft too slowly it will accelerate too quickly and will be at too high a speed, but also it will not climb quite quickly enough and therefore you would not achieve the required gradients. So it is quite a critical manoeuvre. And if you have got a crosswind at that time, you are also transferring from having aileron into wind, to hold the wing down, to allowing the nose of the aircraft to layoff drift, so that you fly along the appropriate path with the ailerons level.

'You then follow the lateral navigation path that has been programmed into the flight management computer. If ATC want you to do anything other than the standard instrument departure; (or SID) that they have cleared you on, they will give a heading and you will then use the autopilot mode 'Heading Select' to fly the appropriate heading. Also, at that point, vertical navigation is engaged and that will follow a pre-programmed acceleration, enabling you to retract flaps.

'Out of London-Heathrow and London-Gatwick, we fly a specific noise abatement procedure, which means that at 1,000 feet above the ground we reduce power to climb-power and at the same time accelerate the aircraft to our Flap Ten speed plus 10 knots. We retract the flaps to Flap Ten and then climb at that speed. The take-off flap setting is twenty. Once we reach 3,000 feet we then accelerate and clean up the aircraft by retracting the flaps, using the various bugs which we pre-computed on the speed tape on the left-hand side of the PFD. Once the aircraft is clean, then our speed is unrestricted by ATC. We also have to bear in mind that if the path we want to follow is a fairly sharp turn, that we do not accelerate the aircraft too quickly because obviously, the faster the aircraft travels, the greater is the radius of turn and this might not be ideal in a crowded terminal control area. We then climb the aircraft using the computed speeds from the flight management computer (FMC), up to the cruising level. The handling pilot will then load in all the meteorological data on the various pages of

the flight plan, so that the FMC can compute a proper ETA at the appropriate altitudes that we are going to fly for the whole of the flight.

'The weight of fuel on this trip is 120 tonnes and a large percentage of this is carried in the wings. When the flaps have been retracted, the fuel system automatically reconfigures so that the centre tank (which is effectively in the middle of the wing inside the fuselage) will be feeding all the engines. The reason for this is that we want to retain the weight of fuel in the wings to provide 'bending relief' (the weight of the engines mounted under the wings also helps relieve the stress in the wings) because obviously, when the 747 is airborne, the wings are producing lift, so the force upwards is bending the wings upwards. Any weight in the wings is bending them downwards, so the more you can keep them in balance, the more the structure is unstressed. So we consume the fuel in the centre tank first and as the aircraft gets lighter it still has weight in the wings from the other fuel.

'Once the centre tank fuel is consumed, we then burn fuel from the two main inboard tanks (tanks two and three) until they equal the amount of fuel in the outboard tanks (one and four). Just before we start running the aircraft on what is called 'straight feed' (when all four tanks are equal), the four tonnes in the reserve tanks, which are the most

outboard tanks in the wings, is run into tanks two and three. This takes place just before we reach the straight feed configuration and basically, that is when there is enough room in the inboard tanks to take the additional four tonnes of fuel.

'We fly on our routing to the east of London, towards the Queen Elizabeth Bridge, then back west again, moving up, past Trent, Manchester, Nevis, Moray Firth and out towards the Western Isles and Stornaway. Our routing does not take us into the oceanic area controlled by Shanwick (the amalgamation of Shannon and Prestwick) because we are routing into Icelandic airspace (we actually obtained our Oceanic clearance as we entered Icelandic air-space). We then route up over Iceland, getting a fantastic view of that and then out over Greenland, before coming in over Labrador, Hudson Bay and across the Canadian border into the United States and on to Denver. As we have said, it is standard procedure in British Airways 747-400s that the handling pilot hands over the controls to the non-handling pilot for the descent, so in this case, as Alan Emery was going to do the landing, I took control of the aircraft for the descent, handing over to him again for the final landing. Again we programme the FMC to give us a vertical navigation profile which we follow, but in fact ATC were somewhat less than helpful and brought us above that

747-436 G-CIVM Nami Tsuru, *or Speedbird 2018, before the departure from Denver, Colorado, for London-Gatwick. The swirling design in blue and grey on the tail is a traditional Japanese art form known as 'Nihon Ga': the original painting on which the design is based is entitled 'Waves and Cranes'. (Author)*

Prior to the return flight to Gatwick the first task for Senior 1st Officer Alan Emery was to carry out the walk-around check on G-CIVM, He checked the nose-wheel gear for possible hydraulic leaks and looked over the tyres for possible cuts and signs of wear and tear and looked inside the RB.211 fan engine to inspect the blades; he then checked the rear cargo hold. He also examined the control surfaces checks that pitots and static vents were uncovered and that access panels were secured, as well as checking for signs of oil leaks and for skin and surface damage caused by foreign object damage (FOD). (Author)

profile - this resulted in an early selection of the undercarriage to increase drag and enable me to increase the rate of descent to get back onto the proper profile. Once we were established on the ILS I handed over to Alan, who continued, eventually disconnecting the autopilot and the auto throttle for a manual, crosswind landing.

'The reason we disconnect the auto-throttle as well as the autopilot when we are manually flying the aircraft, is because under certain circumstances the auto throttle can destabilise the speed. For example, if you pitch the aircraft up, the drag increases as you ask for more lift. The speed starts decreasing, so the auto-throttle would increase power. Now, with the 747, with the engines slung underneath the wing, this increase in thrust pitches the aircraft up. You therefore end up pitching up more than you want to, so you pitch down more. It ends up in what is technically called a 'fugoid'. If you actually control the throttles yourself, then you can co-ordinate more effectively.

'With a crosswind landing, like the one Alan executed perfectly coming in on Runway 25 at Denver, you have the aircraft with drift laid off to maintain the extended centreline of the runway. Then as you approach the flare manoeuvre, at about 30 feet above the ground, the aircraft is pitched up to reduce the rate of descent for a smooth touchdown and then at the same time, a gentle squeezing of downwind rudder yaws the aircraft round so that the fuselage is pointing down the runway. Simultaneously applying into-wind aileron to stop the windward wing pitching up obviously requires a fair amount of co-ordination.

'Once the aircraft has touched down, the nose is lowered towards the runway until the nose-wheel touches down. Simultaneously, the non-handling pilot will move the reverse levers up to the interlock, which makes the cowls translate on the engines and the blocker doors then move across, blocking the fan duct. This drags air from the fan, through a series of cascades - basically removing effective forward thrust. There is not that much of de-celerative component there. A pre-programmed autobrake setting would also have been selected prior to the approach and this will give a programmed amount of deceleration, so that we end up at the appropriate point on the runway to turn off. Once we turn off, the after-landing check is executed, which involves bringing the flaps in, lowering the speed brakes, starting the APU and basically switching off any items which are not required once we have turned off the runway, such as the strobe lights and the transponder. We taxi in towards the gate and at the appropriate time; make a P.A. announcement telling the cabin crew to select the doors to manual so that it is safe for ground crew to open doors without the risk of the slides inflating and causing injury.'

Captain John Downey goes through the pre-flight check-list with First Officer Dominic Boyle for the 16:00 departure to London-Gatwick. Because of the outside air pressure at Denver (which is 5,300 feet above sea level), the Autostart for two engines cannot be used; instead a manual start of each engine is carried out. (Author)

Runway 08 at Gatwick on Speedbird 2018's approach. Dominic Boyle piloting the 747-436 picks up the glide scope level at 3,000 feet, 12 miles out and is over the threshold at 142 knots. Captain Downey then gets a feel of the controls at 1,000 feet and brings the aircraft in for landing. Gear is down at 7.45am and he puts the aircraft down with a slight flare (the 747 is such a stable platform that pilots can flare a few feet (20-50 feet) off the ground. (Author)

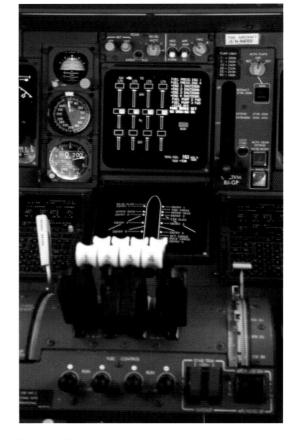

Speedbird 2018's engines are shut down. The two centrally located engine indication and crew alerting system (EICASI display units show the fuel pressures and that all four engines are shut down. The total fuel remaining is 22,266lb. Chock to chock, it has taken 9 hours 2 minutes since leaving Denver, Colorado. (Author)

Footnotes for Chapter 14

72   British Airline Pilots Association.
73   Annually, British Airways was using six million tonnes of fuel, costing £150-£400 per tonne; the cost of which was second only to salaries.

Chapter 16

Towards the 747-8

A380 and 747X are not aircraft in competition with each other - they are aircraft betting on which philosophy for reducing congestion is better-received. Both will receive orders, but Boeing has less committed and has less to lose in case their estimation is wrong; Airbus stands to lose or win big. In 2001 Boeing and Airbus agreed that air traffic would grow 5% annually over the next 20 years, resulting in a demand for at least 15 000 new airliners. The two manufacturers had different predictions for the way the airline industry would deal with the congestion that would result were the current model of air travel to continue. Boeing saw a growth in the number of airports and in direct flights between destinations, while Airbus anticipated the continuation of the hub-and-spoke system of air travel. The two manufacturers developed different solutions to the airport congestion problem to match their predictions of how the airlines would choose to meet the increasing demand on the air traffic system. Boeing, in accordance with its philosophy of improving the network of direct flights, was striving to improve the range on its existing 747 by enlarging and redesigning the wing and slightly stretching the fuselage and an increase in number of passengers would result, but the purpose of the redesign was clearly to increase the range rather than capacity - a gain of only 14 passengers would be made above the capacity of the 747-400. Airbus wanted to avoid overloading airports with aircraft by loading more passengers onto a single aircraft. The A380 would seat 555 passengers in a three-class cabin configuration and could conceivably be brought up to 880 passengers in a high-density layout.

747X vs. A380. How to Reduce Airport Congestion? [74]

The 747-8 (N747EX) on its first test flight on 20 March 2011.

Apart from the short-performance 747s in the Asia-Pacific network of operations, low-level studies conducted in the late 1980s indicated that there was a requirement for another special performance airliner, but at the very opposite end of the scale to the SP. In the 1980s the airline passenger market had not been ready for a big-winged and stretched behemoth; by the end of the decade, though, a combination of high economic growth in Asia (where air travel in 1996 was soaring by up to 10 per cent a year, twice the rate in the West) and dramatic new advances in aeronautical design, indicated

that for the first time there seemed a very real chance that a re-winged and stretched 747 could become a sustainable reality. Airlines now looked to manufacturers to produce an airliner capable of carrying between 600 and 800 passengers at distances of 8,625 statute miles and greater.

In 1988, the product development group at Boeing unveiled its potentially re-winged and stretched 747 design, the '47-X'. It was made possible by features previously denied to earlier development engineers: more efficient engines, composite materials and

The 747-8 flight deck.

747-8F N5017Q the first 747-8 Freighter completes first flight on 8 February 2010.

improved systems were now available. Most important of all, high-aspect wing designs were now so far advanced that reduced sweep angle could be used and huge spans in the region of 240 to 260 feet were possible. Bigger wings meant longer fuselages and a fuselage stretch of about 24 feet using two 12 feet plugs was therefore possible. Longer fuselages meant greater payload, though the new wing would increase gross weight to more than 1,000,000lb. In 1991 United Airlines asked Boeing to carry out studies of an all-new long-range airliner capable of carrying 650 passengers over the vast tracts of the Pacific.

Early in 1992 Boeing invited United and other airlines to form a select group to study data on proposed new large aircraft (NLA) designs provisionally called the N650 or 747-X. In actuality, the designs involved well in excess of one hundred different configurations, the largest of which bore a wing 290 feet wide - 79 feet wider than that used on the 747-400. With wings this wide, folding wing-tips, as developed for the 777, would have to be used if the aircraft was to use gates existing at airports. Take-off weights peaked at an incredible 1.7 million pounds (the -400's gross weight by comparison, is around 870,000lb), with seating for up to 750 passengers in three classes. These would have to be accommodated in rows of seats twelve abreast on the lower deck and eight to nine abreast on the upper deck. The high gross weight would have to be redistributed using a new, main gear design of up to twenty-four main wheels mounted on four main trucks. Even so, after studying the structures of runways and taxiways at seventy of the world's leading airports, it was reckoned that seventeen runways would have to be strengthened and resurfaced. In fact the 747-X was so big that TV cameras, which initially were thought necessary on the very first 747, would have to make their reappearance,

to help the pilots during taxiing at airports.

There were many other important considerations too, not least the greatly increased loading and unloading times, additional meals and galleys that would be needed, the bigger door sizes and increased fuel and so on - but there was also, of course, the usual major stumbling block, the all-important question of suitable engines to power the huge beast! Not only had they to be capable of about 85,000lb of thrust in the climb to lift a 650-seat 747- X into the air, they also had to conform to 'Stage 3 minus' noise parameters and be capable of expansion to power the larger 800-seat 747-X version. The Treble Seven was to show that engines capable of developing the high climb-thrust needed were possible. The three leading engine manufacturers - Pratt & Whitney (PW 4000 series); General Electric (GE90 series) and Rolls Royce (Trent 800 series) - developed more efficient and quieter turbofans to power the Boeing 777. For the initial aircraft, these engines are rated in the 74,000-77,000lb-thrust class. For the longer-range model and the 777-300, these engines are capable of thrust ratings in the 84,000-90,000lb category. These engines could be developed to even higher thrust ratings, depending on future payload and range requirements. Key factors in their performance are new, larger-diameter fans with wide-chord fan blade designs and bypass ratios ranging from 0-to-1 to as high as 9-to-1. Ironically, while the engine technology, for the first time in the 747's operational career, would become available to power this next generation of airliners, there was another technological stumbling block to overcome. By the middle of 1992 two of the three main proposals that emerged from the myriad selection of big-winged and stretched 'super jumbo' designs were stretched developments of the 747-400, but they retained the existing wing design and consequently they would be penalized by the all-too-familiar range restrictions. The basic stretched version, with an increased length of 24 feet achieved by inserting two 12 feet plugs fore and aft of the wing, an empty weight of 438,000lb and seating for up to 480 passengers, would have at least 435 miles less range than the -400.

The third increased stretch variant, 23 feet longer than the -400 and which could potentially carry up to 630 passengers, would have at least 870 miles less range than the -400 and fly only about the same maximum distance as the -200B. Wing-tip winglets (as on the 747-400 series), wing-root extensions and composite materials all offered a modest increase in range, but without a complete wing redesign, it was impossible to dramatically redevelop the 747 configuration further. The third option, therefore - an all-new double-deck NLA - introduced a complete departure from the established 747 design by having four engines mounted on a 258 feet wide high-aspect-ratio-wing, the wing type favoured for use on new-generation airliners such as the Airbus 300 and 310.

One problem with the reduced wing thickness/chord ratio (span, or length, relative to its chord, or breadth) and high sweep-back of the wings as used in the 747 series is that almost all the lift comes from the upper surface just behind the leading edge. The violent acceleration across this area produces intense lift, or suction, but its shape results in supersonic speed being attained at a very low mach number and shock waves build up and cause drag. In the 1960s a wing profile with a reduced curvature, or flatter top, a bulged under-side and down-curved trailing edge, was found to be more efficient than a thinner wing with sweep back. This 'super-critical' (or 'aft-loaded') wing is more efficient in the cruise as the aft-loaded cross-section distributes lift more evenly across the upper surfaces. This creates improved lift because the acceleration across the top of the wing is milder, the onset of supersonic shock-waves is delayed and as a consequence, the cruising speed is greatly increased and the fuel savings are enormous.[75] A thicker wing also enables more fuel to be carried and because much thinner skins are used, there is a marked saving in weight. The higher landing and operating empty weights of the 747-X would have required the use of a thicker-skinned wing then under development for the -400F.

In view of the range penalties associated with the stretch developments on the 747-based versions and the advantages of the all-new aircraft, most in the airline group not surprisingly favoured further study of the

747-8 test aircraft being assembled at Everett.

The massive Boeing Aircraft construction building at Everett - located on the northeast corner of Paine Field, it is the largest building in the world by volume at 13,385,378 m3 (472,370,319 cu ft) and covers 399,480 m2 (98.3 acres).[1] It is where wide-body Boeing 747s, 767s, 777s, and the new 787 Dreamliner are assembled.

NLA. Other aerospace companies, notably Airbus Industrie in Europe and McDonnell Douglas in the US, were, by 1992, showing signs of unleashing their own long-range, high-capacity aircraft. (Airbus carried out studies into a 600-plus ultra high-capacity aircraft (UHCA) by mating two A340 fuselages together side by side and an 800-seater version was even considered. However the projected MD-12 double-deck, long-range design series, planned to become available in six versions and carrying 430-511 passengers over distances of 6,950 miles and 6,260 miles respectively, never left the drawing-board because of the failure to cement links with proposed partner Taiwan Aerospace.) Boeing's all-new double-deck NLA, meanwhile, would offer accommodation for 600 passengers in its primary 235 feet-long configuration, while the stretched configuration, which was more than 300 feet long, would carry more than 750 passengers. Range was anticipated to be in the order of 6,957 miles.

Not for the first time in developments of this magnitude, cost was proving prohibitive. At the beginning of 1993 Boeing tried to spread the huge investment in the NLA by entering into partnership with a consortium made up of four European aerospace companies to develop a very large commercial transport (VLCT).[76] By late 1993, meanwhile, Boeing had arrived at five distinct single- and double-deck NLA configurations, the largest of which could carry 630 passengers. However, having got this far, the NLA finally went the same way as the VLCT when it was decided that the market for the all-new aircraft was too small for the huge investment needed.

It is often said that the only replacement for a DC-3 is another DC-3 and the only improvement on the C-130 Hercules is the next Hercules. By the mid-1990s most of the leading airlines were of the opinion that the only way to improve the 747 was a revamped, re-winged 747, one to carry fewer, not more, passengers than the abandoned NLA, UHCA and VLCT projects. Boeing and the leading carriers knew that the market for very large airliners was not big enough to warrant spending millions of dollars on developing or operating such massive aircraft. Yet soon almost twenty carriers, principally British Airways and Singapore Air Lines and others with substantial 747 fleets, were showing great interest in reviving the 747-X. Not for the first time in

City of Everett *acting as a flying test bed with the Rolls-Royce Trent 800. (Rolls-Royce)*

the 747's long and outstanding career, commonality was a key factor in the decision-making process, not only for the airlines, but for Boeing itself. While the advantages of the 747-X for existing 747 carriers were obvious, the derivative design would also enable Boeing to use many tried and tested components designed for the 747-400 and the 777.[77] This is not to say that the issue was as clear-cut as this: in a way Boeing was by now a victim of its own success. On the international routes their medium-sized 757 and 767 twins were proving more economical for the airlines than a half-empty 747. Whilst commonality with the design of the 747's systems offered many cost savings, the 747-X would require a super-critical wing and also some potential 747-X customers wanted a 747 with appreciably more range, while others wanted much more payload capacity than the 747-400.

Boeing's approach to achieving these aims, while at the same time keeping development, production and end-user costs down, was to use avionics and flight-deck architecture developed for the 747-400 and 777. The super-critical wing for the 747-X would be a 40 per cent scaled-up version of the aft-loaded structure used on the 717 and the gear would be the same six-wheel wing main undercarriage used on the wide-bodied twin-jet. The engines would be a derivative of the Trent 800 which powers the 777. No one airline has exactly the same requirements as another and while this had always been the case with the 747, it was not about to change with the 747-X. Predictably, the gross weight of the -500X and -600X began to rise sharply with increases in the payload demanded by the airlines and engine-thrust would have to rise accordingly.

Finally, a powerplant that was capable of producing between 77,000-80,000lb of take-off thrust (a higher ratio of climb thrust to take-off thrust was needed to provide a higher initial cruise altitude than that of existing 747s) was identified. (Historically, thrust requirements have increased typically by up to 4 per cent a year.) In 1995 there was only one engine entirely suitable and that was the Trent 800 series. Although four Trent 800s would be too powerful for the 747 (in January 1995 this engine was certificated to 90,000lb, by de-rating them, they would then be ideal for the 747-X. The Trent also had two other distinct advantages; it would meet the all-important noise regulation requirements and the 110 inch diameter fan was small enough to fit underneath the 747-X's new wing.

A big fan engine with a high bypass ratio of up to thirteen presents additional problems to the plane makers. Putting four engines with 160 inch fans - 13 feet - on a future, very large aircraft is a nightmare scenario: the size of the landing gear and the additional weight penalty this incurs will be enormous. Another issue that confronts engine designers when planning a powerplant with a bypass ratio of nine and above is the use of a gearbox versus direct drive. John Cundy, writing in 1995, explains: A gearbox allows optimization of the rotational speeds of the fan and the low-pressure turbine that drives it. With direct drive, you have to increase the number of low-pressure stages. For example, an engine with a bypass ratio of ten would require six low-pressure stages. But an engine having a ratio of thirteen would need only three stages if it had a gearbox. However, the reduction gear power for a 100,000lb-thrust engine is 80,000 horsepower. With an assumed transmission efficiency of 99 per cent, the waste heat to be managed in the cooling systems is high - 800hp - that's equivalent

Above: Cargolux 747-8F N5573S over Fresno, California.

Right: Two Cargolux 747-8F freighters on the ramp. (Cargolux)

to the combined power of eight 1.5 litre cars! The trade lies between the weight and cost of the direct drive's increased number of low-pressure stages and the gearbox, with its oil and cooling systems but many fewer stages.'

Left floundering in Rolls' wake, General Electric and Pratt & Whitney announced on 8 May 1996 that they were jointly developing a new powerplant for the 747-500X and -600X. The proposed GP7176 turbofan would involve GE manufacturing the high-pressure part of the engine, including a GE-developed double annular combustor to conform to the latest environmental regulations and P&W would take responsibility for the low-pressure area, including the 110 inch-diameter fan. Rolls responded in July with the announcement that they were developing the Trent 900 for the 747-X. So what had started out as an off-the-shelf and therefore low-cost option had become a race to develop an all-new engine for the 747-X and this only succeeded in substantially increasing the cost of the new airliner.

Bigger airliners were seen as a solution to the already highly congested hubs that would simply be unable to cope with the sheer weight of aircraft movements and slots that are possible. Boeing announced the 747-500X and -600X at the 1996 Farnborough Airshow. The proposed models would have combined the 747's fuselage with a new 251 feet span wing derived from the 777. Other changes included adding more powerful engines and increasing the number of tyres from two to four on the nose landing gear and from 16 to 20 on the main landing gear. The 747-500X concept featured an increased Fuselage length of 18 feet to 250 feet long and the aircraft was to carry 462 passengers over a range up to 8,700 nautical miles (10,000 miles) with a gross weight of over 1.0 Mlb. The 747-600X concept featured a greater stretch to 279 feet with seating for 548 passengers, a range of up to 7,700 nmi (8,900 miles) and a gross weight of 1.2 Mlb. A third study concept, the 747-700X, would have combined the wing of the 747-600X with a widened fuselage, allowing it to carry 650 passengers over the same range as a 747-400. In the mid-1990s British Airways calculated that by 2010 it could double the number of passengers using Heathrow Airport to 36 million passengers by increasing its fleet by just twelve 747-X aircraft. But the cost of the changes from previous 747 models, in particular the new wing for the 747-500X and -600X, was estimated to be more than US$5 billion.

Although the operating costs of the 747-X were 10 per cent lower than that of the 747-400 the development costs escalated from about $1 billion to a staggering $7 billion and the basic 747-X was expected to cost in the region of $200 million. This was way too high when compared to the 'sticker' price of high-tech, fuel-efficient, wide-bodied twins like the 757/767 and the Airbus Industrie A300 series. Apart from the initial outlay, airlines had also to consider the operating costs of the 500X and 600X when compared to the more economical wide-bodied twins such as the 767-200/300ER and A310 and A300-600R. They were making the Transatlantic and long over-water Pacific routes their domain because they could fly directly to their destinations and had no need to use the traditional hubs like New York or London to transfer their passengers. [78] Although the technology was clearly available for a 600-seat airliner powered by four 80,000lb-thrust engines to become reality the airlines, conscious of the fact that it was more profitable to operate medium-size twins on these point-to-point services than to fly sometimes less-than-full 747s, saw 747-X as being uncompetitive in the new order. The 747-X design was less costly than the 747-500X and -600X but it was criticized for not offering a sufficient advance from the existing 747-400. The 747-X family was shelved along with the 767-400ERX in March 2001. Development energies would instead concentrate on the proposed 767-400ERX and 777-200X/300X long-range, high-capacity wide-body twins and the 747-400X being developed concurrently moved into production to become the 747-400ERX. Boeing also

Staircase leading up to the main deck of the 747-8I.

continued to study improvements that could be made to the 747. The 747-400XQLR (Quiet Long Range) was meant to have an increased range of 7,980 nmi (9,200 miles). Changes studied included raked wingtips similar to those used on the 767-400ER and a saw tooth engine nacelle for noise reduction. Although the 747-400XQLR did not move to production, many of its features were used for the 747 Advanced, which Boeing announced early in 2004.

Similar to the 747-X, the stretched 747 Advanced would use technology from the Boeing 787 Dreamliner to modernize the design and its systems. It would be quieter, more economical and more environmentally friendly than previous versions of the 747. On 14 November 2005 as the Airbus A380 was making its demonstration tour in the Asia-Pacific area, Boeing announced that it was launching the 747 Advanced as the 'Boeing 747-8'. Despite initial plans for a shorter stretch than the 747-8F freighter model both the 8I and the 8F feature a fuselage stretch of 18.3 feet over the 747-400, bringing the total length to 250 feet 2 inches, marking the first stretch variant of the 747 family. The 747-8 is the world's longest passenger airliner, surpassing the Airbus A340-600 by approximately 3 feet. With a maximum take-off weight of 975,000lb the 747-8 is the heaviest aircraft, commercial or military, manufactured in the United States. The passenger version is designed to carry up to 467 passengers in a 3-class configuration and fly more than 8,000 nmi at Mach 0.855. This is 51 more passengers and two more freight pallets with 26% more cargo volume than the 747-400. The upper deck is lengthened on the -8I. New engine technology and aerodynamic modifications allow longer range. Boeing has stated that compared to the 747-400, the -8I is to be 30% quieter, 16% more fuel-efficient and have 13% lower seat-mile costs with nearly the same cost per trip. For the 747-8, Boeing has proposed some changes to the interior layout of the aircraft. Most noticeable is the curved stairway to the upper deck and a more spacious main passenger entrance. The 747-8's main cabin uses an interior similar to that of the 787. Overhead bins are curved and the centre row is designed to look as though it is attached to the curved ceiling, rather than integrated into the ceiling's curve like on the 777. The windows are also of similar size to the type used on the 777, which are 8% larger than those on the current 747-400s. The 747-8 features a new solid-state light-emitting diode (LED) lighting system, which can create mood lighting. LED technology also offers improved reliability and lower maintenance costs.

Further down the aircraft, it has been proposed to place cabin-accessible facilities in the 'crown' area, the space above the passenger cabin, previously used for air-conditioning ducts and wiring. The wiring and ducts are moved to the side to create extra space; as a consequence, this area will not have windows. The added space can be used for galleys and crew rest areas, freeing up main deck space for additional passenger seating. During the initial 747-8 marketing phase, Boeing also proposed creating a revenue-generating 'SkyLoft' passenger facility in the crown space. This facility would include 'SkySuites', small individual compartments with sliding doors or curtains, featuring beds, seating and entertainment or business equipment. A common lounge area could also be provided. Boeing also proposed smaller, more modest 'SkyBunks'. Access to the crown area would be via a separate stairway at the rear of the aircraft. Passengers using the SkySuites, sold at a premium price, would sit in regular economy class seats for take-off and landing and move to the crown area during flight. However, pricing feasibility studies found the SkyLoft concept difficult to justify. In 2007 Boeing dropped the SkyLoft concept in favour of upper-deck galley storage options, which were favoured by the airlines. Outfitting the crown space for sleeping remains an option on VIP aircraft.

For airlines seeking very large passenger airliners, the 747-8 and the Airbus A380, a full-length double-deck aircraft now in service, have been pitched as

The 747-8I main deck.

competitors on various occasions. Boeing claims that the 747-8 is more than 10 percent lighter per seat and is to consume 11 percent less fuel per passenger than the A380, translating into a trip-cost reduction of 21 percent and a seat-mile cost reduction of over 6 percent. And, Boeing claimed that it is able to use 210 airports around the world without expensive infrastructure modifications. At its introduction, the 747-8 surpassed the A340-600 as the world's longest airliner and is the largest commercial aircraft built in the United States.

As a derivative of the 747-400, the 747-8 has the economic benefit of similar training and interchangeable parts and was intended to use the same General Electric GEnx-2B67 turbofan and cockpit technology as that of the 787 and partial fly-by-wire. The GEnx is the only engine available for the 747-8. It is one of the two powerplant choices offered for the 787. The 747 engine variant has been adapted to provide bleed air for conventional aircraft systems and feature a smaller diameter to fit on the 747 wing. The flight tests of the GEnx 2b engine fitted to a Boeing 747-100 aircraft at the left inner engine began in March 2009. [79]

Compared to the 747-400, the main changes have been on the wings, which have undergone a complete design overhaul. The sweep and basic structure has been kept to contain costs, but the wing is thicker and deeper, with the aerodynamics recalculated. The pressure distribution and bending moments are different, with the new wing for the passenger version holding 64,225 US gallons (243,120 litres) of jet fuel and the cargo aircraft 60,925 US gallons (230,630 litres). The new wing features single-slotted outboard flaps and double-slotted inboard flaps. Raked wingtips similar to the ones used on the 777-200LR, 777-300ER and 787 aircraft are used on the new 747 variant instead of winglets used on the 747-400. These wingtip structures help reduce the wingtip vortices at the lateral edges of the wings, decreasing wake turbulence and drag and thereby increasing fuel efficiency. Another effort to reduce weight is the introduction of fly-by-wire technology for the majority of the lateral controls. The extra fuel capacity in the redesigned wing compared to the 747-400 eliminates the need to radically change the horizontal tail unit to accommodate auxiliary tanks, further saving costs. The 747-8's vertical tail unit is largely unchanged with a height of 63 feet 6 inches. The lower rudder has changed from single-jointed to double-jointed in order to increase its effect in the event of two engines failing on the same side. Some carbon fibre-reinforced plastic is part of the 747-8's airframe to reduce weight. However, structural changes are mostly evolutionary, rather than revolutionary with respect to

Virgin Atlantic 747-400 G-VAST in flight.
(Virgin Atlantic)

the 747-400.

Cargolux and Nippon Cargo Airlines were the first customers for the 747-8, placing orders for the freighter variant in November 2005. The firm configuration of the aircraft was finalized in October 2006. Lufthansa became the first airline to order the 747-8 Intercontinental on 6 December 2006. Boeing stated firm configuration for the -8I was reached in November 2007. Airlines including Emirates and British Airways considered ordering the 747-8 Intercontinental, but opted to purchase the Airbus A380 instead. Boeing Chairman and Chief Executive Jim McNerney acknowledged in a conference call to Boeing's investors in April 2008 that he would like to see more orders for the passenger version of the 747-8.

The 747 has proven to be a very popular freighter, carrying around half of the world's air freight. In an effort to maintain this dominant position, Boeing designed a freight variant of the 747-8, named the 747-8 Freighter or 747-8F, which is derived from the 747-400ERF. The variant has 16 percent more payload capacity than its predecessor, allowing it to carry seven additional standard air cargo containers, with a maximum payload capacity of 154 tons of cargo but it has less range than the 747-400ERF. When Boeing launched the -400ERF, all of the 35,000 lb increase in

MTOW over the 747-400F 875,000-910,000 lb allowed airlines to take off with more fuel, burn it during flight and land at the same weight as the regular 747-400F. This increased the range of the 747-400ERF compared to the 747-400F. Cargo carriers often move machinery or indivisible loads that require an aircraft with a higher payload and landing capability. As is common with cargo planes, range is given with maximum payload, not fuel. The 747-8s 65,000lb MTOW increase has been directed exclusively to its Zero-Fuel weight or payload capacity. If taking off at maximum payload, the 747-8 takes off with its tanks not full. On trips where the payload is not at maximum, it can take on more fuel and extend its range.

As on previous 747 freighters, the 747-8F features an overhead nose-door to aid loading and unloading. As on the 747-400F, the upper deck is shorter than passenger models; the 18 feet 3$^{1}/_{2}$ inches stretch is just before and just aft of the wing. With a 975,000 lb maximum take-off weight, it is to have a total payload capability of 308,000lb and a range of 4,390 nmi. Four extra pallet spaces were created on the main deck, with either two extra containers and two extra pallets, or three extra pallets, on the lower deck. The 747-8F was expected to achieve a 16% lower ton-mile operating cost than the 747-400F and offer a slightly greater range.

Major assembly of the first 747-8 Freighter began in Everett on 8 August 2008 [80] On 14 November Boeing announced a delay to the 747-8 programme, citing limited availability of engineering resources, design changes and the recent strike by factory workers. In February 2009 only one airline customer (Lufthansa) had ordered the 747-8I passenger model and Boeing chief executive officer Jim McNerney stated that continuation of the project was not a foregone conclusion. The company was assessing various options. On 21 July Boeing released a photograph of the first freighter version, its fuselage and main wing assembled. In October the Company announced that it had delayed the first flight on the 747-8 until first quarter 2010 and delayed 747-8I delivery. Boeing took a US $1-billion charge against its earnings for this delay. In response, launch customer Cargolux stated it still intended to take delivery of the thirteen freighters it had ordered and Lufthansa confirmed its commitment to the passenger version. On 12 November 2009 Boeing announced that Cargolux's first 8F was fully assembled and entering the

Everett plant's paint shop. It would undergo flight testing prior to delivery. On 4 December Korean Air became the second airline customer for the -8 passenger model, with an order for five airliners. The 747-8's first engine runs were completed that same month. Boeing announced the new model had successfully completed high-speed taxi tests on 7 February 2010.

On 8 January 2010 Guggenheim Aviation Partners (GAP) announced the reduction of its -8F order from four to two aircraft. On 8 February, after a 2½-hour weather delay, the 747-8 Freighter made its maiden flight, taking off from Paine Field, Washington at 12:39 PST (Pacific Standard Time) and landed at 4:18 pm PST. Boeing estimated that more than 1,600 flight hours would be needed in order to certify the 747-8. The second test flight in late February, a ferry flight to Moses Lake, Washington, tested new navigation equipment. Further flight testing was to take place in Moses Lake, conducting initial airworthiness and flutter tests, before moving to Palmdale, California for the majority of flight tests, so as to not interfere with 787 flight tests based

out of Boeing Field in Seattle. By 11 March the 747-8F had flown thirteen flights for a total of 33 hours of flying time. Four days' later the second 747-8F first flew from Paine Field to Boeing Field, where it was briefly based before moving to Palmdale to continue flight testing with the first -8F. On 17 March the third -8F made its first flight and joined the test programme. Boeing planned to display the 747-8F at the 2010 Farnborough Air Show, along with the 787, although appearances by both aircraft were contingent on flight testing remaining on schedule. During the flight tests, Boeing discovered a buffet problem with the aircraft, involving turbulence coming off the landing gear doors interfering with the inboard flaps. Boeing undertook an evaluation of the issue, which included devoting the third test aircraft to investigating the problem. The issue was resolved by a design change to the outboard main landing gear doors. In early April 2010 Boeing identified a possible defect in a part at the top of the fuselage called a longeron. According to Boeing, the parts, manufactured by subcontractor Vought Aircraft Industries, were, under

certain loads, susceptible to cracking. Boeing said that the issue would not affect flight testing, but other sources stated that the problem could impact the operating envelope of the aircraft until it is fully repaired. Two other problems were found, with oscillation in the inboard aileron and a structural flutter. Combined, these problems slowed flight testing and used up almost all the margin in Boeing's development schedule. On 19 April the second flight-test aircraft was moved from Moses Lake to Palmdale to conduct tests on the aircraft's engines in preparation for obtaining a type certification for the aircraft. The remaining aircraft in the test fleet were scheduled to be moved to Palmdale during May. It was reported on 3 June that an engine on the second 747-8F was struck by a tug during a ground move. The engine cowling was damaged, but there was no damage to the engine itself. After repairs the aircraft was able to perform fuel efficiency testing.

On 21 April 2010 Jim McNerney announced that Boeing would be accelerating the production of both the 747 and 777 to support increasing customer demand.

747-409(LCF) N708BA Dream Lifter at Anchorage September 2008. The 747-400 Dreamlifter (originally called the 747 Large Cargo Freighter or LCF) is a Boeing-designed modification of existing 747-400s to a larger configuration to ferry 787 Dreamliner sub-assemblies. Evergreen Aviation Technologies Corporation of Taiwan was contracted to complete modifications of 747-400s into Dreamlifters in Taoyuan. The aircraft flew for the first time on 9 September 2006 in a test flight. Modification of four aircraft was completed by February 2010. The Dreamlifters have been placed into service transporting sub-assemblies for the 787 programme to the Boeing plant in Everett, Washington, for final assembly. The aircraft is certified to carry only essential crew and not passengers. (Gerry Manning)

Above: Lufthansa 747-8I D-ABYA.

Main picture: Cargolux 747-8F on the ramp. (Cargolux)

Major assembly of the first 747-8I began on 8 May 2010. The final body join occurred on 15 October 2010, slightly ahead of the projected schedule. It was announced on 14 June that the 747-8 had completed the initial phase of flight-worthiness testing and that the FAA had given Boeing an expanded type inspection authorization for the aircraft. By the end of June the three 747-8Fs that composed the flight-test programme had flown a total of over 500 hours and had completed hot-weather testing in Arizona. Boeing now determined that a fourth -8F aircraft was needed to help complete flight testing and the second production aircraft, RC503, was used to conduct the non-instrumented or minimally-instrumented tests such as HIRF and Water Spray Certifications. The aircraft, painted in delivery customer Cargolux's new livery, first flew on 23 July. On 21 August the 747-8F took off from the Victorville, California runway weighing 1,005,000lbs. Its design

maximum take-off weight (MTOW) is 975,000lbs. (The fifth 747-8F joined the flight-test effort with its first flight on 3 February 2011). On 30 September Boeing announced a further postponement, with the delivery of the first freighter to Cargolux planned for mid-2011. (The first freighter version was delivered to Cargolux on 12 October). As of December the 747-8 had received 106 total orders, including 70 for the -8F and 36 for the -8I. [81]

Assembly of first 747-8I was completed in February 2011, before being unveiled at a roll out ceremony in Everett, Washington on 13 February. At the time, deliveries were set to begin in late 2011. In March Korean Air converted options into a firm order for two additional -8 freighters. Gauntlet ground testing of the -8I, which tests systems by simulating flight conditions, took place on 12 and 13 March. The 747-8I's first flight occurred on 20 March from Paine Field in Everett, Washington, the second 747-8I flying on 26 April. The 747-8F received its amended type certificate jointly from the Federal Aviation Administration (FAA) and European Aviation Safety Agency (EASA) on 19 August. Freighter deliveries were to begin on 19 September. Then on 17 September Cargolux announced that it would not accept the first two 747-8Fs scheduled for delivery on September 19 and 21 September 2011, due to 'unresolved contractual issues between Boeing and Cargolux' with the aircraft. Boeing handed over the first 747-8F to Cargolux in Everett, Washington on 12 October. The freighter then flew to Seattle-Tacoma International Airport and picked up cargo before flying to Luxembourg. At its six-month service mark, Boeing announced that initial 747-8F operators had achieved a l-percent reduction in fuel burn over projections.

On 25 October 2011 the 747-8I flew to Grantley Adams International Airport in Barbados to begin flight testing in the tropical climate of the Caribbean to determine its effects on the aircraft. The Boeing 787 Dreamliner preformed similar testing at Barbados the previous week. One test -8I was used for an evaluation by Lufthansa in early December before first delivery in early 2012. Three 747-8I aircraft had taken part in flight testing by December 2011 and the 14th of the month the 747-8I received its type certificate from the FAA. At that time, -8I deliveries were planned to begin in early 2012. The first 747-8 Intercontinental was delivered to a VIP customer on 28 February 2012. It is to be outfitted with a VIP interior before entering service in 2014. (In 2010 South Korea government sources indicated that the country was considering purchasing the 747-8 to serve as the country's presidential aircraft). After resolving their contractual issues, Lufthansa received its first 747-8I on 5 May 2012 and began operating the 747-8I on flights from Frankfurt to Washington, DC on 1 June. Flights from Frankfurt to Delhi, Bangalore, Chicago and Los Angeles were added later.

The US Air Force is seeking to upgrade Air Force One by replacing the Boeing VC-25 (two heavily modified 747-200Bs). Boeing is reported to be exploring a 747-8 proposal, along with a Boeing 787 Dreamliner variant.

Footnotes for Chapter 15

74 Geoffrey Buescher AOE 4984, *Configuration Aerodynamics* 22 March 2001.

75 Whereas the 707 has a ratio of 7, the A310 reaches 8.8 and the A320, 9.4.

76 The potential market for such a large aircraft was finally deemed too small and in July 1995 the VLCT project was put on hold.

77   The latter, the world's largest twin-jet, was first delivered in May 1995

78 In 1998 eighteen 747s were produced and in 1999 fourteen were finished.

79 In September 2012 the Federal Aviation Administration issued an airworthiness directive, ordering immediate inspections of 787 Dreamliner and 747-800 GEnx 1B and 2B engines after three GEnx engine failures in three months that could potentially lead to the loss of the aircraft. Two Dreamliners assembled but not yet delivered to customers were still being operated by Boeing in July and August when fractures in the fan mid shaft were discovered. On 11 September a 747-800 Airbridge Cargo flight, with the same GEnx engines experienced an engine shutdown during the takeoff roll from Shanghai Pudong International on September 11. The AirBridge engine had accumulated 1,200 hours and 240 cycles. The takeoff was aborted and damage was found in the low pressure turbine along with broken fan blades and was similar to the damage seen on the first Dreamliner engine failure during a test flight in July at the Boeing assembly plant in Charleston. The GEnx is the first with carbon fibre fan blades and fan case and performs with 15 percent reduction in fuel burn. It is also cleaner and quieter.

80 The aircraft first left Boeing's Everett factory on 12 November 2009

81 On 7 March 2011 it was announced that Air China had agreed to purchase five 747-8Is, pending approval by the Chinese government. On 20 June 2011 at the Paris Air Show, Boeing announced that it had received two orders and 15 commitments from two different undisclosed users for the -8I. Then GE Capital Aviation Services (GECAS) agreed to buy two freighters the next day. On 6 October Arik Air was announced as the customer for two 747-8Is; the airline was previously identified as an unidentified customer for the order at the Paris Air Show. On 8 November 2011 it was reported that Transaero had preliminarily agreed to purchase four 747-8Is.

Appendices

Appendix I: 747-100 Characteristics

Engine	JT9D-7A	JT9D-7AW	JT9D-7A	JT9D-7AW*
Takeoff thrust, sea level (lb)	46,950	48,57C)	46,950	48,570
Max taxi weight (lb)	713,000	713,000	738,000	738,000
Max brake release gross weight (lb)	710,000	712, 000	733,000	735,000
Design landing weight (lb)	564,000	564, 000	564,000	564,000
Max zero fuel weight (lb)	526,500	526,500	526,500	526,500
Operating empty weight (lb)	356,900	357,400	357,100	357,600
Structural payload (lb)	169,600	169,100	169,400	168,900
Cargo/baggage volume (cubic feet)	6,190	6,190	6,190	6,190
Fuel capacity (gallons)	47,210	47,210	47,210	47,210

Appendix II: Specification - 747-100

Powerplant:	Four 43,500lb Pratt & Whitney JT9D-3, 52,000lb General Electric CF6-S0E or 50,100lb Rolls-Royce RB211-534B; fuel capacity 47,210-53,160 US gallons.
Weights:	Empty 348,8I6-370,8I6lb; gross 710,000-735,000lb.
Dimensions:	Length 231 feet 4 inches; height 63 feet 5 inches; wingspan 195 feet 8 inches; wing area 5,500 square feet.
Performance:	Cruising speed 604mph .Ceiling 45,000 feet. Range 5,527 miles.
Capacity:	374-490 passengers (typical), 516 passengers (maximum).

Appendix III: 747-100 Total Production List

Construction No	Series	Customer	Number built
19637/661	-121	Pan Am	24
19967/678	-131	TWA	12
19725/27	-146	JAL	3
19729/30	-143	Alitalia	2
19733/35	-124	Continental	3
19744/45	-148	Aer Lingus	2
19746/48	-130	Lufthansa	3
19749/52	-128	Air France	4
19753/57	-122	United	5
19761/66	-136	British Airways	6
19778/87	-151	Northwest	10
19875/83	-122	United	9
19896/98	-132	Delta	3
19918/19	-135	National	2
19925/28	-122	United	4
19957/58	-156	Iberia	2
20007	-190	(Alaska Airlines)	not built
2013/15	-133	Air Canada	3
20080/83	-131	TWA	4
20100/109	-123	American	10
20207	-127	Braniff	1
20208	-101	Wardair	1
20235	-121	Boeing prototype	1
20246/47	-132	Delta	2
20269/73	-136	British Airways	5
20284	-136	British Airways	1

20305	-101	Continental	1
20320/22	-131	TWA	3
20323/26	-123	American	4
20332	-146	JAL	1
20337/39	-147	(Western Airlines)	not built
20347/54	-121	Pan Am	8
20355	-128	Air France	1
20376/78	-128	Air France	3
20390/91	-123	American	2
20401/02	-129	SABENA	2
20528	-146A	JAL	1
20531/32	-146A	JAL	2
20541/43	-128	Air France	3
20708	-136	British Airways	1
20767	-133	Air Canada	1
20798/800	-128	Air France	3
20809/10	-136	British Airways	2
20829	-198	(Air Zaire)	not built
20881	-133	Air Canada	1
20952/53	-136	British Airways	2
20954	-128	Air France	1
21029	-146A	Japan Asia Airlines	1
21141	-128	Air France	1
21213	-136	British Airways	1
			Total: 167

Appendix IV 747-100B Total Production List

		Registration	Customer
21759	-1868	EP-IAM	Iran Air
21760	-1868		(Iran Air) not built
21761	-1868		(Iran Air) not built
21762	-1868		(Iran Air) not built
22498	-1688	HZ-AIA	Saudi Arabian Airlines
22499	-1688	HZ-AI8	Saudi Arabian Airlines
22500	-1688	HZ-AIC	Saudi Arabian Airlines
22501	-1688	HZ-AID	Saudi Arabian Airlines
22502	-1688	HZ-AIE	Saudi Arabian Airlines
22747	-1688	HZ-AIG	Saudi Arabian Airlines
22748	-1688	HZ-AIH	Saudi Arabian Airlines
22749	-1468	HZ-AII	Saudi Arabian Airlines

Appendix V Characteristics with JT9D-7A engines

Maximum taxi gross weight (lb)	523,000	603,000*	713,000*
Maximum brake release gross weight (lb)	520,000	600,000	710,000
Design landing weight (lb)	505,000	525,000	564,000
Zero fuel weight (lb)	475,000	485,000	526,000
Operating weight (lb)	345,000	345,000	345,000
Structural payload (lb)	130,000	140,000	181,000
Cargo/baggage volume (cu ft)	6,190	6,190	6,190

* = options

Appendix VI Model 747-100SR Production List

C/No	Series	Registration	Customer
20781	SR-46	JA8117	JAL
20782	SR-46	JA8118	JAL
20783	SR-46	JA8119	JAL

20784	SR-46	JA8120	JAL
20923	SR-46	JA8121	JAL
21030	SR-46	JA8124	JAL
21032	SR-46	JA8125	JAL
21033	SR-46	JA8126	JAL
21604	SR-81	JA8133	Nippon Airways
21605	SR-81	JA8134	Nippon Airways
21606	SR-81_	JA8135	Nippon Airways
21922	SR-81	JA8136	Nippon Airways
21923	SR-81	JA8137	Nippon Airways
21924	SR-81	JA8138	Nippon Airways
21925	SR-81	JA8139	Nippon Airways
22291	SR-81	JA8145	Nippon Airways
22292	SR-81	JA8146	Nippon Airways
22293	SR-8J	JA8J47	Nippon Airways
22294	SR-81	JA8148	Nippon Airways
22594	SR-81	JA8152	Nippon Airways
22595	SR-81	JA8153	Nippon Airways
22709	SR-81	JA8156	Nippon Airways
22710	SR-81	JA8157	Nippon Airways
22711	SR-81	JA8158	Nippon Airways
22712	SR-81	JA8159	Nippon Airways
22066	SR-146B	JA8142	JAL
22067	SR-146B	JA8143	JAL
23150	SR-146B	JA8164	JAL

Appendix VII: Specification 747-200B

Powerplant:	Four 54,750lb Pratt & Whitney JT9D-74R4G2, 52,500lb General Electric CF6-50E2 or 53,110lb Rolls-Royce RB211-524D4-B; fuel capacity 47,210-53,160 US gallons (178,690-201,210 litres).
Weights:	Empty 374,700-383,600lb; gross 775,000-833,000lb
Dimensions:	Length 231 feet 10 inches; height 63 feet 5 inches; wingspan 195 feet 8 inches; wing area 5,500 square feet.
Performance:	Cruising speed 600mph+. Ceiling 40,000 feet. Range 7,940 miles.
Capacity:	Up to 550 passengers.

Appendix VIII 747-200B Characteristics with JT9D-7AW engines

Max taxi gross weight (lb)	778,000	788,000*
Max brake release gross weight (lb)	775,000	785,000
Design landing weight (lb)	564,000	564,000
Zero fuel weight (lb)	526,500	526,000
Operating empty weight (lb)	365,800	365,800
Structural payload (lb)	160,700	160,700
Cargo/baggage volume (cubic feet)	6,190	6,190
Fuel capacity: gallons (US)	51,430	51,430
pounds (@ 6.7lb/gallon)	344,580	344,580

Appendix IX Specification 747-300S

Powerplant:	Four 54,750lb Pratt & Whitney JT9D-74R4G4, 55,640lb General Electric CF6-80C2B1 or 53,000lb Rolls-Royce RB211-524D4.
Weights:	Empty 383,400-393,500lb; gross 775,000-833,000lb.
Dimensions:	Length 231 feet 10 inches; height 63 feet 5 inches; wingspan 195 feet 8 inches; wing area 5,500 square feet.
Performance:	Cruising speed 619mph. Ceiling 45,000 feet. Range 6,502 miles.
Capacity:	496 passengers (typical) 563 (maximum).

Appendix X: Specification 747-200SP

Powerplant:	Four 43,500-53,000lb Pratt &Whitney JT9D, 52,500lb General Electric CF6-50E or 50,100lb Rolls-Royce RB211-524B; fuel capacity 47,210-53,160 US gallons (178,690-201,211 litres).
Weights:	Gross 660,000-690,000lb.
Dimensions:	Length 184 feet 9 inches; height 65 feet 5 inches; wingspan 195 feet 8 inches; wing area 5,500 square feet.
Performance:	Cruising speed 619mph. Ceiling 45,000 feet. Range 10,222 miles.
Capacity:	305 passengers and 20,000lb cargo.

Appendix XI: 747SP Production Totals

Reg	Model	Customer	No. Built
EP-IAA	SP-86	Iranair Fars	2
EP-IAB	SP-86	Iranair Kurdistan	
N530PA	SP-21	Pan Am *Clipper Mayflower*	5
N531 PA	SP-21	Pan Am *Clipper Liberty*	
N532PA	SP-21	Pan Am *Clipper Constitution*	
N533PA	SP-21	Pan Am *Clipper Freedom*	
N534PA	SP-21	Pan Am Clipper Great Republic	
21027	SP-21	(Pan Am)	not built
21028	SP-21	(Pan Am)	not built
EP-IAC	SP-86	Khuzestan	1
ZS-SPA	SP-44	SAA *Matroosberg*	3
ZS-SPB	SP-44	SAA *Outeniqua*	
ZS-SPC	SP-44	SAA *Maluti*	
YK-AHA	SP-94	Syrian Arab *November 78*	2
YK-AHB	SP-34	Syrian Arab *Arab Solidarity*	
ZS-SPD	SP-44	SAA *Majuba*	3
ZS-SPE	SP-44	SAA *Hantam*	
ZS-SPF	SP-44	SAA *Soutpansberg*	
B-1862	SP-09	China Airlines	1
N536PA	SP-21	Pan Am *Clipper Lindbergh*	5
N537PA	SP-21	Pan Am *Clipper High Flyer*	
N538PA	SP-21	Pan Am *Clipper Fleetwing*	
N539PA	SP-21	Pan Am *Clipper Black Hawk*	
N540PA	SP-21	Pan Am *Clipper White Falcon*	
HZ-HM1	SP-68	Saudi Arabian	1
EP-IAD	SP-68	Iranair	1
21785/86	SP-27	Braniff	2
21932/34	SP-J6	CAAC Beijing	3
21961/63	SP-31	TWA	3
21992	SP-27	Braniff	1
22298	SP-09	China Airlines	1
22302	SP-27	CAAC Beijing	1
22483/84	SP-85	Korean Air	2
22495	SP-38	QANTAS	1
22503	SP-68	Saudi Arabian	1
22547	SP-09	China Airlines	1
22672	SP-38	QANTAS	1
22750	SP-68	Saudi Arabian	1
22805	SP-09	China Airlines	1
YI-ALM	SP-70	Iraqi *Al Oadissiya*	1
A6-ZSN	SP-Z5	Abu Dhabi	1

Total 45

Appendix XII: 747-200F Characteristics with JT9D-7AW engines

Max taxi gross weight (lb)	778,000	788,000*
Max brake release gross weight (lb)	775,000	785,000
Design landing weight (lb)	630,000	630,000
Zero fuel weight (lb)	590,000	590,000
Operating empty weight (lb)	337,000#	337,000#
Structural payload (lb)	253,000	253,000
Cargo/baggage volume (cubic feet),	23,630	23,630
Fuel capacity: gallons (US)	51,430	51,430
pounds (@ 6.7lb/gallon)	344,580	344,580

* options   # includes 16644lb tare weight

Appendix XIII: Iranian Air Force 747s

C/N	Series	Source	Iranian AF Serial Nos.
19733	-124/SCD	ex-Continental	5-289/5-8110
19734	-124/	ex-Continental	5-290
19735	-124/SCD	ex-Continental	5-291/5-8112
20080	-125/SCD	ex-EAL/TWA	5-282/5-8103
20081	-125/SCD	ex-EAL/TWA	5-284/5-8105
20082	-125/SCD	ex-EAL/TWA	5-286/5-8107
20083	-125/SCD	ex-EAL/TWA	5-288/5-8109
19667	-131/SCD	ex-TWA	5-280/5-8101
19668	-131/SCD	ex-TWA	5-285/5-8106
19669	-131/SCD	ex-TWA	5-287/5-8108
19677	-131/SCD	ex-TWA	5-283/5-8104
19678	-131/SCD	ex-TWA	5-281/5-8102
21486	-2J9F		5-8113/EP-NHN
21487	-2J9F		5-8114/EP-NHQ
21507	-2J9F		5-8115/EP-ICB
21514	-2J9F		5-8116/EP-ICC

• not taken up

Appendix XIV: E-4/C-25A/SP (Military/VIP) Series

C/N	Series	Unit	Serial No
20682	E-4A	USAF/1st ACCCS/55th Wing	73-1676
20683	E-4A	USAF/1st ACCCS/55th Wing	73-1677
20684	E-4A	USAF/1st ACCCS/55th Wing	74-0787
20949	E-4B	USAF/1st ACCCS/55th Wing	75-0125

C/N	Series	Unit	Serial No.
23824	C-25A	89th ALW	86-8800/82-8000
23825	C-25A	89th ALW	86-8900/92-9000

C/N	Series	Operator
21652	SP-68 HZ-HM1	Saudi Royal flight RSAF/1 Squadron
21785	SP-27 A40-S0	Govt of Oman
21961	SP-31 A6-SMR	Govt of Dubai (op by Dubai Air Wing)
21963	SP-31 A6-SMM	Govt of UAE (op by Dubai Air Wing)
22750	SP-68 HZ-AIJ	Saudi Royal Flight
23610	SP-Z5 A6-ZSN	Govt of Abu Dhabi

Appendix XV: Specification 747-400

Powerplant: Four 56,000lb Pratt & Whitney 4056, 57,900lb General Electric CF6-80C2BIF or 58,000lb Rolls-Royce RB211-524G.

Weights:	Empty 391,000-393,000lb; gross 800,000-870,000lb.	
Dimensions:	Length 231 feet 10 inches; height 63 feet 5 inches; wingspan 211 feet 5 inches/213 feet fully fuelled; wing area 5,650 square feet.	
Performance:	Cruising speed 612mph. Ceiling 45,000 feet. Range 8,400 miles.	
Capacity:	496 passengers (typical), 630 (maximum).	

Principal Characteristics

	747-400 Domestic	747-400 Combi		747-400 Freighter	
		All Pax	7 Main Deck Pallets	Basic	Maximum
Weights (lb)					
Maximum takeoff gross weight	600,000***	870,000*		800,000	870,000
Maximum landing weight	574,000	630,000		652,000	666,000
Maximum zero fuel weight	535,000	565,000		610,000	635,000
Typical operating empty weights:					
General Electric engines	386,600	409,300	403,900	366,400	366,400
Pratt & Whitney engines	386,600	409,200	403,800	366,800	366,800
Rolls-Royce engines	412,000	406,600		369,900	369,900
Fuel capacity US gallons /litres					
General Electric engines	53,765/203,500	57,065		53,765	57,065
Pratt & Whitney engines	53,985/204,330	57,285		53,985	57,285
Rolls-Royce engines		57,285		53,985	57,285
Dimensions (feet-inches)					
Length	231ft 10 ins	231 ft 10 ins		231 feet 10 ins	
Wingspan	195 ft 8 ins	211 ft 5 ins		211 feet 5 ins	
Height	63 ft 8 ins	63 ft 8 ins		63 feet 8 ins	
Engines					
Type	CF6-80C2B7F	CF6-80C2B7F		CF6-80C2B7F	
Thrust (lb)	61,500	61,500		61,500	
Type	PW4062	PW4062		PW4062	
Thrust (lb)	62,000	62,000		62,000	
Type		RB211-524H		RB211-524H	
Thrust (lb)		60,600		60,600	
Design range **					
General Electric engines	1,720 nmi	7,055	6,620	3,150	4,335
Pratt & Whitney engines	1,690 nmi	6,985	6,550	3,105	4,275
Rolls-Royce engines		6,920	6,485	3,120	4,295

* MTOW of 875,000lb available with loading restrictions; ** Based on 210lb per passenger and baggage; *** Maximum design take-off weight is 833,000lb.

Appendix XVI: 747-100B-747-8I

	747-100B	747-200B	747-300	747-400 747-400ER	747-8I
Cockpit crew	Three	Three	Three	Two	Two
Typical seating capacity	SR: 550 (1st class) 539 (1st-class, high density) 490 (1st Class) 452 (2nd-class) 366 (3rd-class)		539 (1st-class) 496 (2nd-class) 412 (3rd-class)	660 (1st-class) 524 (2nd-class) 416 (3rd-class)	605 (max) 467 (3rd-class)
Length	231ft 10 in	231ft 10 in	231ft 10 in	231ft 10 in	250ft 2 in
Interior cabin width	20 feet	20 feet	20 feet	20 feet	20 feet
Wingspan	195 ft 8 in	195 ft 8 in	195 ft 8 in	211 ft 5 in	224ft 7 in
Wing area	5,500 ft^2	5,500 ft^2	5,500 ft^2	5,650 ft^2	5,963 ft^2
Wing sweep	37.5°	37.5°	37.5°	37.5°	37.5°
Aspect ratio	6.9	6.9	6.9	7.9	8.5
Tail height	63 ft 5 in	63 ft 5 in	63 ft 5 in	63 feet 8 in	63ft 6 in

Op empty weight	358,000lb	383,000lb	392,800lb	393,263lb ER: 406,900lb	472,900lb
Max takeoff weight	735,000lb	833,000lb	833,000lb	875,000lb ER: 910,000lb	975,000lb
Cruising speed (at 35,000 feet altitude)	Mach 0.84 (555 mph)	Mach 0.84 (555 mph)	Mach 0.84 (555 mph)	Mach 0.85 (567 mph) ER: Mach 0.855 (570 mph)	Mach 0.855 (570 mph)
Max speed	Mach 0.89 (594 mph)	Mach 0.89 (594 mph)	Mach 0.89 (594 mph)	Mach 0.92 (614 mph)	Mach 0.92 (614 mph)
Required runway at at MTOW*	10,466 feet	10,466 feet	10,893 feet	9,902 feet ER: 10,138ft	10,138 feet
Maximum range at MTOW	5,300 nmi	6,850 nmi	6,700 nmi	7,260 nmi ER: 7,670 nmi	8,000 nmi
Max fuel capacity	48,445 US gals	52,410 US gals	52,410 US gals	57,285 US gals ER: 63,705 US gals	64,225 US gals
Engine models	PW IT9D-7A/-7F/-7J RR RB211-524B2 RR RB211-524D4	PW IT9D-7R4G2 GECF6-50E2 RR RB211-524D4	PWJT9D-7R4G2 GE CF6-80C2B I	PW 4062 GE CF6-80C2B5F RR RB211-524G/H ER: GE CF6-80C2B5F	GEnx-2B67
Engine thrust (per engine)	PW 46,500 lbf RR 50,100 lbf	PW 54,750 lbf GE 52,500 lbf RR 53,000 lbf	PW 54,750 lbf GE 55,640 lbf RR 53,000 lbf	PW 63,300 lbf GE 62,100 lbf RR 59,500/60,600 lbf ER: GE 62,100 lbf	66,500lbf

Appendix XVII: Specification 747 Dreamlifter

Wing Span: 211.5 feet Length: 235 feet, 2 inches Height (fin tip): 70 feet, 8 inches Swing Tail Cargo Door: Hinge on aft section of the fuselage
Cruise Speed: Mach 0.82
Cargo Capacity: 65,000 cubic feet
Maximum Takeoff Weight: 803,000lbs
Aircraft Purchased: 4

Appendix XVIII: 747 Orders and Deliveries

Year	Orders	Deliveries	Year	Orders	Deliveries	Year	Orders	Deliveries
1966	83	-	1982	14	26	1999	35	47
1967	43	-	1983	24	22	2000	26	25
1968	22	-	1984	23	16	2001	16	31
1969	30	4	1985	42	24	2002	17	27
1970	20	92	1986	84	35	2003	4	19
1971	7	69	1987	66	23	2004	10	15
1972	18	30	1988	49	24	2005	48	13
1973	29	30	1989	56	45	2006	68	14
1974	29	22	1990	122	70	2007	25	16
1975	20	21	1991	31	64	2008	2	14
1976	14	27	1992	23	61	2009	5	8
1977	42	20	1993	2	56	2010	1	0
1978	76	32	1994	16	40	2011	-1	9
1979	72	67	1995	32	25	2012	-	
1980	49	73	1996	56	26	Total	1524	1431
1981	23	53	1997	36	39			
			1998	13	53			

Appendix XIX: 747-8 Firm Orders and Deliveries

Date of Initial order	Customer	747-8I	747-8F	Delivered
15 November 2005	Cargolux Airlines	-	13	4
15 November 2005	Nippon Cargo Airlines	-	14	1
30 May 2006	Business Jet /VIP	9	-	4
11 September 2006	Atlas Air	-	9	4
30 September 2006	Dubai Aerospace Enterprise	-	10	-
30 November 2006	Volga-Dnepr Airlines	-	5	2
6 December 2006	Lufthansa	20	-	2
28 December 2006	Korean Air Cargo	-	7	1
8 November 2007	Cathay Pacific Cargo	-	10	5
7 December 2009	Korean Air	5	-	-
15 June 2011	Arik Air	2	-	-
29 July 2011	GE Capital Aviation Services	-	2	-
		36	70	-
	Totals	106	106	23

Appendix XX: 747 Airframe Losses and Incidents

Date	Reg	Series	Carrier	Fate
6 September 1970	N752PA	-121	Pan Am	Blown up by terrorists, Cairo, Egypt following hijack.
24 July 1973	JA8109	-246B	JAL	Hijacked on a flight from Amsterdam to Anchorage, Alaska. It flew to Dubai, then Damascus, before ending its journey at Benghazi, Libya. The occupants were released and the aircraft was blown up. One of the hijackers was killed.
20 November 1974	D-ABYB	-130	Lufthansa	Took off from Nairobi, Kenya with leading-edge flaps retracted. 59 casualties.
12 June 1975	F-BPVJ	-128	Air France	Destroyed by fire after undercarriage fire, Bombay, India. No casualties.
9 May 1976	5-8104	-131F	IIAF	Crashed near Madrid due to structural failure of its left wing in flight, killing the 17 people on board. The accident investigation determined that a lightning strike had caused an explosion in a fuel tank in the wing, leading to flutter and the separation of the wing.
27 March 1977	N736PA	-121	Pan Am	N736PA struck by PH-BUF in fog at Los Rodeos, Tenerife, CO when the KLM aircraft took off prematurely.
	PH-BUF	-206B	KLM	see above
1 January 1978	VT-EBD	-237B	Air India	Dived into sea off Bombay following ADI failure, killing all 213 on board. All passengers and crew were killed. Many residents of seafront houses in Bombay witnessed the disaster. The cause was lack of situation awareness on the captain's part after executing a banked turn.
19 November 1980	HL7445	-2B5B	Korean Air	Touched down 300 feet short of runway in fog at Seoul, RoK. Fourteen passengers died.
4 August 1983	N738PA	-121	Pan Am	Karachi International. No casualties.
31 August 1983	HL-7442	-230B	Korean Air	Shot down, Sakhalin, Sea of Japan by Soviet Air Force Su-15
27 November 1983	HK-2910	-283M	AVIANCA	Near Madrid, Spain. Inaccurate approach. 181 killed.
16 March 1985	F-GDUT	-383	UTA	Caught fire, Paris CDG, France. No casualties.
23 June 1985	VT-EFO	-237B	Air India	Terrorist bomb in the forward cargo hold, Atlantic

Date	Registration	Type	Operator	Details
				Ocean, off Ireland while en route from Montreal-London. 329 killed.
12 August 1985	JA8119	SR-46	JAL	Crashed into Mount Osutaka, Japan after rupture of the aft Pressure bulkhead following improper repair. 520 killed.
2 December 1985	F-GCBC	-228M	Air France	Ran off runway at Rio-Galeao, Brazil and damaged beyond economical repair.
28 November 1987	ZS-SAS	-244M	SAA	Intense fire developed in the right-hand foward pallet while en route from Taipei to Mauritius; crashed into Indian Ocean.159 fatalities.
21 December 1988	N739PA	-121/SCD	Pan Am	Exploded over Lockerbie, Scotland. Terrorist bomb. All 259 killed plus 11 on the ground.
19 February 1989	N807FT	-249F	Flying Tigers	In flight collision with terrain, Puchong, Malaysia. Four killed.
7 May 1990	VT-EBO	-237B	Air India	*Emperor Vikramaditya*. Landing accident, New Delhi. Destroyed by fire.
2 August 1990	G-AWND	-136	British Airways	Impounded by Iraqi forces. Kuwait City. Destroyed by shelling. Kuwait International Airport on 27 February 1991.
29 December 1991	B-198	-2RF	China Airlines	No.3 engine separated from wing soon after take-off, Taipei, Taiwan. Five fatalities.
4 October 1992	4X-AXG	-258F	El Al	No.3 engine separated from wing, crashed Bijmermeer, Netherlands.
12 September 1993	F-GITA	-428	Air France	Veered off runway at Papeete.
4 November 1993	B-165	-409	China Airlines	Overran runway, Kai Tak. Instructional airframe at Xiamen, PRC.
20 December 1995	N605FF	-136	Tower Air	Aborted take-off at New York JFK. Aircraft cannibalised, January 1997.
17 July 1996	N93119	-131	TWA	Lost in Atlantic off Long Island, NY 11½ minutes after take-off. Suspected fuel-tank ignition.
12 November 1996	HZ-AIH	-1688	Saudi Arabian	Mid-air collision in cloud at Charkhi Dadri, 30 miles west of Delhi with IL-76 UN-75435 of Kazakstan Airlines, whose crew 'lacked English language skills' and who were relying entirely on their radio operator for communications with ATC. He in turn did not have his own flight instruments and had to look over the pilots' shoulders for his readings. The pilot was measuring his height in metres (as is the norm in the former Soviet Union) rather than feet, which is the norm in the rest of the world. Now it is forbidden into fly into airports, Delhi included, without airborne collision avoidance systems (ACAS).
6 August 1997	HL7468	-385	Korean Air	Flight 801 with two pilots, a flight engineer, 14 flight attendants and 237 passengers departed Seoul-Kimpo International Airport (now Gimpo Airport) at 8:53 pm on 5 August for Antonio B. Won Pat International Airport, Guam. The aircraft crashed while on approach to the airport killing 223 people, including 209 passengers and 14 crew members (3 flight crew and 11 cabin crew). Of the 31 occupants found alive by rescue crews, two passengers died en route to the hospital and three other passengers died of their injuries within 30 days of the crash. There was heavy rain at Guam so visibility was

significantly reduced and the crew attempted an instrument landing. The glideslope ILS on runway 6L was out of service; however, the captain believed it was in service and at 1:35am managed to pick up a signal which was later identified to be from an irrelevant electronics device on the ground. The crew noticed that the aircraft was descending very steeply and noted several times that the airport 'is not in sight'. Despite protestations from the flight engineer that the detected signal was not the glide-slope indicator, the captain pressed on and at 1:42 am the aircraft flew into Nimitz Hill (at the edge of Mount Macajna and the Sasa Valley) about 3 nautical miles (5.6 km) short of the runway, at an altitude of 660 feet (200m).

28 December 1997	N4723U	-122	United Airlines	Inadvertent flight into adverse weather conditions and over-ocean turbulence, 956.3 miles ESE of Tokyo over the Pacific Written off (damaged beyond repair).
5 August 1998	HL7496	-4B5	Korean Air	Korean Air Flight 8702 departed Tokyo-Narita at 16:50 for a Flight to Seoul-Kimpo, scheduled to arrive there at 19:20. Bad weather, including heavy rainfall, at Seoul forced the flight crew to divert to Cheju. The aircraft took off from Cheju at 21:07 for Seoul. On landing, the 747 bounced and slid 100 metres off the runway before coming to a stop in a grassy area on the edge of a platform.
5 October 1998	ZS-SPF	SP-44	SAA	Shortly after takeoff from Maputu, Mozambique, the No. 3 engine suffered an uncontained failure. Flying debris caused damage to the No. 4 engine and the wing. A fire erupted, but could not be extinguished immediately. An emergency landing was carried out. Written off (damaged beyond repair).
6 March 1999	F-GPAN	-2B3F	Air France Asia	Madras-Chennai Airport, India. After travelling 700 feet along runway, nose-wheel collapsed, overran runway and destroyed by fire. Five crew escaped (one injured jumping to ground).
22 December 1999	HL7451	-200B5F	Korean Air Cargo	Took off from London-Stansted bound for Milano-Malpensa Airport and crashed into Hatfield Forest near the village of Great Hallingbury. All 4 crew on board were killed.
31 October 2000	9V-SPK	-412	Singapore Airlines	Crashed at Chiang Kai-Shek International Airport while attempting take off from the wrong runway during Typhoon Xangsane. Aircraft destroyed killing 83 of the 179 occupants,
5 November 2000	TJ-CAB	-2H7B	Cameroon Airlines	Paris CDG.
25 May 2002	B-18255	-209B	China Airlines	Lost 28.1 miles NE of Makung, Penghu Islands in the Taiwan Strait with all 225 passengers and crew. Likely due to the structural failure in the aft lower lobe section of the fuselage.
23 August 2001	HZ-AIO	-368	Saudi Arabian	Aircraft rolled into a drainage ditch at Kuala Lumpur and toppled forward causing severe damage to the nose section. Was taxied to the departure gate to board 319 passengers for Jeddah,

				Saudi Arabia, reportedly, by a ground engineer on the no. 2 and 3 engines. When trying to make a turn brakes and steering had no effect and the aircraft continued into the ditch. It is said that the auxiliary hydraulic pumps switches were in the off position.
27 November 2001	9G-MKI	-246F	MK Airlines	Crashed about 700m short of the runway at Port Harcourt, Nigeria. The front section broke away from the fuselage. A fire erupted in the main fuselage. One fatality.
25 May 2002	B-18255	-209B	China Airlines	near Penghu.
29 November 2003	ZS-OOS	-258C	Hydro Air Cargo	Written off (damaged beyond repair) landing at Lagos-Murtala Muhammed Airport (LOS). ZS-OOS was operating on a cargo flight from Brussels to Johannesburg (JNB) with an intermediate stop at Lagos. A Notam stated that runway 19R, a 3900 x 60 meters asphalt runway, was closed because of resurfacing work. During the descent the controller at Lagos told the crew that 19R was in use. After a query by the Hydro crew he made the correction and reported that the runway in use was 19L. Apparently the approach controller cleared the flight to land on 19R. On landing the 747 struck stacks of asphalt and slewed left with the first engine in contact with the surface until the nose wheel came to rest in a drainage ditch. No injuries to the 9-man crew.
14 October 2004	9G-MKJ	-200F	MK Airlines	Flight 1602 crashed into a rock quarry shortly after takeoff from Halifax Stanfield International Airport on a cargo flight bound for Zaragoza, Spain with a load of fish and lobster. Initial reports indicate that the aircraft's tail struck the runway for approximately the last 1,000 feet of the takeoff roll, with the tail becoming separated from the fuselage upon impacting a berm at the end of the runway. Weather at the time of the accident was reported as good, with clear skies and unlimited visibility.
7 November 2004	TF-ARR	-230F (SCD)	Air Atlanta	Sharjah Airport. The cause of this accident was the termination of the take-off at a speed above V1 with insufficient runway remaining to stop the aircraft safely as a result of the commander's interpretation that there was smoke and 'fire'. Written off (damaged beyond repair).
24 January 2005	N808MC	-212BSF	Atlas Air	Operated on a cargo flight to Düsseldorf on behalf of Emirates. After landing on the snow covered runway 23L the 747 overran runway, hitting the localizer antenna and some poles of the approach lighting system. The No.2 engine caught fire and sustained damage. The aircraft was withdrawn from use at Düsseldorf until being scrapped there in April 2006.
19 August 2005	N627US	-251B	Northwest	Written off (damaged beyond repair) after landing at A. B. Won Pat International Airport with the nose gear retracted.
7 June 2006	N922FT	-2U3BSF	Tradewinds Int	Rionwgro/Medellín-José María Córdova Airport, Colombia. Take-off, at a speed higher than 12 knots

calculated for the existing conditions, was aborted because of No.1 engine failure. Aircraft could not be brought to a halt on the wet runway and overran into a field. The nose gear was sheared off completely and the 747 came to rest about 150m past the 3500m long runway. Written off (damaged beyond repair).

Date	Reg	Type	Operator	Notes
2 February 2008	N527MC	-2D7B	Atlas Air	Cargo broke loose during takeoff from Lome (LFW) and broke through the bulkhead, causing severe damage. No crew injuries.
25 March 2008	TF-ARS	-357	Saudi Arabian	Flight SV810 made an uneventful landing at Dhaka-Zia International, Bangladesh. During the landing roll the tower controller reported seeing a fire on the right hand wing. Upon exiting runway 14 the crew received a fire indication for engine No.3. The fire extinguisher was activated and all engines were shut down. The fire could not be extinguished and the 747 was evacuated. Investigation determined a fuel leak where the fuel enters the front spar for engine #3. The aircraft was written off (damaged beyond repair).
25 May 2008	N704CK	-209F	Kalitta Air	Broke in three parts when it overran R20 at Brussels Airport Belguim on departure for Bahrain International Airport. The five crew members were uninjured.
7 July 2008	N714CK	-209BSF	Kalitta Air	Crashed into a farm field near the small village of Madrid, Colombia shortly after takeoff from El Dorado International Airport. Crew had reported an engine fire and were attempting to return to the airport. One of the engines hit a farmhouse, killing 3 people inside.
3 August 2008	JA8955	-481D	All Nippon	The aircraft had received maintenance at Bangkok-Don Muang. Was being cleaned internally after maintenance. An inflammable cleaning agent was being used, which led to a fire in the forward cargo hold.
27 October 2008	OO-CBA	-228F(SCD)	Cargo B	Brussels-Zavantem.Tail strike on take-off from runway 25R, Returned to land. The aircraft was withdrawn from use as a result of the damage and finally scrapped in January 2011.
3 September 2010	N571UP	-44AF/SED	UPS	Near Dubai International Airport. 2 crew members killed.
28 July 2011	HL7604	-48EF	Asiana	Destroyed when it crashed into the sea off Jeju, South Korea. Both pilots were killed in the accident. The flight departed Seoul-Incheon International Airport (ICN) at 03:05 on a cargo flight to Shanghai-Pudong International Airport (PVG), China. About one hour after take-off the crew radioed ATC that a fire had broken out in the hold and that the jet had to divert to Jeju. The jet carried 58 tonnes of cargo, including 0.4 tonnes of hazardous materials such as lithium batteries, paint, amino acid solution and synthetic resin.
29 April 2013	N949CA	-400BCF	National	Stalled and crashed shortly after take-off from Bagram airfield, Afghanistan. All 7 crew died.

INDEX

ABL Program   166
ACC (Aerial Aircraft Carrier)/AWACs proposals   165, 170-171
ACESS   179
Admiral Richard E. Byrd   94
Aerial refuelling tanker proposal   171
AFDS
AGM-86 ALCM   165
Airborne Laser (YAL-1A/AL-1A)   171-172
Airbus Industrie   173, 225, 229, 232
Aircraft
   Airbus
      A300   82
      A300-600R   232
      A310   232
      A320   173
      A330   173
      A340-600   173, 232
      A380   50, 233
   Antonov
      An-124   50
      An-225   50
   Boeing
      707   22-23, 25-26, 35, 156
      707-320B   27, 31-32
      707-820/505   27
      727-100   21-23
      727-200   23, 89
      737 Series   23, 31, 58-59, 76, 177
      747 Advanced   222
      747 CMCA (Cruise Missile Carrier Aircraft)   172
      747-100   32, 37-38, 43, 58-59, 80, 90, 149
      747-100/'747B' Two Phase Programme 80-82
      747-100SR   163
      747-121SCD   68
      747-122   82
      747-127   72
      747-200 Evergreen Supertanker   168
      747-200B   29, 38, 82, 90-91
      747-200F (C-33A)   165, 150, 155-156
      747-200F ICBM launch platform proposal   169, 172
      747-236B   35-36
      747-2G4B   168
      747-300 Series   23, 45, 88, 91
      747-357   94
      747-400 Combi   183, 188
      747-400 freighter   171, 184
      747-400 high-capacity Domestic 188
      747-400 Series   167-192
      747-400ERF   225
      747-400ERX   232
      747-400F   225
      747-400XQLR   232
      747-500X/600X   232
      747-8 Series   225-240
      747-Combi   91, 94 (-300 'Big Top'), 187-188
      747SP Series   117-132, 169
      747SR Series   82, 117-132, 163
      747-X   225, 232
      757   173, 177, 197
      767   82, 173, 177
      767-200/300ER   232
      767-400ER   232
      767-400ERX   232
      777-200X/300X   232
      7X7   119

AL-1A   172
B-1 Lancer   165
B-17 Flying Fortress   33
B-47 Stratojet   19-20, 22, 24
B-52 Stratofortress   35, 38, 44
B-9   17
C-19A   167-168
C-33A (747-200F) airlifter   171-172
Dash 80   20, 58-59
Dreamlifter (747-409 LCF)   237
Dreamliner (787)   228, 233, 237, 240
E-4/4A/B   29, 164-167
KC-135   160
KC-33A   171
KC-33A   165
KC-747 (Iran)   165
Model 200 Monomail   16
Model 214 (Y1B-9)   17
Model 215 (YB-9)   17
Model 247   16-17, 21, 58
Model 314   17
Model 367 Stratofreighter   21
Model 367-80   21-22
Model 377 Stratocruiser 18-19, 37
Model 473-60C   22
Model 733 (2707-2000   22
VC-137C (707-320C)   168
VC-25A/ VC-25 (747-200B) 168-170, 240
XBA7   19
YAL-1A   171-172
Convair
   CV-880   27
   B-58 Hustler   27
Douglas
   C-54 Skymaster   33
   Dakota (C-47)   229
   DC-7C   22
   DC-8 series 22, 26, 28, 76, 117, 123, 156
   DC-9   23
   DC-10-30 Advanced Cargo Transport Aircraft
      (ACTA)   171
   DC-10-30/40   38, 46, 82, 118, 120, 156, 173
Lockheed
   C-130 Hercules   129-130, 229
   C-141 Starlifter   27
   C-5A Galaxy   27, 29-30, 35, 62, 90, 170-171
   L-1011 TriStar   38, 46, 82, 117-118, 120-121, 132, 156
   P-3 Orion   113
   SR-71 Blackbird   169
McDonnell Douglas
   C-17 Globemaster III   171
   C-19A   162
   C-54   33
   DC-10   38, 46, 132
   DC-10-30 Advanced Cargo Transport Aircraft
      (ACTA) 171
   DC-10-30/40   114, 117-120
   DC-8-50/60 Series   22, 26-28, 119
   KC-10A Extender   171
   MD-11   173
   MD-12   229
ALCM   164
Allen, William 'Bill' McPherson 22, 29-30, 33, 37, 39, 50, 54, 60
Amsterdam   69, 103, 153
Amsterdam-Schiphol Airport   29, 90, 197-202

Anchorage Airport, Alaska   8, 103, 107, 123, 153, 193-194
Andrews AFB, Maryland   165, 168, 170
Arab Solidarity   126, 129
Athens, Greece   85
Atlantis Space Shuttle   162-163
Auburn   41
Auckland, New Zealand   94

Bagram airfield, Afghanistan   252
Bangkok   145, 180, 183, 188, 191-193, 252
Bangladesh   252
Barajas Airport, Madrid   153
Basuta, Jaswant   133-134, 136
Bauer, Eugene E.   161,
Beijing   184
Bendix Aerospace   169
Benghazi, Libya   87
Bennett, Paul   53
Bern   91
BF Goodrich   176
Bijlmermeer   153
BOAC (now British Airways)   72, 78-79
BOAC brochure   64-67
Boeing Field   56, 237
Boeing, William E.   15
Boeing-Renton   23, 25, 64, 68, 186
Boeing-Wichita   40, 147, 149, 170, 172
Borger, John   31, 37
Boston Belle   140-141
Boullioun, 'Tex'   57, 64
Boyle, Dominic   214-224
Bracknell, Berkshire   207
Bradley   160
Brown, Rowland 'Row' E.   30, 32
Brussels, Belgium   252

Cairo, Egypt   73, 248
Calgary   186
California Girl   104
Canadian Pacific Air Lines' Disaster   107-108
Cargo door failure   82-83
Cebu   111
Charkhi Dadri mid-air collision   249
Charles A. Lindbergh   189
Château du Reduit   124
Chek Lap Kok International Airport (Hong Kong)   203, 211
Chula Vista, California   46
Civil Air Reserve Fleet (CRAF)   108
City of Belfast   139
City of Birmingham   116
City of Canberra   90
City of Cardiff   190
City of Darwin   104
City of Edinburgh   94-95, 98-102, 106
City of Elgin   106
City of Everett   27, 116, 230
*City of Gold Coast Tweed*128
City of Hong Kong   198-199, 200-202
City of Hull   213
City of Johannesburg   199
City of Newcastle   191-192, 195-196
City of Paris   71
City of Sydney   185
Clipper America   73-74
Clipper Bostonian   72
Clipper Champion of the Seas   69
Clipper Constitution   36, 62, 72, 119-120, 123
Clipper Derby   71
Clipper Flying Cloud   69
Clipper Fortune   73
Clipper Freedom   123

Clipper Great Republic   124
Clipper Juan T. Trippe   87, 116
Clipper Liberty Bell   124
Clipper Liberty   120, 124
Clipper Maid of the Seas   134-136
Clipper Mayflower   121, 124
Clipper Mercury   105, 132, 156
Clipper Nautilus   70
Clipper New Horizons   124, 132
Clipper Ocean Express   62
Clipper Ocean Telegraph   61, 68
Clipper Red Jacket   72
Clipper Rival   71
Clipper San Francisco   132
Clipper Sea Lark   87
Clipper Storm King   60-62, 68
Clipper Victor   62, 69, 74-78
Clipper White Falcon   132
Clipper Young America   62-63, 69, 132
Clipper Young American   47
COIL   171-172
Cokely, Ralph   64, 68
Collins AFDS   183-184
Collins CMC   178
Colum   181
Columbia   252
Combi crashes   157-158
Comet, de Havilland   22, 35
Concorde   23, 57
Continental Airlines   66
Conway, Rolls-Royce Mk.508   27, 35
Cronin, Captain David   82-84
Cundy, John   35, 230-231
CX-HLS project   25, 27-30, 33, 37-38

Denver International Airport, Colorado   213, 220-224
'Desert Shield'   171
'Desert Storm'   171
Diego Garcia   113
Don Meung International Airport   191-193, 252
Douglas Aircraft   21
Downey, Captain John R. MRIN   213-224
Dreamlifter   236-237, 247
Dryden Flight Research Facility   132, 161, 163
Dubai International Airport   252
Dubai, Government of   120
Dulles International Airport, Washington DC   69
Dunsfold   116
Düsseldorf   251
Dyer, Captain Calvin Y.   73-74, 87

East Hanford   44
Edwards AFB   90, 161, 163, 171
EFIS electronic flight instrument system   180
EICAS engine indication and crew alerting system   180-181
Eldorado   97
Embakasi Airport, Nairobi   78-80
Emery, Senior First Officer Alan   214-224
Emmly Masanabo   181
Emperor Ashoka   81
Emperor Kanishka   110-111
Emperor Vikramaditya   249
Engine mounting problems   152-154
Engines
    de Havilland
        Ghost turbojet   35
    General Electric
        CF6   35, 76, 82, 159, 165
        CF6-45A2/50E2Series   119, 155
        CF6-80C2 Series   162, 165, 168, 176, 181, 186, 188
        CF6-50 Series   38, 90-91, 94, 151, 155

CJ-805   27
GE90 Series   217, 227
GEnx-2B67 turbofan   234
GP7176 turbofan   221
J47   19
TF-39   28
GP7176 (joint GE and P&W) turbofan   231
Pratt & Whitney
   JR9D-7R4G151, 155
   JT3D Series21, 27, 35
   JT3S-15   27
   JT9D Series   27, 43-46, 50-51, 54, 57, 60, 69, 80,
     82, 89, 149, 152, 155, 165
   JT9D-3A/AW   80, 89, 161
   JT9D-7/7A/W   80, 82, 89
   JT9D-7F/7FW   152
   JT9D-7R-62   89, 91
   JT9D-7R4G2   152
   PW4000 Series   171, 176, 181, 186-187, 227
   Wasp   17
Rolls-Royce
   Conway Mk.508   27
   RB.200-524 Series   82
   RB211 Series   28, 35-36, 38, 82, 90, 176, 186, 217
   Trent 800 Series   227, 230

Engines (general)   241, 243-247
Engine mounting problems   153-154
E-Systems   130, 165
Euphrates   95
Everett, Washington   39-41, 44, 46-48, 50, 53, 58, 64, 90,
   105, 150, 156, 170, 236-237, 240
Evergreen 747-200 Supertanker   162, 166
Evergreen Aviation & Space Museum   116
Evergreen Aviation Technologies Corporation, Taiwan   237
Evergreen International Airlines   105, 153, 237
Eyjafjallajökull volcano   103

FAA   227
FADEC   170
Fairchild Hiller   41
Farnborough Air Show   231, 237
Fitch, Dennis E.   132
Fitzgerald   96
Flower, Scott   37
Frankfurt   133, 136, 138, 142, 193
Freighter losses   159-160
Freighters   147-160
Fritz   91

Galunggung, Mount   98, 102, 106
Ganges   94
Garrett (Allied Signal)   177
Garrett GTCP331   169
Gatwick (LGW) Airport   59, 140-143, 213-216, 220, 223-224
General Dynamics F-111   169
GMD Program   166
Grantley Adams International Airport, Barbados   240
Greenland   217, 221
Grubbs, Captain Victor   75-77, 88
Guam   82, 114-115, 249
Guggenheim Aviation Partners   236
Gulf War   171
Gwinn, Bill   39

Halaby, Najeeb   60
Halifax Stanfield International Airport   160, 251
Haneda (Tokyo) Airport   123, 127, 189
Hantam   125
Hatfield Forest   159
Hawthorne   41

Heathrow Airport (LHR)   61-62, 69, 71, 75, 84, 94, 110, 121,
   123, 133-134, 138, 142, 166, 180-181, 195, 211, 220
Heinemann, Milt   32
Helderberg, The   112-114, 157
Hessen   78-80
Highlander   94
Hollingsworth, David   182-183
Honeywell (Sperry) FMCS   183
Hong Kong   187, 191
Honolulu Airport, Hawaii   82-83, 86
Houston, Texas   199
Huge Viking   104
Hughes H-4 Hercules 'Spruce Goose'   50

Iberia   65-66
Iceland   216
Imperial Iranian Air Force (IIAF)   164-165, 169
Israel   168

Jakarta, Indonesia   98-99
JAL 123 (JA8119) disaster   127-131
Johannesburg   113

'Kneecap', (NEACP) flying command post   164-165
Kai Tak Airport, Hong Kong   122, 127, 151, 155, 158-159,
   182, 187, 190-191, 203-212, 249
Kauffman, Sanford   37
Kazakstan Airways (UN-75435 mid-air collision)   249
KC-135/EC-135   165, 169
Kennedy John F. International Airport (JFK)   38, 75, 85,
   107, 124, 133, 249
Kimpo Airport   107-108, 249
Knutson, Don   64
Korean Air Lines' disaster   103-106
Krack, Captain Christian   80
Krueger leading-edge flap   22
Kuala Lumpur   94, 101
Kuter, General Larry S.   37

Lake Washington   58
Las Palmas airport   75
Leonardo da Vinci International Airport, Rome   85
Lindbergh, Charles   64
Lockerbie, Scotland   135-136, 249
Lockheed bankruptcy   38
Lockheed-Martin   172
Loesch, Dix   62
Lombard, Adrian   35
London-Stansted   159, 250
Long Island disaster   249
Los Angeles International Airport (LAX)   190-191, 194-195
Los Rodeos Airport, Tenerife   75-78, 248
Luxembourg-Findel Airport   159

MacQuarrie, Captain James Bruce 134
Mactan-Cebu airport   107
Madras-Chennai Airport, India   250
Madrid   140, 153, 157, 248
Malta   136
Maluti   124
Manchester   155
Manila   196
Maputu. Mozambique   250
Marana, Arizona   105
MATS (Military Air Transport Service)   29
Mauritius   157
MC747 ICBM launch Project   169-170
McDonnell Douglas   29, 229
McNerney, Jim   235, 237
McQuarrie, Captain James Bruce   134, 136
Melbourne   94, 195

Meurs, Klaus   76
Miami Maiden   94
Miami   85
Minuteman ICBM   169
Moody, Captain Eric   94-103
Moses Lake, Washington   24, 187, 236-7
Mount Carmel   168
Mount Redoubt   103
Mulanje   118, 121
Museum of Flight, Seattle, WA   116
Museums   116

Nairobi Airport   79-80, 248
Nami Tsuru   220-222
Narita International Airport   107
NASA   130, 161-167
Neumann, Gerhard   35
Nixon, Pat   69
NLA proposal   227-229
Nordrhein-Westfalen   71, 96
Northrop Noorair Division   41
Northrop-Grumman TRW   166
November 16   126, 129

Okinawa   139
Oklahoma City Air Logistics Center   160
Olympic Flame   92
Oman, Royal Flight of   123
Osaka-Itami   127, 132
Osutaka, Mt, Japan disaster   249
Outeniqua   118, 121

Paine Field   39, 51, 123, 186, 237, 240
Palmdale   237
Pan Am Building   39
Pan Am Flight 103 disaster   133-136
Pan Am, bankruptcy   136
Papeete   190
Paris Air Show   56, 173, 240
Paris-Charles-de-Gaulle Airport   85, 106, 248
Paris-Le Bourget   64
Pasay City, PI   111
'Peace Station' in-flight refuelling tanker (IIAF)   169
Pennell, Maynard   21-22
Perth   94, 101
Phuket   191
Port Harcourt Airport   159, 251
Pratt & Whitney Canada (P&WC) APU   177
Princess Juliana Airport, St, Maarten   103

Raytheon   130
Reina Sofia airport, Tenerife72
Rendezvous   213
Reyes, Captain Eduardo 'Ed' 111-112
Rigg, Captain Mike   203-212
Rijn (Rhine)   75, 77
Rio de Janeiro, Brazil   157
Robert F. Six   104
Roberts, P. J. de   64
Rohr Corporation   41, 46
Roll-Out, 747   46-48
Rolls-Royce bankruptcy   38
Romeo Vachon   104
Roswell, NM   187
Rushmore, Mt   170

Sakhalin Island   109, 248
San Francisco International Airport   73-74
Sasaki, First Officer Yutaka   127-129
Schiphol Airport   69, 84, 197-202

Schwartz, Lieutenant General Norton   194
Seattle-Tacoma (SeaTac) International Airport   64, 240
Seoul   107, 159, 252
Sharjah   129, 188, 251
Singapore-Changi Airport   194
Sioux City, Iowa   132
Sir Frank Whittle   200
SkyBunks   233
Skyliner   142
SkyLoft concept   233
SkySuites   233
Snow Leopard   125
Snyder, George   29
SOFIA   130, 132
Space Shuttle   161-163
Spijkers   185
Spirit of Sir Freddie   94, 215
SST (Supersonic Transport) Programme   22, 30, 70
St. Maarten   103
Stamper, Malcolm T.   39, 47, 64
Stansted (*see* London-Stansted)
Steiner, Jack   22
Sutter, Joe   25-26, 29-31, 33, 35, 43, 54, 57, 61, 64, 117, 121
'Sutter's Balloon'   121
Suzie   96
Swissair   91

Taipei   112-113, 194-195
Taiwan Aerospace   219
Taiwan   132, 189, 194
Takahama, Captain Masami   127-129
Taormina   97, 156
Tashkent   159
Tenerife disaster   75-78
Tokyo(Haneda)   66, 107, 110-111, 127
Top Gear, BBC TV Series   116
Tower Air   78
Toyko-Narita Airport   86, 114
Trippe, Juan Terry   18, 22, 30, 33-37, 39, 47, 50, 70
Tubular Belle   142

UHCA project   229
United Airlines   58, 66, 80
UTA   91, 97
Uys, Captain Dawid Jacobus   112-113

van Zanten, Captain Jacob Veldhuyzen   75-78, 88
Vickers VC-10   27
Victorville, California   239
VLCT Project   229
Vought Aircraft Industries   237

Waddell, Jack   51-57, 60, 123, 186
Wallick, Jess   64, 186
Wallner   96
Webb, Everette L.   45, 61
Weeks, Captain Robert M.   63, 69
Wells, Ed   33, 35
Whitehorse, Yukon, Canada   194
William M. Allen   58, 70
Wilson, Thornton A.   47, 62
World Trade Center attacks   193-194
Wygle, Brien   51, 54, 186

Yeager, Chuck   161
Yokota Air Base   129-130

Zanten Captain van (*see* van Zanten)
Zaragoza Airport, Spain   160
Zurich   156